THE HISTORY OF ANTI-SEMITISM

From the Time of Christ to the Court Jews

LÉON POLIAKOV

THE HISTORY OF
ANTI-SEMITISM

translated from the French by Richard Howard

SCHOCKEN BOOKS · NEW YORK

First SCHOCKEN PAPERBACK edition 1974
Second Printing, 1976
Copyright © 1965, by Léon Poliakov
Library of Congress Catalog Card Number: 65-10228
Published in France under the title:
Histoire de l'Antisemitisme: Du Christ aux Juif de Cour
Published by arrangement with Vanguard Press, Inc.

EDITOR'S NOTE: Passages originating in another language, quoted by the author in French, have usually been translated directly from the French.

Manufactured in the United States of America

Foreword

A very simple fact provides a point of departure for the present book—the first in a series of four devoted to the problem of anti-Semitism. A look at the globe shows that Israel, the center from which the Jewish Dispersion took place, is approximately equidistant from Greece and Mesopotamia, from western Europe and India, from New York and Tokyo. Thus, this Dispersion, which continued to the four points of the compass, resulted in the creation of Jewish colonies in Mesopotamia, India, and China at the same remote times that the first Jews established themselves in North Africa, Gaul, and Germany. These settlements exist today, and through the centuries contact between them and the Jewish communities of the Mediterranean and northern Europe has never been broken. But in contrast to what happened in the West, the Jews in the East have never been—to use the image of Judah Halevi—"the aching heart of nations"; that is, they have not been a disturbed and disturbing ferment, they have not shocked the world by a history of torment and massacre nor expiated its imperfections, they have never played a role disproportionate to their numbers or distinguished themselves in intellectual or economic activities, nor have they assumed any role other than their own. In short, not having caused streams of ink or rivers of blood to flow, they have lived the lives of happy men and have had no history. Those in China disappeared a generation or two ago; those in India, an inconspicuous sect among thousands of others, lead humble lives as farmers or artisans.

To explain this continuing disparity, there are two kinds of hypotheses:

1) *The supernatural explanation.* By virtue of the mysterious designs of Providence, the Jews, having been assigned a special role among nations, play it first among the so-called Noachian peoples—those practicing a religion that derives from the Old Testament. It will be noted, as a matter of fact, that Judaism's area of diffusion in its "intense" form coincides exactly with the area of diffusion of its daughter religions, Islam and Christianity. I see no particular reason for rejecting such an hypothesis a priori, provided we have first exhausted, in accordance with what I judge to be the duty of an investigatory and comparative method, all the natural explanations—that is, those based on what we know from other sources about the behavior of human societies and groups.

2) *Natural explanations.* These may be of two kinds:

a) An explanation derived from human environment, ignoring the relationship between Judaism and its daughter religions.

b) Explanations derived from collective psychology, especially religious psychology, essentially based on this relationship.

The present work is an attempt to interpret both the Jewish phenomenon and the anti-Semitic phenomenon in the light of this latter explanation, without ignoring the difference between Christianity, which regards the Jews as the deicidal race, and Islam, for which the Crucifixion was not relevant. Hence the general plan of the work:

1) A first part, the present volume, is concerned with the Jews known as Ashkenazim, whose history has been confined to Christian territories, down to their emancipation.

2) A second part will deal with the Jews who have lived by turns in Christian and in Moslem territories (Sephardic Jews), or exclusively in Moslem territories.

3) A third part will be devoted to the phenomenon of

Jewish "assimilation," characteristic chiefly of the last century, as well as to the recrudescence of anti-Semitism, characteristic chiefly of our epoch.

4) Lastly, appendices will present additional data on our subject by such auxiliary human disciplines as anthropology, genetics, and social psychology. These appendices are brief, but in the elaboration of our hypothesis, their role has been an essential one.

I should add that the proposed analysis is not entirely new. Its schema may be found more or less clearly formulated by various authors of the past. The first of these was Immanuel Kant, who in a little-known passage of *Religion Within the Limits of Mere Reason* examined the case of the Jews in India and China and drew the following conclusions: "Hence we find no Jews outside the countries referred to [that is, the Christian and Islamic regions] if we except the few on the coast of Malabar and possibly a community in China (and the former could have been in continual commercial relationship with their coreligionists in Arabia). Although there is no doubt that they spread throughout those rich lands, yet, because of the lack of kinship between their faith and the types of belief found there, they completely forgot their own. . . . To base edifying remarks upon this preservation of the Jewish people is very hazardous, for both sides [that is, Christians and Jews] believe they find therein confirmation of their own opinions."

There is a story, for example, that when Frederick II of Prussia asked his physician to give him a proof of the existence of God, the latter replied: "The Jews, Your Majesty!" While the argument has not always been so over-simplified, the uniqueness of the Jews' destiny has tenaciously been regarded, down through the ages, as the direct and explicit expression of the divine will, and this as much by the world at large as by the Jews themselves. Many people in our own times have not abandoned this point of view. Faith in the divine destiny of the Jews has been an important influence on their truly strange fate.

With the advent of the rationalist spirit, other views found expression. Their authorship was extremely diverse: among others, the name of Baruch Spinoza stands out. Spinoza's violent attacks on Judaism contributed not a little to the spread of the notion, among the thinkers of the Enlightenment, that the Jewish religion was nothing but crude superstition and that the old Jehovah was merely a God of hatred.[1] From this it followed quite naturally that the Jewish people were ignorant and fundamentally perverse not only since the Crucifixion but throughout all time. (Voltaire was a clever propagandist of "anti-Semitism" in this form.) At a period when the nascent sciences of biology and anthropology classified living beings in fixed and immutable genera and species, such views contained the germ of a racism *avant la lettre*. Thus the grandiose edifice of the Church was breached, and a historian of ideas could readily reconstruct the thread that leads from Spinoza to Herder, Fichte, and Hegel, and also to Schleiermacher and Harnack. It is in this context that the "divine" interpretation was replaced by the "racial" one: the prerogative of an elite in the eighteenth century, the property of the masses in the nineteenth, and in the twentieth affording an ideological justification for the crematory ovens. Such may be the fatal consequences of an insufficiently informed opinion, and the enormous responsibilities of philosophers. But Spinoza and his philosophical descendants did not have access to the enormous body of information, borrowed from the various social sciences, that we possess today and that permits us to ac-

---

[1] In the *Tractatus Theologico-Politicus* we find, among passages characterized by the greatest serenity, paragraphs such as the following: "Thus the love of the Hebrews for their country was not only patriotism but also piety, and was cherished and nurtured by daily rites until, like their hatred of other nations, it was absolutely perverse (as it very well might be, considering that they were a peculiar people and entirely apart from the rest). Such daily reprobation naturally gave rise to a lasting hatred, deeply implanted in the heart: for of all hatred, none is more deep and tenacious than that which springs from extreme devoutness or piety, and is itself cherished as pious" (Chap. 17).

count for the uniqueness of the Jewish destiny not by means of a "rigid" hypothesis, but by employing an "evolutionist" hypothesis of the kind that has long since prevailed in science. Thus the present work is an attempt to co-ordinate these many elements as they relate to anti-Semitism.

The undertaking has been completed under the aegis and thanks to the co-operation of the History Department of the Centre National de la Recherche Scientifique. Such sponsorship increases my own responsibility and makes it even more essential for me to consider a possible criticism that I have not explored my subject sufficiently, and that although I have expressed my personal views, I have attempted to treat the history of two thousand years in three hundred pages without producing enough documents and facts to support my theses. To this I can only reply that an author's capacity for work has limits, as does a publisher's dedication, and that I have been concerned not with producing a definitive work but a useful one, likely to provoke controversy but also thought. May I hope that my errors, if they exist, will be fruitful ones. Some of my interpretations may be disputed, and certain details revised and corrected: but with regard to the essential point—that is, the relationship between anti-Semitism and the Jews, viewed sometimes in a reciprocal relationship, sometimes in isolation from each other—I believe I have followed a valid method and have unearthed a number of unknown or forgotten facts.

It remains for me to thank the teachers, colleagues, and friends whose counsel I have sought during these years on questions of detail as well as on the structure of the entire work; on points of history as well as on the countless sociological, psychological, or literary problems that arose in the course of this study. The list of names is long, and it would be arduous for me to make it a complete one, so numerous were my benefactors; may they all be assured of my sincere gratitude.

L. P.
Paris

Who is he that hideth counsel without knowledge?

Job 42 : 3

CONTENTS

PART FOUR | THE AGE OF THE GHETTO

PART ONE
FROM GOLGOTHA TO THE CRUSADES

one

Anti-Semitism
in Pagan Antiquity

Rivalries among clans, tribes, and peoples have occurred at all periods and in all regions. With respect to ancient Israel, it would be utterly futile to attempt to ascertain, by means of the traditional documents at our disposal, whether the hostility expressed toward Israel by neighboring peoples already assumed some special significance in Biblical times, whether some particular virulence entered into it. Whatever the merits of the Old Testament as an historical source book, its involvement in the very notion of a covenant, of a unique role providentially devolving upon the people of Israel, the grandiose inspiration of the *lekh lekha,* of the "Get thee out of thy country, and from thy kindred, and from thy father's house," makes this point necessarily ambiguous and keeps us from seeing to what degree the destiny of Israel, eschatologically claimed to be special, was actually so from the beginning. Egyptian and Babylonian inscriptions are of no help here; and as for the Greeks, who were the first to study history in the sense in which we understand it, their authors make no mention of the Jews until the century of Alexander the Great, although, as archaeological discoveries prove, Greek influence was already powerful in Palestine at a much earlier period. From this silence we can only conclude that Greek travelers, for all their curiosity, found nothing special to say about the people of Judea, who in no way struck them as noteworthy or roused their imaginations.

Of course, the Maccabees' stubborn resistance to Hellenization attracted the attention of their contemporaries. And in the first century B.C., the Stoic Posidonius of Apamea, recounting the siege of Jerusalem by Antiochus VII, imputes to him the intention to annihilate the Jewish race completely, ". . . for, alone among all nations, this one refused to have any intercourse with the other peoples, and regarded them all as enemies" (1).* However, such remarks have always served to illustrate long and pitiless conflicts, and the *delenda est Carthago*, which dates from these same years, may stand here as a counterpart.

Indeed, the outlines become clear only when the majority of Jews, having willy-nilly left the territory of Judea after the wars that periodically laid waste to the region, were living in the Dispersion alongside and among other peoples, and when documentation of some validity is made available. To realize this more clearly, let us turn to a period closer to us and more familiar, when, under Caesar and Augustus, Rome established her domination over the Mediterranean world. In this period the Jews, who still retained their territorial and spiritual center in Palestine, were already swarming throughout the Roman Empire and even beyond its borders. As the only people to profess the belief in one God, they were singularly distinguished from all the other subjects of the empire. May we, then, infer the existence of a generalized "anti-Semitism," that is, of an effective *sui generis* attitude of the gentiles regarding the Jews, an endemic hatred pregnant with explosive outbursts, reducing the children of Israel to pariah status and exposing them, as traditional scapegoats, to numberless and endless massacres?

The question has been widely debated, but though it has been the object of much research, particularly in recent years, the ancient texts on which this research is based are not very numerous. The "Jewish question" does not seem to have had more than secondary importance for the men of those times. It is equally difficult to reach a valid conclusion on the basis of the few writings that have come down to

* For numbers in parentheses, see Notes.

us, just as it would be for an historian of the future to judge contemporary anti-Semitism from only *Mein Kampf*, the writings of Édouard Drumont, and a few works of general history. We shall return later to the relevant Greek and Latin texts; let us try now to establish our investigation on more positive bases.

What, then, was the importance of the Jews in the Roman Empire? Numerically, the most reliable estimates speak of one million Jews inhabiting Palestine proper, and from three to four million Jews in the Dispersion, from Asia Minor to Spain: seven to eight percent of the empire's total population.[1] Racially, the matter concerned the ancients very little, and the retrospective hypotheses of today's anthropologists bring no clarity to this point. The problem is rendered still more complex as the result of an extremely active proselytism, converting Egyptians, Greeks, and even Romans to Judaism. We shall return to this subject later. As to the Jews' trades and occupations, these were extremely varied, but in the Dispersion, as in Palestine, they gained their livelihood chiefly by the sweat of their brow. As Marcel Simon notes: ". . . considering the whole of the empire, the Jewish population included a large majority of poor people. . . . What the Jews are most frequently criticized for is not being covered with gold but rather with filthy rags . . ." (2). In Egypt and Asia Minor they were generally agricultural colonists; elsewhere, they were widely represented in all the trades of the period, particularly weaving and dyeing, which they virtually monopolized in certain regions. They were also goldsmiths, glass blowers, and workers in bronze and iron. As the monk Cosmas Indicopleustes was to write later, in the sixth century, "God . . . gave them knowl-

[1] This is the figure adopted by Arthur Ruppin (cf. his study, "The Jewish Population of the World," in *The Jewish People, Past and Present,* New York, 1946, Vol. 1, p. 348). It is also the average of the sometimes divergent estimates of such specialists as R. Beloch, A. Harnack, J. Juster, J. Klausner, Ch. Guignebert, etc. See also the extremely detailed note by Salo W. Baron in *A Social and Religious History of the Jews,* 2nd ed., New York, 1952, Vol. 1, pp. 370-72.

edge and filled them with the divine spirit, and instructed
them that they might conceive and perform all kinds of un-
dertakings, working gold, silver, and bronze, and the dye of
hyacinth, and the purple, and the application of crimson to
stuffs, fine linen, stones and wood . . . and it is found that
even to this day such trades are practiced the most by
Jews" (3). Others were simple laborers, still others engaged
in commerce and the professions, but as the historian J. Juster astutely observes, "No pagan author has ever characterized them as merchants; nowhere do we come upon that
identification of Judaism with business that, a few centuries
later, will seem so natural" (4). Still others were professional—and highly esteemed—soldiers, fighting or mount-
ing guard along all the marches of the empire.[2] There were
also Jewish officials, sometimes of high rank; in the imperial
hierarchy, we find Jewish knights and senators, Jewish leg-
ates, and even Jewish praetors.[3] If we add that the Jews of the
Dispersion regularly adopted the language as well as the
costume of the province they inhabited, that they were rapidly "assimilated" from every point of view, even Helleniz-
ing or Latinizing their names, we seem justified in drawing
this first conclusion: that they did not seem to suffer any special animosity, and that nothing, except their worship, sin-
gled them out from the mosaic of peoples that comprised the
population of the empire.

Nothing except their worship. But it was just this worship,
unlike all others, that imperiously prescribed certain duties
strikingly different from practices universally required of all

---

[2] See in this connection the abundant documentation collected by J. Juster in *Les Juifs dans l'Empire romain*, Paris, 1914, Vol. 2, pp. 265-78. The
exemptions from military service granted the Asian Jews by Julius Caesar
and Dolabella, mentioned by Josephus, must have been of a purely local
character.

[3] Herod Agrippa I had obtained the praetorian insignia from Caligula,
and Claudius granted them to Herod Agrippa II. Josephus mentions the existence, in Palestine itself, of several Jews who were Roman knights. See in
this connection the considerable epigraphic material collected by J. Juster,
op. cit., Vol. 2, pp. 246-50.

other Roman subjects. "Thou shalt have no other gods before me," the first commandment, forbade the Jews any religious act toward the gods of the empire and of the city, and
toward the living gods—the deified monarchs. The fourth
commandment sometimes had consequences just as weighty:
"The seventh day is the sabbath of the Lord thy God: in it
thou shalt not do any work, thou, nor thy son, nor thy
daughter. . . ." Faced with Jewish intransigence in this matter, the Romans, skillful administrators that they were, rapidly settled on certain compromises, especially one exempting the Jews from offering sacrifices to the emperors. Such
privileges in fact constituted a source of jealousy and
possible conflict, especially in the great cities of the East,
where the population was extremely mixed. This is easy to
understand; furthermore, we have a valuable description of
the situation in the Book of Esther (written in the second or
first century B.C.) (5). The text describes the jealousy of the
minister Haman when confronted with the spirit of independ-
ence shown by Mordecai, who ". . . bowed not, nor did him
reverence. . . . And Haman said unto king Ahasuerus,
There is a certain people scattered abroad and dispersed
among the people in all the provinces of thy kingdom; and
their laws are diverse from all people; neither keep they the
king's laws . . ." (Esther 3: 5, 8).

But there were not only jealous courtiers. Another text reveals the scornful and exasperated attitude of a noble Roman
faced with Jewish stubbornness. This is a speech attributed
to Flaccus, prefect of Egypt, when he tried in the year 38
to forbid the Alexandrian Jews to celebrate the Sabbath,
despite explicit orders from the capital:

"If a sudden enemy invasion, an overflow of the Nile, a
conflagration, a thunderbolt, a famine, a plague, an earthquake or any other disaster occurred on Saturday, would you
still remain calmly in your homes? Or, according to your custom, would you stroll through the streets, your hands hidden
in your clothing so as not to be tempted to give aid to those

who are doing the rescuing? Or would you remain in your synagogues in solemn session, reading your sacred books, explaining obscure passages and making long-winded lectures about your philosophy? No! Without wasting a moment, you would seek to shelter your parents, your children, your fortune, and all that is dear to you. Now, even thus am I all these together: tempest, war, flood, thunderbolt, famine, earthquake, and disaster, and this not in the abstract but as a present and potent force" (6).

Furthermore, the sign of a special covenant with God—the practice of circumcision—doubtless raised disturbing echoes: *curtis judaeis,* wrote Horace; *recutitus,* Martial quipped; and Catullus speaks of *verpus priapus ille.* There were also other regulations that expressed Jewish separateness, the isolating force of the Law: "Neither shalt thou make marriages with them; thy daughter thou shalt not give unto his son, nor his daughter shalt thou take unto thy son" (Deuteronomy 7:3). Hence Jewish monotheism involved consequences of a purely sociological order, varying with times and places.

In the period of antiquity—and apart from the situation in Alexandria—there are scarcely any examples of popular outbursts against the Jews. The masses were not concerned with them and harbored no special prejudice against them. As for professional writers, they were already noting the close solidarity of the Jews (which gained them the reputation of misanthropy: they were said to be united among themselves and hostile to the pagans), as well as a combative spirit that we find described by many pagan authors. Let us now consider the texts these authors have left us.

It should be noted that the most violent anti-Jewish texts have not reached us directly: we know them only through the Jewish historian Flavius Josephus, who collected them in his polemical work, *Against Apion.* Most of their authors were natives of Alexandria, the city where a very important Jewish colony had been established and where conflicts between Jews and the Greek population were frequent and bitter. What, then, do the grammarian Apion and the other authors quoted by Josephus hold against the Jews?

In the first place, they refer to a certain number of legends about the Jews' origin, depicting them as corrupt beings, lepers whom the Egyptians, at some indeterminate period, had driven from their country. Manetho, an Egyptian historian and priest of the third century B.C., was the first to popularize this idea, which is merely a malicious parody of Exodus. "The king caused all the sick to be gathered together, in number, it is said, eighty thousand, and imprisoned them in quarries on the east bank of the Nile in order that they might labor there along with other Egyptian captives: there were among them illustrious priests also tainted with leprosy." And subsequently, having recounted the freeing of the prisoners and their flight into the land of Canaan: "Their lawgiver, a priest from Heliopolis named Osarsiph, after the god Osiris worshiped in that city, having changed his nationality, took the name of Moses." With variations in detail, Lysimachus of Alexandria, Posidonius of Apamea, and others repeated this legend. This is interesting insofar as the accusation of spreading leprosy, that is, of being untouchable, is linked to another accusation: that of being unsociable. There are numerous texts on this subject. Among those Josephus quotes, here is a characteristic passage by Lysimachus: "Moses . . . exhorted them [the Jews] to show kindness to no one, to follow only the worst counsels and to overthrow all the sanctuaries and altars of the gods they might come upon." Even an author who speaks well of the Jews and their institutions—Hecataeus of Abdera—makes this observation: "He [Moses] instituted a kind of life opposed to humanity and to hospitality." Other Greek authors (Diodorus of Sicily, Philostratus), as well as certain Latin writers (Trogus, Juvenal) repeat the same accusation, which we find again, concisely summarized, in this celebrated passage of Tacitus: ". . . the Jews . . . reveal a stubborn attachment to one another, an active commiseration, which contrasts with their implacable hatred for the rest of mankind. They sit apart at meals, they sleep apart, and though, as a nation, they are singularly prone to debauchery, they abstain from intercourse with foreign women. . . ."

A completely logical conclusion that several ancient authors drew from this—though one that surprises us—was that the Jews were an atheistic people. Their outspoken horror of other divinities, their eternal *contemnere deos*, their refusal to sacrifice to the emperors, already sufficed to characterize them as an impious race; furthermore, what was their God? Had not Pompey remarked, when he had boldly entered their temple in 63 B.C., that "inside there was no image of the gods, the place was empty and the secrets of the sanctuary were nought"? [4]

The other accusations against the Jews, which were sometimes contradictory—an obstinate, rebellious, audacious people; or a cowardly and contemptible people, a nation born for slavery—all proceed more or less from those we have quoted. However, special consideration must be given to the indignation of certain ancient authors with regard to the Jews' extremely active proselytism. Horace and Juvenal in their satires ridicule the Jewish neophytes; Valerius Maximus accused the Jews of "corrupting Roman morals by the worship of Jupiter Sabazios"; and Seneca states that the "practices of this villainous nation have so greatly prevailed that they are accepted throughout the universe; the vanquished have given laws unto the victors." It is important to note that such proselytism had already been practiced for a long time in the ancient world; one finds premonitory signs ever since the times of the prophets. Had not Jonah been ordered by the Lord to go to preach repentence in the city of Nineveh? The perfect proselytes—those who submitted to the baths of purification and to circumcision—were accepted by the Jewish congregations on a basis of complete equality and were regarded as "sons of Abraham." This was not true of the "semiproselytes," the *metuentes* or "God-

---

[4] *Nulla intus deum effigie, vacuam sedem et inania arcana.* Tacitus, *Historiae*, V, 9.

fearers," also called "proselytes of the porch," who, not daring to take the definitive step, observed one or another Jewish custom, such as the Sabbath. Yet their sons often became perfect proselytes. One of Juvenal's satires, ridiculing the "parents whose examples corrupt their childen," suggests that conversions were quite common.[5] Anticipating the triumphant success of Christian propaganda, the Jewish variety won many adherents at this period. This may lead us to think twice about the exact origins and ancestry of what came to be called "the Jewish race."

In short, apart from legends, we see that the ancient authors reproached the Jews for certain peculiarities of morals and behavior expressly imposed by the Old Testament—as had already been observed by the unknown author of the *Sibylline Oracles* ("And you shall fill all the lands and all the seas; and each shall be enraged by your customs": III, 271). On the other hand, these authors invariably allude to the Jews' martial valor and their family spirit: "This nation is terrible in its wrath," writes Dio Cassius, and even the hostile Tacitus observes: "It is a crime among them to kill any newborn infant. They hold that the souls of all who perish in battle or by the hands of the executioner are immortal. Hence a passion for propagating their race and a contempt for death."

Thus from this rapid scrutiny we may draw certain conclusions. On the one hand, we observe in pagan antiquity none of those collective emotional reactions that would subsequently render the lot of the Jews so hard and so precarious. We may add that, in general, the Roman Empire in

[5] Satire 14. Juvenal continues: "He who happens to have had a father who observed the Sabbath will adore only the clouds and the spirit of the sky; he will as soon eat human flesh as that of swine, from which his father abstained; soon he will even be circumcised. Raised in scorn of the Romans, he learns, observes, reveres only the Judaic law, all of which Moses transmitted to his followers in a mysterious book: [he is taught] not to show the way to the traveler who does not practice the same rites, and to lead only the circumcised to the fountain. And all this because his father passed every seventh day in sloth, without taking any part in the duties of life!"

pagan times knew no "state anti-Semitism," despite the frequency and violence of Jewish insurrections (the sole exception being the anti-Jewish edicts of Hadrian in 135, after the Bar Kokheba rebellion; these edicts were repealed three years later by Hadrian's successor, Antoninus). On the other hand, the attention of contemporaries, especially of the "intellectuals" of the period, was attracted by what was singular about Judaism. This inquiring attention oscillates between two poles: aversion to Jewish "exclusiveness," and an attraction to the monotheistic religion, that "strange charm," as Renan calls it, whose proof is furnished by the successes of Jewish proselytism.

Hence, as Josephus proudly asserted in the *History of the Jewish War,* "For many years the people have shown an ardent desire to adopt our religious practices: there is no Greek city, no barbarian people, no nation to which our custom of abstaining from work upon the seventh day has not spread, and where the fasts, the lighting of the lamps, and many of our dietary prohibitions are not observed."

It is commonplace today to contrast the jealous exclusivism of Jehovah with the tolerance of the pagan gods. When we consider the matter more closely, things are not so simple. The tutelary gods of the ancient city-state heeded only their own worshipers; a foreigner could not count on their protection, but remained bound to the gods of his ancestors. Thus, while acknowledging alien gods, local or regional worship remained exclusive and intolerant within its own bounds. On the other hand, though the universal God of the Jews tolerated no rivals, the congregation of the chosen people was open to all, and its protection was extended to all men. As the prophet expressed it: "Also the sons of the stranger . . . even them will I bring to my holy mountain, and make them joyful in my house of prayer . . . for mine house shall be called an house of prayer for all people" (Isaiah 56: 6-7).

We may observe, in this connection, that under the powerful influence of Hellenic culture, Judaism developed in its own fashion, gradually reducing its ritualism and absorbing ideas borrowed from Greek thought and philosophy. In the Talmudic tradition, in the school of Gamaliel, five hundred young men studied the Torah and another five hundred the wisdom of the Greeks. As a result, we find Hellenized Jewish thinkers, like Philo of Alexandria, seeking to harmonize the doctrine of the Stoics with the precepts of the Torah. These developments obviously facilitated the ascendancy of Jewish proselytism and at the same time prepared the ground over which Christian propaganda was to extend its influence. The latter, in turn, affected the Jews' status. But before examining the situation thus created, we must look briefly at the fate of certain Jewish communities scattered among peoples destined to remain outside the orbit of the daughter religions of Judaism. West of Judea, the God of Abraham had ultimately compelled recognition and had triumphed; yet what is the course of events when He remains a minor or a local divinity?

In the first centuries of the Jewish Dispersion, the Jews had settled far beyond the geographical limits of the Mediterranean world. Thus, while the main threads of Jewish history, especially after the rise of the great monotheistic religions that were the heirs of Judaism, were woven upon the warp of Christianity and Islam, certain communities did persist among polytheistic peoples in India, in China, and perhaps even in Japan. Let us consider whether their development under such conditions can be related and compared with what they experienced in the Roman Empire.

We mention the existence of the Jews in Japan only incidentally, for there is no way of ascertaining the facts about this subject, though certain etymological assumptions are of interest.[6] The case of the Jews in China, on the other hand, deserves closer consideration.

[6] There exist, as a matter of fact, near Yamako, two villages, Goshen and Manasseh, whose names have nothing in common with current Japanese etymology; an abandoned temple located nearby bears the name

Some years ago there still existed in Honan Province, at Kai-feng-fu, a handful of Chinese who refrained from eating pork and who remembered that their fathers had been circumcised. The ruins of a synagogue were also found in the vicinity. These were the last vestiges of several once-prosperous and important communities. The best information as to their history comes from the Jesuit missionaries who visited them in the seventeenth and eighteenth centuries and who inquired about their sacred books and the details of their worship. It appears from their accounts that toward the middle of the eighteenth century, the Kai-feng-fu community, although already declining, still numbered about a thousand members. The Jews of China had seen better days: As Père Domenge puts it, ". . . for a long time, they played a great role in China. Several were governors of provinces, ministers of state, bachelors and doctors. There were some who possessed great landed wealth. But today nothing of this former glory remains to them. Their settlements in Ham Chow, Himpo, Peking, Ning-hyo have disappeared . . ." (7). Some inscriptions discovered on commemorative steles[7] confirm these remarks, as does a sentence from Marco Polo, who mentions the prosperity and the influence

---

"David"; in the neighboring city of Usumasa, the word "Israel" is carved on a well several centuries old. There has also been an attempt to relate the word "samurai" (according to tradition, the samurai were descendants of a tribe that had come from deep in the Asian continent several centuries before Christ) to "Samaria," and this has been made the point of departure for speculations on the Japanese as descendants of the ten lost tribes. (Cf. *The Universal Jewish Encyclopedia*, London, 1904, Vol. 6, article "Japan," and Dr. S. Oyabe, *Origin of Japan and of the Japanese*, Yale University Press, 1926.) During the last century, such speculations were sufficiently attractive for Ranke to write: "The Jewish type is frequently encountered among the Japanese nobility, including the imperial family. The crown prince has a Jewish physiognomy . . ." etc. Even early in this century, Werner Sombart, speaking of the "extraordinary resemblance between the Japanese nature and the Jewish nature," returned to this naïve hypothesis.

[7] These steles were unearthed in 1824 near the city of Lo Yang. One of the inscriptions, written in 1512 by a Chinese mandarin, states that "the Jews excel in agriculture, commerce, law, and the military arts; they are greatly esteemed for their integrity, their loyalty, and their piety."

of the Jewish settlements in China (1286), and accounts of Arab travelers dating from the ninth century. This last source asserts that "the Jews have been settled in China since time immemorial" (8); thus, without going back as far as King Solomon, as some have attempted to do, it seems reasonable to grant, with the Jewish historian Graetz, that the first Jewish settlements in China date from the first centuries of the Christian era.

The significant fact in all this is that for at least ten centuries the Jews of China—their customs and ethnic group purely Chinese—led a peaceful and uneventful existence, harmoniously combining the practices of Jewish ritual with the respect due to Confucius, ". . . convinced that the latter were purely civil and political ceremonies," as Père Domenge informs us (9). The Jews were not the object of persecutions and in no way intruded upon the attention of the people or the government. Cut off entirely from their co-religionists for an extraordinarily long period, their loyalty to their faith apparently must be attributed, in the absence of other ethnic or social or economic explanations, to the peculiar isolating power of Jewish monotheism. Yet even this was not an indestructible mortar, and ultimately it yielded to the erosion of time. Other conditions, it appears, are essential in order to assure the persistence and multiplication of the Jewish people among the nations.

Closer to the traditional centers of Judaism, the Jews of India, where immigration occurred in several successive waves, have maintained themselves in considerable numbers to our own day. There are still some tens of thousands of them, the olive-skinned "Beni Israel," in the vicinity of Bombay and, farther south, Jews of Cochin or Malabar, called "black Jews"; ethnically, neither group shows any distinction from the surrounding population. Their first settlement dates from about the first centuries of the Christian era. In the course of the Middle Ages, other Jews settled in India, coming either overland from Mesopotamia or by sea from Europe; the latter kept rigidly apart from the native

Jews. Though commerce was the usual occupation of these latest arrivals, the Beni Israel and the Jews of Cochin were generally farmers and artisans. The history of the Beni Israel, also called "Shauvar Telis" (pressers of Saturday oil), is very obscure, and we may conclude from this that they were happy, since happy peoples, it is said, have no history. In any case, in modern times these humble people have provoked no hatred and experienced no persecution. Curiously enough, in India there is a religious group that for centuries has assumed the economic role inherited by the Jews in Europe. These are the Parsis, the last modern representatives of ancient Persian Zoroastrianism. Numbering approximately a hundred thousand, they live in the city and region of Bombay, and commerce is their chief if not exclusive occupation. Living in comfort, they are known for the purity of their family habits, as well as for their remarkable group solidarity. If one adds that Zoroastrianism is, in the opinion of historians of religion, the sole monotheistic creed to appear independently of Judaism, one may make an interesting comparison, without, of course, being able to venture the slightest hypothesis for the historical reasons that have led the Parsis (and not the Jews) to assume the role of "the Jews of India."

two

Anti-Semitism
and Early Christianity

Deriving from Judaism and calling upon the God of Abraham for its authority, a new teaching appeared and after three centuries of struggle triumphantly imposed itself upon the whole of the Roman world. It is quite inconceivable that such an event should not have influenced the position of the Jews who had remained faithful to the old Law: its repercussions were as swift as they were substantial, and we must consider in some detail a development that from its inception is extremely complex and sometimes contradictory.

We shall not discuss here the question of the exact degree of "historicity" attributable to the Gospels nor express any opinion concerning related controversial questions: the biography of Jesus, the authenticity of the sayings attributed to him, the precise nature of his teachings, and so forth. It seems, indeed, as if the word "objectivity" loses its meaning as soon as we approach these questions, each author treating them with some preconceived idea: the agnostic unable to refrain from doubt, the believer unable to deny belief. But let us remark, for the point is an important one, that the Gospel accounts of the trial of Jesus afford enough contradictions and improbabilities for even Christian Biblical criticism to have called several points into question. Thus the Protestant historian Hans Lietzmann writes: ". . . It is highly unlikely that Mark's account of the deliberation of the Sanhedrin during the night is based on Peter's testimony; from all appearances, this is a subsequent Christian conjecture. . . . We may wonder whether in this account distant recollections of a real past are preserved . . ." (10). As for freethinking historians, they have a marked tendency (if they do not completely deny the existence of Jesus) to write bluntly, as does Charles Guignebert: ". . . this trial appears to be merely an artifice, clumsily introduced in order to shift the principal responsibility for Jesus' execution onto the Jews. . . . What remains likely is that the Nazarene was arrested by the Roman police, tried and condemned by the Roman procurator, Pilate or some other" (11).

As a matter of fact, nothing in the Nazarene's teachings (even though they may have shocked many a doctor of the Law) constituted formal heresy from the Jewish point of view: even at the end of the first century, a doctor of the Law, Rabbi Eliezer, considered that Jesus, too, would have a place in the world to come (12). Furthermore, the members of the first Christian community, that of Jerusalem, were Jews who observed the Law strictly and who desired to continue to do so. They seem to have suffered no rebuffs or systematic persecutions,[1] and went into exile from Jerusalem only after the fall of the Temple in the year 70. Traces of these "Judeo-Christians," as they were subsequently called, occur as late as the following century. These first Christians obeyed the commandments of the Law to the last detail and chose to recruit adherents only among the Jews. It was not until Christian propaganda spread beyond the borders of Palestine, extending to the Dispersion and affecting the Jewish colonies in Syria, Asia Minor, and Greece, that true Christianity, as we know it, was born. We have seen that these Hellenized colonies were surrounded by a kind of fringe of "semiproselytes"—"sympathizers" we would call them today—considered to be Jews of a very in-

---

[1] Indeed, the famous episode of Stephen's being stoned, as related in Acts, seems to have been merely the consequence of an internal conflict between the "Hebrews" and the "Hellenists" of the young community. Cf. Acts 6: 1-6, and Lietzmann's interpretation in his *Histoire de l'Eglise ancienne*, Vol. 1, pp. 70-71.

ferior class because they were unwilling to conform to all observances. When Christians began preaching in this atmosphere, so different from that of Palestine, Saint Paul, as the New Testament informs us, made the crucial decision to exempt Christian proselytes from the commandments of the Law and from circumcision—and thereby changed the course of the world's history.

This decision was imposed upon the first Christian communities only after prolonged struggle, and the conflicts between the orthodox partisans of the Christian Church of Jerusalem and the innovators of the Dispersion are reflected in Acts and in the Pauline epistles.[2] The decision suddenly transformed the Christians from harmless followers of Judaism into grave heretics against whom we may see a reaction in the solemn malediction of apostates, apparently inserted in the Eighteen Benedictions about the year 80.[3] This decision, finally, by exempting the new converts from the arduous duties imposed by the Law and abolishing all distinction between the "sons of Abraham" proselytes and the semiproselytes, tremendously enlarged the range of Christian propaganda. Saint Paul expresses the matter as follows: "And unto the Jews I became as a Jew, that I might gain the Jews; to them that are under the law, as under the law, that I might gain them that are under the law; To them that are without law, as without law . . . that I might gain them that are without law; To the weak became I as weak, that I might gain the weak. . ."[4] Henceforth the new teaching gained ground with increased rapidity.

The original source and center of the Church remained

---

[2] Acts 13: 44-47; 15: 1-29; Galatians 2: 1-14, etc.

[3] Twelfth Benediction: "And may there be no hope for the apostates, and may all those who do evil be destroyed in an instant, and may they all be uprooted and torn, and the arrogant be humbled speedily. Cast them down and humble them speedily in our days. Blessed art thou, O Lord, who breakest the enemies and humbles the arrogant." Cf. Marcel Simon, *Verus Israël*, Paris, 1948, "The Christians in the Talmud," pp. 214-38. We may note in this connection that since the late Middle Ages, the word "apostates" (*minim*) has been replaced by the word "informers" (*malshinim*).

[4] 1 Corinthians 9: 20-22.

the Jewish colonies of the Dispersion, but converts were increasingly sought among the gentiles. Yet Jew and Christian both claimed the God of Abraham as authority; both claimed to be the sole faithful interpreters of that God's will; both revered the same sacred book, though each interpreted the text in his own light. We may add that the Roman authorities appear to have made little distinction between them initially (the oldest Roman texts we know simply identify them).[5] Rarely has there been, it would seem, a situation so propitious to the creation of implacable hostility.

It is quite probable that the Jews of the Dispersion, in the pride of their ancient privileges, attempted to stand apart from their rivals, that on occasion they even denounced to the authorities those whom they regarded as dangerous heretics. As for the Christians, these dissidents from Judaism discovered with irritation that their propaganda among the chosen people was not bearing much fruit. Henceforth, it would be their concern to prove to the world that God had withdrawn from this people the privilege of His favor, shifting it to a new Israel. The Jewish war and the destruction of the Temple afforded them, from this point of view, a perfect argument. Did not such a dreadful catastrophe, which could only be a divine punishment, prove that God had turned away from His people forever? (Certain Jewish texts of the period express the same notion, but interpret quite differently the reasons for the punishment. According to Ben Azzai, Israel was dispersed for having denied the one God, circumcision, the commandments, and the Torah.[6]) Furthermore, the New Church, while addressing itself increasingly to the gentiles and gradually absorbing pagan influences, lost no time in attributing to Jesus a divine nature. Consequently his death inevitably became a deicide, the crime of crimes; and this abominable sin, just as inevita-

[5] For instance, Suetonius, in *The Twelve Caesars:* "Because the Jews at Rome caused continuous disturbances at the instigation of Chrestus [i.e., Christ], Claudius expelled them from the city" (Claudius, 25).

[6] *Midrash on Lamentations,* I, 1.

bly, was upon the heads of the Jews who had denied him. The demonstration of their loss of grace was thus complete. (Perhaps it was also politic to exonerate the Romans, who were in power, from all responsibility.) Thus everything was accounted for and made clear: crime and punishment, rejection and new election. For the organization of Christianity, it was essential that the Jews be a criminally guilty people.

Thus, from the first centuries, the various motifs of the original antagonism between Jews and Christians become interwoven, now in rivalries for proselytes, now in the effort to conciliate officialdom for its own advantage, or in the exigencies of theological thought; they are the nucleus of a strictly Christian anti-Semitism. We shall review them briefly here.

The attitude of the Roman authorities toward the Jews on the one hand, and toward the Christians on the other, varied many times in the course of the first three centuries. Letters of Tacitus and of Pliny the Younger (13) inform us that by the beginning of the second century Rome already made a distinction between them. At the time of Hadrian's prohibition of circumcision and of the bloody Bar Kokheba rebellion in 135, the first Christian apologists were attempting to prove that the Christians, having no link with Israel and the land of Judea, were irreproachable subjects of the empire (14). Antoninus, Hadrian's successor, re-established freedom of worship for the Jews, and in the second century, confronted with the growing successes of Christian teaching (numerous active communities already existed in all the provinces of the empire), initiated the age of the great persecutions of the Christians, supported by the popular hatred provoked by Christian exclusivism. In the eyes of the pagans, the worshippers of Jesus did not even have the excuse of belonging to a religion. Judaism was obviously absurd and exasperating, yet it at least possessed claims to nobility based upon a national tradition going back to the dawn of time.

Christians were disturbing newcomers, the *genus tertium:* "*Usque quo genus tertium!*" shouted the mob at the circus. Hence they were the victims of a real "transfer of hostility": the legends of a Manetho or an Apion about the ignominy of Jewish worship were now applied to Christian practices. As Lietzmann writes: ". . . each time a public disaster occurred, a plague or a famine, the furious mob screamed for the death of the Christians: 'Throw them to the lions!' " (15). (For a Jewish author, these lines echo with a strangely familiar ring.) It was scarcely surprising if, under these circumstances, the Jews sought what advantage they could and sided with the pagan camp—though there are records of many cases of Christian martyrs being buried in Jewish cemeteries, and as Tertullian says, the Jews sometimes offered the threatened Christians the asylum of their synagogues (16). A new reversal occurred, of course, once Christianity became an officially recognized religion. We shall return to this subject later.

The rivalry for proselytes also set Jews and Christians against each other. Though Christian preaching rapidly appeared to be more effective than Jewish, it did not follow that Judaism lost its attraction, and its propagandists did not give up quickly. On the contrary, some texts suggest that in the second and third centuries they were quite as active as before, if not more so. In about 130, Juvenal ridiculed "parents whose examples corrupt their children." When, a few years later, Antoninus re-established the freedom of the Jews to worship, he took the precaution of maintaining the prohibition against circumcising non-Jews, under pain of death or banishment, in order to oppose the spread of Judaism. Some Jewish sources state that rabbinical tradition regarded some of the most prominent doctors of Israel of this period as proselytes.[7] They also mention solemn reception ceremonies for proselytes in the third century, and public lectures in which the Torah was eulogized (17). To whom was such

[7] In particular Shemaiah, Abtalyon, Rabbi Meir, as well as the famous Rabbi Akiba himself.

proselytism addressed? It is logical to assume that it was directed equally toward converts to Christianity and toward pagans. And, in fact, were not the Jews the people of the Old Testament? Were not their doctors its most qualified interpreters? Do we not find the first Christian exegetes, even Saint Jerome, seeking instruction from the rabbis? Did not the Christians follow the Jewish calendar for more than two centuries? Thus certain contacts were established that sometimes proved dangerous for the stability of the new faith. We must recall that for the first two or three centuries the Christian Church was not yet hierarchized and recognized no universally supreme institution: each community could interpret the sacred texts in its own way. Countless sects and heresies appeared, often conforming more or less to Judaism, and thus the prestige and influence of the people of the Book prevailed on many occasions. The social status of the Jews was still far from being such that they could be used as a contrast. And the dilemma still remained: to interpret the Old Testament correctly, who was better qualified than the people to whom it had been given and who had preserved it down through the centuries? Consequently, whereas Christians and Jews continued to compete among the gentiles, Judaism was also able to confuse and to attract many a follower of nascent Christianity. And this brings us to the strictly doctrinal rivalry that finds its ultimate expression in what has been called "theological anti-Semitism."

From the beginning of the third century, the thesis of the divine punishment of the Jews was explicitly formulated by Origen: "We may thus assert in utter confidence that the Jews will not return to their earlier situation, for they have committed the most abominable of crimes, in forming this conspiracy against the Saviour of the human race. . . . Hence the city where Jesus suffered was necessarily destroyed, the Jewish nation was driven from its country, and another people was called by God to the blessed election" (18). On the occasion of anti-Christian persecutions, the Jews were to reverse the argument ironically: "Is there not, then, among you even one man whose prayers are accepted by God, so that your miseries may cease?" (19)

If we wish to examine more closely the gradual rise of a "theological anti-Semitism," the slow development of the paschal liturgy offers a striking example. According to the *Didascalia Apostolorum,* one of the oldest ecclesiastical documents that has come down to us, the chief reason for the celebration of Easter was not only to commemorate the Passion of Christ, but to obtain forgiveness for the guilty and unfaithful Jews: "Know, then, my brothers, in the case of the fast that we practice for Easter, that you will fast for our brothers who have not obeyed, even when they shall hate you. . . . We must fast and mourn over them and over the judgment and destruction of the nation . . . because when our Lord came among the Jewish nation, they did not believe him when he did teach them . . ." (V, 14, 23). But the majority of Christians rapidly rejected such a point of view. At the same time that the new reasons for the festival (the Passion and Resurrection of the Lord) were clarified, many communities, and especially that of Rome, advocated changing the date and calculating it independently, so as not to suffer a humiliating subordination to the Jews. On Good Friday prayers were offered for gentiles as well as for Jews; and ultimately, from the ninth century on, certain sacramentaries of the Roman liturgy expressly directed: *Pro Judaeis non flectant* ("Do not genuflect to the Jews").[8]

In the Gospels one already sees the beginning of such a development. The Gospel According to Saint John, the last to be written, is also the one most hostile to the Jews. Another example from the Gospels: the fact that the name of the apostle to betray his Lord appears to be derived philologically from Judea, the fatherland of the Jews, might of course be merely a coincidence. But the coincidence is too remarkable not to suggest a deliberate desire to symbolize the opprobrium henceforth heaped upon the chosen people.

It is not at all surprising, in this situation, that beginning

[8] Cf. p. 32.

with the fourth century, and especially in the East, where the Jews were more numerous, many preachers attacked them with the utmost violence: "Murderers of the Lord, assassins of the prophets, rebels and detesters of God, they outrage the Law, resist grace, repudiate the faith of their fathers. Companions of the devil, race of vipers, informers, calumniators, darkeners of the mind, pharisaic leaven, Sanhedrin of demons, accursed, detested, lapidators, enemies of all that is beautiful . . ." (Gregory of Nyssa) (20). "Brothel and theater, the synagogue is also a cave of pirates and the lair of wild beasts. . . . Living for their belly, mouth forever gaping, the Jews behave no better than hogs and goats in their lewd grossness and the excesses of their gluttony. They can do one thing only: gorge themselves with food and drink . . ." (Saint John Chrysostom) (21).

Thus a Byzantine tradition of anti-Semitism was established. From it, in particular, was to emerge the superstitious fear of the Jews so characteristic of the Muscovite Empire a thousand years later. In Western Europe, on the other hand, the development was to be more complex and more bizarre. And it is the Christian West that we shall now consider.

three

The Western Jews
in the High Middle Ages

Apart from a few more or less legendary episodes, not much
is known about the way in which Christianity spread to
Roman Gaul; nor is anything known of the circumstances
under which the first centers of Judaism appeared there. In-
stinctively, there is a tendency to take quite divergent
views toward these movements: whereas the fiery words of
some of the apostles supposedly brought about conversions
to a gradually spreading Christianity, Judaism was manifested only by the immigration of Jews and the handing
down of Jewish beliefs from father to son. But the historian
must sometimes mistrust instinctive reactions, so often subject to the common error of viewing past ages through the
lens of the present. One might equally well advance an opposing hypothesis: that Christianity and Judaism took root
in the West in an identical fashion, essentially through conversions; Judaism, moreover, preceding Christianity and
providing it—as in the East—with an essential vehicle. We
shall discuss later the considerations that lead us, in the absence of any valid documentation, to decide in favor of this
second hypothesis. First, though, let us consider what is
known of the first Jewish settlements in Gaul.

Nothing certain is known concerning the Roman period,
except for a few comments about Jewish merchants in Marseilles, Arles, or Narbonne. In the Frankish period, however,
when the clergy took over the writing of history, the outlines
become clearer. Many Church council decisions of the fifth

and sixth centuries have reference to the Jews and their influence. They forbid Christians, both clerics and laymen, to
eat with Jews; they oppose mixed marriages; give warnings
about the observation on Sundays of the countless Sabbath
prohibitions; and forbid the Jews to mingle with Christian
crowds during the Easter festival.[1] Such resolutions, by their
very nature, were intended primarily to prevent the believers from accepting the Jewish faith and rituals, and to
counter the dangerous Judaizing heresies that one sees so
often among populations recently evangelized and still uncertain in their faith. Similarly, the only text of an anti-
Jewish polemic of the period that has come down to us, that
of the Gaul Evagrius (22), constitutes more of a warning
to Christians than an attempt to evangelize Jews. All of this
suggests that at this time the Jews of Gaul were numerous,
influential, and, since they lived on good terms with the
Christians and mixed freely with them, of concern to Church
leaders by very reason of this association with their flock.
More detailed information is afforded, at the end of the sixth
century, by Gregory of Tours. His various writings give us a
detailed picture of the Jews of his time. We learn, for instance, that they were merchants, landowners, officials,
physicians, or artisans, and that, mingling with the "Syrians"
(whom the author mentions in the same context), they were
numerous in the cities, where, as cosmopolites, both sects
must have lorded it over the local barbarians. The Syrians,
however, were Christians; the Jews represented for the
Church the enemy par excellence, as evidenced by certain
turns of phrase used by the good bishop: "Liars to God";
"close-minded, ever-incredulous race"; "wicked and perfidious nation."

Nonetheless, the highest ecclesiastical dignitaries occasionally requested their services and even maintained

[1] Councils of Vannes (465), of Agde (506), of Épone (517), of Orléans (533), of Clermont (535), of Mâcon (583), etc. Cf. on this question:
R. Anchel, *Les Juifs de France*, pp. 27-29.

friendly relations with them. Gregory of Tours relates at length[2] the frank theological discussion that he himself had occasion to enter upon in 581 with the Jew Priscus, a favorite of King Chilperic. From the conclusion of the story, it appears that a year later Priscus was killed, as he was passing unarmed[3] into the synagogue, by Phatir, a converted Jew. Shortly afterward, Phatir was murdered by Priscus' family. Thus the Jews of this period carried arms and knew how to use them. Other episodes mentioned by Gregory confirm that the Jews constituted, in the open society of the period, a portion of the population quite self-confident, prosperous, and not the object of any special unfavorable prejudice. The names they bore—Armentarius, Gaudiocus, Priscus, Julius—are for the most part Gallo-Roman, and it seems that they conducted their rites to some extent in the vernacular (23). At times the Church, which constantly warned against their pernicious influence, tried to convert them by force, seeking help in so doing from the kings, while the excited crowds would occasionally turn against them. It is significant that the best-known of these forced conversions was provoked by the aggression of a Clermont Jew at Eastertime against an apostate (24). In short, the incidents related by Gregory of Tours, as well as certain others (forced conversions in Arles and Marseilles), can be regarded as part of an interdenominational rivalry in which Judaism still confronted Christianity on equal terms.

Other than the priceless information of Gregory of Tours, we have no further concrete details about the status of the Jews in Gaul. Such silence, if it means anything at all, suggests that their status was little changed. A few rare Hebrew inscriptions on stone (25) only reinforce this supposition: they imply that the expulsion of the Jews under King Dagobert, mentioned by one chronicler (26), was either legendary or was never carried out. Later, at the beginning of the

---

[2] In Book VI (5, 10) of the *Historia Francorum.*

[3] . . . *nullum in manu ferens ferramentum* . . . , which we can translate as "weapons."

ninth century, the field of our study is suddenly illuminated by numerous, precise, and extremely revealing documents.

Starting in the reign of Pepin the Short in the eighth century, ecclesiastical letters, legislative directives, and even the accounts of Arab travelers note the presence, within the Carolingian Empire, of a number of prosperous Jews: great merchants (the Carolingian ordinances mention *negotiatores judeai et alii:* Jewish merchants and others), great travelers ("they speak Persian, Arabic, Greek, as well as the languages of the Franks, the Spanish, and the Slavs. They travel from west to east and from east to west, both by land and by sea . . .") (27), and landowners and farmers (28). Under Louis the Pious (Holy Roman Emperor Louis I) they were granted "letters of protection," authorizing them to live according to their own laws and especially prohibiting the baptism of their slaves. In favor at court, they managed on occasion to recruit proselytes among the Christians, which provoked the clergy to increasingly violent polemics against them. Archbishops Agobard and Amolon of Lyons were ready to resort to open combat. It may be an exaggeration to claim, with the Protestant historian Wiegand, that "all the anti-Semitism of the Middle Ages has its source in Agobard." At any rate, his campaigns may be regarded as a point of departure during a period when evangelization, functioning in depth, called for the "recrudescence of religious feeling in men's souls." The numerous anti-Jewish texts of Agobard and Amolon, almost all preserved intact, enable us to discover the status of the Jews in the Carolingian Empire and the attitude of the Christians toward them, as well as the specific reasons for the renewal of ecclesiastical hostility. Hence we shall examine them in some detail. But first let us consider the background of the conflict that centered in Lyons.

Archbishop Agobard (778-840), "the most enlightened man of his age," according to Henri Martin, belonged to the host of learned and active reformers of what has been called the "Carolingian renaissance." Greatly disturbed by the influence over his flock acquired by the Jewish colony of Lyons, he appealed to Emperor Louis the Pious, reminding him of the traditional council decisions and begging him for authorization to baptize the slaves of the Jews. Far from granting this request, the emperor expressly confirmed the privileges of the Jews and sent the *magister judaeorum*[4] Everard to Lyons to ensure their being upheld. The quarrel soon grew bitter. Puffed up with his own importance, exiled to Nantua, the fiery prelate Agobard (who, in the conflict between Louis the Pious and his sons, had sided with the latter) did not consider himself beaten and, year after year, continued to return to the attack. It was under such conditions that he wrote the five anti-Jewish epistles we possess (29), and thus we know that the Jews lived freely among the people of Lyons, kept open house, had Christian servants, and, far from permitting themselves to be won over by the archbishop's preaching or permitting their pagan slaves to be baptized, they managed to win followers even among the Christians. But let us hear Agobard himself:

"No matter how kindly we treat them, we do not succeed in drawing them to the purity of our spiritual faith. On the contrary, several among us, willingly sharing with them the food of the body, have also allowed themselves to be seduced by their spiritual nourishment." In effect, ". . . matters have reached the point where the ignorant Christians claim that the Jews preach better than our own priests. . . . Some Christians even celebrate the Sabbath with the Jews and violate the blessed day of rest. Many women live as domestics or as paid laborers of the Jews, who lure some from their faith. Laborers and peasants are inveigled into such a sea of errors that they regard the Jews as the only people of God, so that only among them is to be found the observance of a pure religion and of a faith far more certain than our own. . . ." And Agobard goes on to complain bitterly of the sacrilegious fables that the Jews spread abroad concerning

[4] Apparently this title referred to the official in charge of relations with the Jewish communities and the protection of their rights.

Jesus, the Virgin Mary, and the apostles. He confronts the emperor with his responsibilities: "The Jews, abusing the naïveté of the Christians, deceitfully pride themselves on being dear to your heart, because of the patriarchs from whom they are descended. . . . They exhibit orders and warrants bearing your gold seal and containing words that I cannot believe to be true. They display the dresses that their wives, they claim, have received from your family and from the ladies of the palace; they boast of having received from you, contrary to the law, the right to build new synagogues."

Corresponding to this ascendancy over souls is the Jewish influence upon manners and customs. "So that the Jews might celebrate freely their Sabbath, the 'missi' [regional administrators] have ordered the market to be transferred from Saturday to another day, leaving to the Jews even the choice of the day of the week. . . ."

Yet for all Agobard's impassioned indignation, nowhere does he accuse the Jews of those diabolical practices—profanation of the Host, ritual murder, poisoning of wells—that in later times will constitute the leitmotiv of the anti-Jewish campaigns. Agobard's argument is entirely on the level of a theological polemic; it is "Jewish superstitions" that he attacks. The remedies he advocates, intended to protect the souls of his flock from the contagion of Judaism, are limited to assuring a better separation between Christians and Jews, aided by a strict observance of the old decisions of the council. He deals with putting an end to meals taken in common, of forbidding the Jews to own Christian slaves or servants, and so on. Twenty years later his successor, Amolon, was to reiterate and stress these exhortations: ". . . cursing the infidelity of the Jews and seeking to protect the Christian people from contagion, I have thrice publicly asked that our faithful draw aside from them, that no Christian serve them either in the cities or in the villages, letting them perform their labor with the help of their pagan slaves; I have also forbidden the eating of their food and the drinking of their liquors. And I have published several other severe injunctions, in order to tear out the evil by the root and to imitate the example of our pious master, shepherd, and predecessor Agobard . . ." (30). The bishops Hincmar of Rheims, Vanilo of Sens, and Rodolphe of Bourges lent their support to Amolon, and in 848 the Council of Meaux demanded the enforcement of the ancient canonical decisions and of the edicts of Theodore II.

It will be noted that such decisions, if enforced, would inevitably have brought about a deterioration in the Jews' economic status. We have not yet reached this point, and the directives issued by Agobard, Amolon, or Hincmar to the temporal powers do not seem to have been very effective. Furthermore, the time was not yet ripe for vigorous action. This is the period of the Treaty of Verdun (843) and the chaotic feudal parceling out of land that followed. This is also the time of an innovation that was to have grave consequences. It was in the course of the ninth century (it is not possible to specify the exact date) that we note a significant modification of the Roman Catholic liturgy, in the section referring to the Jews. Hitherto, in the Good Friday prayers, the custom was to pray successively, and in the same terms, for the catechumens, the Jews, and the pagans, kneeling after each prayer. The missal was now changed to read: *Pro Judaeis non flectant* ("Do not genuflect to the Jews"). Thus it was emphasized that the Jew belonged to a category apart, that he was different from, and more than a simple infidel, thereby introducing a concept whose full effects were to be felt several centuries later.[5]

[5] According to M. Louis Canet ("The *Pro Judaeis* Prayer in the Roman Catholic Liturgy," *Revue d'Études Juives* [cited hereafter as *R.E.J.*], Vol. 41, 1906, p. 213), the modification appears for the first time in the sacramentary of Rethel (or of Saint-Vaast-en-Corbie), where a marginal note reads: *Hic nostrum nullus debet modo flectere corpus ob populi noxam ac pariter rabiem.* Hence it was the people who had insisted on the abolition of the genuflection. As M. Canet writes: "As far as can be judged, the practice had arisen by itself, and we must regard it as a manifestation of popular anti-Semitism." Even if this is the case, it is interesting to note that the effects of his kind of anti-Semitism make themselves felt for the first time in the century of Agobard and Amolon.

This concept begins to open up an entirely new field. This was the period in which the dramatic art of the Middle Ages, issuing, as we know, from the liturgy, took its first tentative steps. For centuries, ecclesiastical authorities had forbidden the transformation of the great religious festivals into spectacles and had prohibited singing and dancing in front of the churches. Now these prohibitions were dropped. The church service was extended into the courtyards of the cathedrals, a stage setting was roughly suggested, and thus was born the religious theater, whose favorite subjects at Easter were to be the Crucifixion and the Resurrection, as well as the Church's victory over the Synagogue. Was the license thus granted to humor the masses an indication of the impotence of the clergy to eradicate the vestiges of paganism? Was this the celebration of the eternal myth of spring's victory over winter, to which the Church had to adapt itself and which it proceeded to symbolize? It matters little. The fact is that henceforth the anti-Semitic theme took hold. It will also be found in the art of many sacramentary and ritual objects where the Church and the Synagogue are personified, the former with the features of a resplendent young woman, the latter as a widow with bandaged eyes. This had been a theme familiar to the Doctors of the Church since the time of Augustine, but one that had not penetrated to the masses. But now they were being indoctrinated as vigorously as possible with the idea of a unique and special role of the Jews. However, we must also note that it was only Jewish unbelief and arrogance that were being attacked: not a single text of this period mentions the wickedness and perfidy of the deicidal race.

Thus, we may draw the following conclusions:

The very terms of anti-Jewish propaganda in the ninth century show that at this time there was no trace of a specific, popular anti-Semitism. On the contrary, it seems that Judaism still exerted a definite attraction for the Christian population. In general, one may say that so long as a solidly dogmatized Christianity had not established its complete ascendancy over men's souls, these remained receptive to Jewish propaganda. Indeed, we find the same state of affairs in the East in the third and fourth centuries, in the West in the high Middle Ages, and, as we shall see, in Russia during the fifteenth century.[6] Once the rudiments of Jewish history are impressed upon newly converted populations, many persons "regard the Jews as the only people of God . . . cherished because of the patriarchs from whom they are descended" (Agobard). This point of view, which, granted, is not without a naïve logic, leads converts to lend an attentive ear to the arguments of the Jews. In Carolingian France, conversions to Judaism must have been even more frequent, since the Jews' privileged economic status enabled them to exert pressure upon their slaves and servants. There are no statistics, of course, but even some high dignitaries of the Church were won over by the Jewish "seduction," as is shown by the famous example of Deacon Bodon, confessor to Louis the Pious, who was converted to Judaism and fled to Spain, where, adopting the name Eleazar, he married a Jewess (829). It is in this light that we must consider the campaigns of his contemporaries Agobard and Amolon.

Furthermore, the close juxtaposition of Jews and Christians gave rise to frequent intermarriages, as we already noted in imperial Rome. Actually, we are dealing with a true amalgamation; extending over some ten centuries, it led a Renan or a Leroy-Beaulieu in the last century to assume that the Jews were at least partially of European ancestry. In the absence of any precise statistical data, we can advance merely a hypothesis. In our times (see Appendix A), research in genetics permits one to conclude that this was a complete amalgamation, a total "panmixia" (which amounts to saying jokingly that M. Israel Levy is as likely as his concierge to be a direct descendant of Vercingetorix). This observation has a certain piquancy about it, if we think of the stubborn persistence of "racial" interpretations of the Jewish ques-

[6] Cf. Chap. 12.

tion by authors who are sometimes far from being anti-
Semites!

The favorable status of the Jews in Carolingian Europe
led to a rapid multiplication of Jewish settlements. Prosperous communities appeared in Champagne, in Lorraine, in
the Rhenish villages, and as far away as Prague. Colonization proceeded eastward, and until the twelfth century
French was the usual language of the Jewish communities
in Germany, as well as in France.[7] Kings, nobles, and bishops granted the Jews a broad autonomy: thus they administered their own communities and lived according to their
own laws. Talmudic scholarship flowered again on the banks
of the Rhine and the Seine at the very period when it was
falling into decay in Babylonia. In Troyes, the celebrated
Rashi wrote commentaries on the Bible and the Talmud that
even today form an integral part of traditional Jewish education. As in the preceding centuries, the Jews constituted a
commercial guild par excellence, with vast international connections, and while they preferred to establish themselves in neighborhoods of their own, they continued to mix
freely with the Christian populations and to live on excellent terms with them. It is true that, increasingly, the chroniclers of the period tend to couple with the word "Jew" some
pejorative epithet, and the accusation of witchcraft becomes

[7] This is particularly evident from the Biblical and Talmudic commentaries written in eastern France in the eleventh and twelfth centuries, in
which we find many French words (glosses) transcribed in Hebrew characters. Such texts constitute a valuable source of information as to the
pronunciation of the vulgar French of the period. It was only very gradually
that German replaced French as the normal speech of the German Jews, and
certain French locutions have lasted down to our own day; traces of them
are to be found in the Yiddish of the Polish Jews. We might cite, for example, *tcholnt* (hot dish), which comes from the old French verb *chaloir,* as
well as the given name *Yenta* (Jeannette). Similarly, the characteristic expression *bobbe-mayseh* (tall story) takes its origin from the adventures of
the Sire de Beauvais; under the name *Bova-Buch,* these were very popular
among the German Jews of the Middle Ages.

a commonplace. Yet these molders of public opinion were all churchmen, writing with a definite purpose: all the more significant, then, that until the eleventh century, no chronicles mention outbursts of popular hatred of the Jews (31).

But shortly after the year 1000, vague rumors began to agitate Christendom. At the instigation of the Jews, the "prince of Babylon" had caused the destruction of the Holy Sepulcher; he had also launched countless persecutions against the Christians of the Holy Land and had caused the patriarch of Jerusalem to be beheaded. Whatever the truth of the Eastern accounts[8] (in reality, the intolerant Emir Al-Hakim oppressed the Jews as much as the Christians), in the West, princes, bishops, and villagers immediately began to seek revenge against the Jews. In Rouen (32), in Orléans (33), in Limoges (1010) (34), in Mainz (1012) and doubtless other Rhenish villages (35), and apparently in Rome as well (36), Jews were converted by force, massacred, or expelled, and the imaginative monk Raoul Glaber even assures us that "throughout the world, Christians were unanimous in deciding that they would drive all the Jews from their lands and their cities." This was an obvious exaggeration, for the wave subsided as quickly as it had arisen; this was merely the premonitory sign of that tide of religious enthusiasm that, though it was to serve as indispensable mortar to the structure of medieval Christianity, would also give the signal for the great persecutions. The status of the Jews remained sufficiently enviable for noteworthy conversions to Judaism still to be made,[9] and when, in 1084, Rüdiger, bishop of Speyer, granted the Jews a charter, it stated that their presence "greatly increases the renown of the city,"

[8] Perhaps the legend has its source in an historical fact, mentioned by several Arabic chroniclers, that had occurred four centuries before: In 614 the Jews of Jerusalem, persecuted by the Christians, surrendered the city to the Persians. (Cf. J. Juster, *op. cit.*, Vol. 2, p. 213.)

[9] For example, that of Vécelin, chaplain of Duke Konrad, a relative of the Holy Roman Emperor Henri II (1005) (Pertz, *Monumenta*, Vol. 2, p. 93); or that of Renant, Duke of Sens (1015) (Glaber, *Les Histoires*, III, 6).

and authorized them, in defiance of traditional prohibitions, to keep Christian servants and serfs, to own fields and vineyards, and to carry arms (37).

Rüdiger's charter is dated 1084. It would certainly have been inconceivable a few decades later. We have reached the eve of that crisis in the development of Christianity, the Crusades.

PART TWO
THE AGE OF
THE CRUSADES

four

The Fateful Summer
of 1096

Few dates are as important in Western history as that November 27, 1095, when, at the Council of Clermont-Ferrand,
Pope Urban II undertook to preach the First Crusade—without suspecting, we may well believe, the enormous chain of
events his appeal would set off throughout Christendom. The
great role the Crusades were to play in the development of
medieval civilization is well known: a general awakening of
commercial and intellectual activities, followed by the rise
of the urban bourgeoisie and, above all, that growing self-
awareness of Christian Europe already reflected in the chronicles of the first Crusades (38). But less attention is usually
paid to the consequences of the great enterprise on the
destiny of the Jews, which destiny was henceforth to be
singular and unique in Europe.

And yet here the historian finds himself in a privileged
position, so numerous and eloquent are the texts. Let us try,
then, to imagine ourselves in this heroic, chaotic age, in
which, with the battle cry *Dieu le veult,* knights, monks,
and commoners, having abandoned their families and their
homes, pursued their course toward a legendary destina-
tion. On their clothing they sewed the sign of the Cross.
Whatever they did, eternal felicity had been promised
them; they were God's avengers, appointed to punish all infidels, whoever they might be. The chroniclers state this explicitly: *Omnes siquidem illi viatores, Judaeos, haeretios,
Sarracenos acqualiter habeant exosos, quos omnes Dei ap-
pelant inimicos* (39). Therefore, what could be more nat-

ural than to take revenge, along the way, upon the various infidels living in Christian territories? Would not anything else be "to start the whole affair backward" (as the Crusaders were to say in Rouen)?[1] This reasoning was not without its cruel logic, and we shall hear it again in other times and other places.[2] Especially for the scum that always rises to the surface during great revolutionary movements, it served as a pretext for easy and lucrative pillaging. Thus the perpetrators of the chief massacres of Jews were not the organized armies of the barons but the formless mobs that preceded them.

Of course, not all the details have come down to us. As for France in particular, only one massacre in Rouen is known with certainty. But some chronicles allude to other brutalities—for example, Richard of Poitiers (". . . before journeying to these places, they [the Crusaders] exterminated by many massacres the Jews of almost all Gaul, with the exception of those who accepted conversion. They said in effect that it was unjust to permit enemies of Christ to remain alive in their own country, when they had taken up arms to drive out the infidels abroad") (40)—and this is confirmed by Jewish sources. In an urgent letter, the French Jewish communities warned their coreligionists in Germany of the danger that threatened them. We also know the latters' answer. Though the German Jews prayed for their brothers in distress, they were confidently assured that for their own part they had nothing to fear (41). An unwarranted optimism, if ever there was one. It was in Germany, in this very Rhine Valley whose Jewish communities were probably the most

[1] As reported by the chronicler Guibert de Nogent, the Rouen Crusaders said: "We desire to go and fight God's enemies in the East; but we have before our eyes certain Jews, a race more inimical to God than any other: this is to start the whole affair backward" (Guibert de Nogent, in Migne's *Patrologiae* [Latin], Vol. 156).

[2] As among the French revolutionaries of 1792, eager to press on to the borders: "Each exclaimed: 'On to the enemy! But our enemies are here; they are in Paris as in Verdun; they are in the prisons. Shall we leave our wives, our children, our old parents at the mercy of these criminals? To the prisons, exterminate all the monsters! . . .'" (From a newspaper of the period).

numerous in Europe at the period, that the most systematic and bloody massacres were perpetrated.

As for Peter the Hermit, that fiery preacher of the People's Crusade—the First Crusade—he seems to have operated quite realistically, abstaining from futile excesses and limiting himself to levying contributions on the Jews in order to assure money and supplies for his troops (42). Quite different was the case of the various bands led by French as well as German lords—Guillaume le Charpentier, Thomas de Feria, and especially Emicho von Leiringen ("a most noble and powerful man," according to Albert of Aix) (43)—who, traveling down the Rhine Valley, massacred in a systematic and regular manner.[3]

The spirit of pillage that characterized the undertaking resulted from Emicho's methods; occasionally, before putting Jews to death, Emicho ransomed them in order to "protect" them. The religious aspect is emphasized by the alternative with which the Jews were inevitably confronted: baptism— or death. A first attempt at a massacre occurred at Speyer on May 3, 1096, but thanks to the swift intervention of Bishop Jean of that city, who forced Emicho's men to disperse, only eleven Jews were killed. Matters turned out differently at Worms, two weeks later.

When the news of the events at Speyer reached Worms, one part of the Jewish community sought refuge in the palace of Bishop Adalbert; other Jews remained in their homes, the burghers of the city having promised to help them. All met the same fate. Those who had remained at home were massacred first, on May 18; subsequently, Adalbert's protégés, refusing to accept Christianity, were killed by the bishop

[3] Various historians (especially H. Graetz, in his monumental *History of the Jews*, as well as F. Chalandon in his *Histoire de la Première Croisade*, Paris, 1925) have tried to reconstruct Emicho's itinerary. Taking the chronology of the massacres into account, it appears that Emicho's troops descended the Rhine Valley from Speyer to Mainz, where at least part of the band, instead of following the valley of the Main River (toward Hungary), continued up the Moselle (Trier and Metz massacres). But, for example, nothing is known of the perpetrators of the Cologne massacres.

himself on May 25. But let us hear the story from the Jewish chronicler Solomon bar Simeon:

"On the twenty-fifth day of the month Iyar, the terror fell upon those who were living in the episcopal palace. The foe killed them even as the others, putting them to the sword. They sustained themselves by the example of their brothers, let themselves be massacred and hallowed the Name. . . . They fulfilled the words of the prophet: 'The mothers are laid upon their children, the father fell upon his sons.' This one killed his brother, that one his parents, his wife, and his children; the betrothed killed each other, even as the mothers killed their children. All accepted with a full heart the divine verdict. Recommending their souls to the Eternal, they cried: 'Hear, O Israel, the Eternal is our God, the Eternal is the One God.' The enemies stripped them naked and dragged them off, granting quarter to none, save those few who accepted baptism. The number of the slain was eight hundred in these two days. . . ."

Two days later came the turn of the Jews of Mainz, who briefly attempted to defend themselves, according to Albert of Aix. (The striking parallel between the two accounts should be noted: the indignation of the Christian chronicler is scarcely less than that of the Jewish narrator):

"Emicho and all his men, having taken counsel, proceeded at sunrise to attack the Jews with lances and axes. . . . Having broken the locks and knocked in the doors, they seized and killed seven hundred who vainly sought to defend themselves against forces far superior to their own; the women were also massacred, and the young children, whatever their sex, were put to the sword. The Jews, seeing the Christians rise as enemies against them and their children, with no respect for the weakness of age, took arms in turn against their coreligionists, against their wives, their children, their mothers, and their sisters, and massacred their own. A horrible thing to tell of—the mothers seized the sword, cut the throats of the children at their breast, choosing to destroy themselves with their own hands rather than to succumb to the blows of the uncircumcised! Only a small number of Jews escaped this cruel massacre, and a few accepted baptism, much more out of the fear of death than from love of the Christian faith."

The Jews of Cologne had a month's respite, having been able to take shelter for some days with their Christian neighbors and friends. With the help of the archbishop, they then sought refuge in nearby localities,[4] where they were surprised by the Crusaders at the end of June. Faced with the obligatory choice, most of them resorted to the supreme defiance of suicide. Those of Trier for the most part sought salvation in baptism, in this following the example of Rabbi Micah, who declared that "it was better to be a Christian than to tremble for one's life day and night" (44). Those of Regensburg, baptized forcibly in the Danube, immediately recanted after the departure of the Crusaders. Massacres occurred at Metz and Bamberg, as well as in other German cities impossible to identify.[5]

It is important to note that almost everywhere, counts and bishops (Adalbert in Worms, Archbishop Ruthard in Mainz, Archbishop Hermann III in Cologne, the Count of Mörs, etc.) attempted, sometimes even at the peril of their lives, to protect the Jews, yielding to the Crusaders only under constraint and the show of force. As for the people, sympathy and horror seem to have been their first reactions, and we see from the example of Cologne that they occasionally afforded the Jews effective support. Only the dregs of the population everywhere joined the slaughterers.

A final massacre occurred in Prague, despite the efforts of Bishop Cosmas. The total number of victims, variously estimated according to the sources used, amounted to several thousand at least.

[4] Neuss, Altenahr, Wevelinghofen, Kerpen, Hanten, Mörs (Aronius, *Regesten*, Nos. 190-96).

[5] To reconstruct the map of the massacres of the First Crusade, the historians proceed by checking Jewish against Christian sources. Since the Jewish chronicles were written in Hebrew, the names of certain localities, transcribed in Hebrew characters, have remained indecipherable.

But numbers are irrelevant, for here we confront a decisive moment of our history. Obstinate, heroic (some will say fanatical), the Jews of the Rhine Valley, unlike those of Spain or the Oriental countries, preferred to die rather than yield to even the semblance of a conversion. How explain this difference in attitude? Is it because they despised the boors and bandits who tried to preach an abhorred gospel to them? Or more simply because, faced with a brutal alternative, they simply had no time for those gradual concessions, those secret compromises characteristic of the ·*anusim* of North Africa or the marranos of Spain? In any case, just as a glowing steel blade suddenly thrust into icy water acquires great toughness and strength, similarly the sudden ordeal of the summer of 1096, a thunderbolt out of a blue sky, had the effect of forging the power to resist, characteristic henceforth of the European Jews. It matters little that on certain points our sources remain vague, that we may dispute endlessly the exact number of victims, which, in any case, compared to the holocausts of the centuries to come, seems insignificant. What does matter is that during these months a tradition took root: that of a heroic and complete refusal by a tiny minority in opposition to the majority; that of the sacrifice of life "to hallow the Name"—a tradition that was to serve as inspiration and example for future generations.

The squall once past, and the figures of the Crusaders blurring in the distance, our information once again becomes scanty. All we know is that on his way back from Italy, Emperor Henry IV expressly authorized the Jews who had been baptized by force to return to their former faith (and thus began a special relationship between the Holy Roman emperor, the designated protector, and the Jews under obligation to him, which was subsequently to lead to the theory of the "bondage" of the German Jews). We also know that in a letter to the bishop of Bamberg, Pope Clement III strongly opposed the position of Henry IV (thereby expressing a fundamental tenent of the Catholic Church that has remained immutable down to our own day).[6] We know, lastly, that two years after the massacres, the Jews of Prague attempted to flee to Poland and to Hungary—an attempt that failed and that served as an excuse for Duke Bratislas to authorize new pillaging. It is not known if other attempts of the same nature were made elsewhere. At Mainz, several chroniclers report long disputes on the subject of the stolen goods of massacred Jews, which Henry IV accused Archbishop Ruthard of having appropriated—while he regarded himself as the legitimate heir. Elsewhere, apparently, the status of the Jews returned, at least outwardly, to what it had been. Protected by the emperors, they resumed their habitual occupations, chiefly as merchants. For several decades there is virtually no mention of persecutions against them in either Germany or France, or in England, where they had meanwhile estab-

[6] The canonical theory of "forced baptism" is one of great subtlety. Even in the twelfth century, it was commonly thought that for baptism to be invalid, it was not enough to have been secured by force or threat, but that an express declaration of protest or unwillingness had to be made at the precise moment of that baptism.

This is expressed in the bull of Innocent III in September, 1201:

"Assuredly, it is contrary to the Christian faith that one who is unwilling and totally opposed to it be constrained to adopt and observe Christianity. For this reason, some make a distinction, which is valid, between those who are unwilling and those who are constrained. It is thus that he who is led to Christianity by violence, by fear, and by torture, and who receives the sacrament of baptism to avoid harm (even as he who comes falsely to baptism), receives indeed the stamp of Christianity and can be obliged to observe the Christian faith, even as he who expresses a conditional will, although in absolute terms he is unwilling. It is in this fashion that the decree of the Council of Toledo must be understood, which stated that those who previously had been forced to become Christians, as was done in the time of the most pious Prince Sisebut, and their association with the divine sacraments having been established, by the grace of the baptism received, they themselves having been anointed with the holy oil and having participated in the body of the Lord, must be duly constrained to abide by the faith they had accepted by force. However, he who has never consented, but has altogether opposed it, has received neither the stamp nor the purpose, for it is better to object expressly than to manifest the slightest consent . . ." (A. Potthast, *Regesta Pontificum Romanorum*, Berlin, 1875, No. 1479).

Since those who "objected expressly" to a forced baptism were generally executed on the spot, all cases of baptism became valid in practical terms.

lished a compact and prosperous community. They seem to have associated with clerics on a friendly basis. We even find a bishop of Prague reproaching himself on his deathbed for having been too intimate with them.[7] We also find an abbé of Cologne receiving Jewish men and women on friendly visits (45). The same impression of an excellent relationship is communicated by a curious little work in which the monk Hermann, a converted Jew, writes his autobiography and examines his conscience (46).

Such was the case until the gradual weakening of the free states of the Levant and the fall of Urfa (Edessa) impelled Pope Eugenius III and Saint Bernard of Clairvaux to preach a new Crusade in 1146. We know that this second expedition, though better prepared and more disciplined than the first, led by the king of France and the emperor of Germany in person, provoked no great popular movement comparable to that of 1096. Still, its preaching was accompanied by excesses against the Jews, perpetrated in many places on a vast scale. And what had been only a popular and spontaneous outbreak fifty years before was this time doctrinally exploited by fiery monk-preachers. Thus Abbé Pierre of Cluny in France: "What is the good of going to the end of the world, at great loss of men and money, to fight the Saracens, when we permit among us other infidels who are a thousand times more guilty toward Christ than the Mohammedans?" (47). Thus the monk Rudolf in Germany: ". . . First avenge the Crucified upon His enemies living here among us, and then go off to fight against the Turks!" (48). Such propaganda had less immediate consequence than the popular excesses of 1096. The times were already more orderly, so that princes and bishops generally managed to protect the Jews from the rage of crowds, while Bernard of Clairvaux personally called

[7] *Vae mihi quia silu, quia apostatricem genetem non revocavi, nec in gladio anathematis pro Christo dimicavi; sed me ipsum et populum christianum passus sum per tactum manus cum gente non sancta pollui . . .* (Cosm. Chron. Boem, 4, Cap. 49, *Monumenta Germaniae Historia* [hereafter referred to as *M.G.H.*], *Scripta Sanctorum* [hereafter, SS], Vol. 9, p. 125).

the popular agitators to task, showing them the theological danger of the undertaking. (Did they not risk, by provoking the extermination of the Jews, eliminating the Church's great hope of their conversion?) (49). The chronicle refers to incidents and massacres only in Cologne, Speyer, Mainz, and Würzburg in Germany, and in Carentan, Ramerupt, and Sully in France; the number of victims this time reached only several hundred at most. But the chronicles also relate something else: It was precisely at this period that there appeared for the first time, in two different places —in an obscurely defined form in Germany, more clearly in England—the accusation of ritual murder, followed by the accusation of the profanation of the Host. (These two imputations constitute only one in reality, since the murder of a Christian child and the offense against Christ substantialized are both dominated by the same concept of sacrilege.) From this point of view, too, 1146 marks a new age.

Thus, each time medieval Europe was swept by a great movement of faith, each time the Christians set out to face the unknown in the name of the love of God, hatred of the Jews was fanned into flame virtually everywhere. And the more the pious impulses of the heart sought satisfaction in action, the worse became the Jews' lot.

Virtually every time a Crusade was preached, the same consequences could be anticipated. In 1183 (the Third Crusade), there were great massacres in England—in London, York, Norwich, Stamford, and Lynn; twenty years later, at the time of the Albigensian Crusade, there were persecutions in the Midi. When a Crusade was ineffectually preached in 1236, massacres also occurred in western France, in England, and in Spain, which the good Benedictine Dom Lobineau describes thus:

"There were few lords who in the first fervor of the preaching did not find the Cross light to bear; but to many it became a burden thereafter. To remedy this discomfort, they were permitted to renounce the vow they had made to serve against the Infidel. . . . The greatest and the first expedition of these crusaders was to massacre the Jews, who were not the cause of the evils which the Saracens were inflicting upon the Christians in the East. The Bretons, Angevins, Poitevins, Spaniards, and English were conspicuous in this cruel expedition of the year 1236 . . ." (50).

Once the era of Crusades organized by nobles and lords was past, there followed the massacres perpetrated amid the final outbreaks of popular fanaticism, in the general context of the social crisis of the early fourteenth century: mass uprisings in Germany at the time of the abortive Crusade of 1309, and massacres in Cologne, the Low Countries, and Brabant; the "Shepherd's Crusade" in the Midi in 1320, and massacres in Bordeaux, Toulouse, Albi, and even Spain (the striking description is given on pp. 102 ff). The broad outlines of the story always remain the same: looting; desperate flight; inability of the princes to protect the Jews when "multitudes inconsolable for the offense to the living God rushed to slaughter them" (51); asylums or fortresses taken by assault; mass suicides. This permanent Calvary was unlikely to inspire, in the hearts of those Jews whom, theologically, it was so important to convert, the love of Our Lord Jesus Christ. While the reaction of the Jews was undergoing gradual crystallization, these events also brought great changes in the attitude of the Christians toward the Jews.

The first great persecutions and public opinion

As we have said, mention of the Jews, so rare in the centuries preceding the First Crusade, becomes much more frequent with it. We possess nearly a dozen narratives by various chroniclers referring only to the massacres of 1096. It is true that these are the accounts of clerics, the intellectuals of the period; what the barons or the masses may have thought we can only guess, but let us recall that our informants are the very men who helped form the public opinion of their times.

Let us try, then, to discover the impression these events left upon them.

One anonymous chronicler, writing a kind of journal in his Prague monastery, condenses into a few words what seemed to him the most salient event of each year. In 1094 this event was a dynastic change: his king, Wratislas, died and was succeeded by Bratislas. In 1095 it was the ordination of his bishop, Cosmas. And in 1096 it was the massacre of the Jews: "There has been a massacre and Jews were baptized," he notes laconically (52). (As for the Crusade as such, it is not even mentioned.) In other words, the event in question is one that vividly appealed to the imagination of certain of his contemporaries.

As for what they themselves thought of the massacre, some chroniclers mention it in a placid and disinterested tone, discussing the facts "objectively," as we would say today, like the Prague chronicler or this annalist of Würzburg in Bavaria: "An enormous host, coming from all regions and all nations, went in arms unto Jerusalem and obliged the Jews to be baptized, massacring by thousands those who refused. Near Mainz, 1014 Jews, men, women, and children, were slaughtered, and the greatest part of the city burned . . ." (53).

Others do not conceal their satisfaction. Thus the monk Bernhold, speaking of the Jews of Worms:

"While the crusaders awaited their reply without, the Jews, tempted by the Devil and under the rule of their own obduracy, killed themselves in the apartments of the bishop" (54).

Or the chronicler Fruitolf:

"In the villages they traversed, the latter [the Crusaders] killed or forced baptism upon what remained of those impious Jews, who are truly enemies which the Church tolerates in its bosom. Of these there was a certain number that returned to Judaism, even as dogs to their own vomit . . ." (55).

Still others condemn the massacres with more or less violence. "It may, forsooth, appear wonderful that in a single day but one massacre animated by the same mystical fervor can have taken place in various and numerous places," comments the monk Hugon. "This occurred despite the fact that the clergy was hostile to it and despite the sentences of excommunication by many ecclesiastics and the threats of numerous princes" (56). The criticism is much more violent in an anonymous Saxon chronicle:

". . . the enemy of mankind lost no time sowing tares among the wheat, raising up false prophets, mingling untrue brothers and licentious women with the army of Christ. By their hypocrisy, by their lies, by their impious corruptions, they caused dissension in the army of the Lord. . . . They decided to avenge Christ upon the pagans and the Jews. This is why they killed 900 Jews in the city of Mainz without sparing the women and children. . . . Indeed, it was pitiful to see the great and many heaps of bodies that were carried out of the city of Mainz on carts . . ." (57).

Stronger still, as we have seen above (pp. 44 f.), was the indignation of Albert of Aix, who attributed the defeat of the "People's Crusade" to divine punishment, seeing in it a just retribution for excesses committed on the way. In general, it might be said that the Crusaders were far from being universally approved by the authors of our chronicles. Their violence and plundering generally disturbed these peaceful clerics. Emicho von Leiringen, the German baron who was the architect of the principal massacres, had a particularly bad press. (Furthermore, two of our sources[8] suggest that this "beast" was a converted Jew, but there is no convincing support for this hypothesis, such rumors appearing regularly concerning the great persecutors of the Jews.[9] However, this

[8] Ekkehardt and the anonymous Saxon.

[9] Among others, Adolf Hitler. It has been claimed that the Führer was the illegitimate son of an Austrian Jew; that his minister of justice, Hans Frank, was assigned, even before the Nazis came to power, to deal with the blackmailers who possessed proofs of this descent, etc.

presents an interesting clue: it was not unthinkable, in 1096, that a converted Jew should become a plundering baron, a great captain!)

We may say, then, that at the start public opinion appears disturbed and divided. But primarily, the events just described had as their principal effect a recrudescence of hostility toward the Jews. This is a phenomenon we shall encounter many times in the course of our study, one that is readily explained. The killers, in general, only hate their victims more; the simple witnesses decide that there must be a reason for the killing; finally, the profiteers, the pillagers and looters great and small, fear the return of those who have escaped. In this context, the massacres of 1096 mark the beginning of the gradual deterioration of the status of the Jews. Furthermore, another causal link, also connected with the Crusades, had the same result. Once the eastern routes were open to Europeans, Italian merchants increasingly supplanted the Jews as businessmen, and the rise of the urban bourgeoisie in the rapidly growing cities was to effect a similar displacement.

We shall deal further with this fundamental aspect of the question; let us here confine ourselves to observing how this development began to be reflected in contemporary public opinion.

National literatures first appear in France and Germany during the twelfth century, written in the vernacular and addressing an audience much larger than the limited public of the clerics. In religious inspirational works, Jews appear quite frequently, but the way in which they are represented is still ambivalent. Thus many of the "miracles" are concerned with the conversion of Jews: the obdurate, those who do not accept baptism, are described with great loathing. For example, in Gautier de Coincy:

Plus bestial que bestes nues	More bestial than naked beasts
Sont tuit Juif, ce n'est pas	Are all Jews, without a
doute . . .	doubt . . .

Moult les hair, et je les haiz,	Many hate them, as do I,
Et Dieu les het, et je si faiz	And God hates them, as well I wist,
Et touz li mons les doit haïr (58).	And everyone must hate them indeed.

On the other hand, the Jewish child touched by grace is depicted by the same author as:

Mieus antendant et moult plus bel	Wiser still and much lovelier
De tous les autres Juiti-aus . . .	Than all the other Jews . . .
Aus enfants chrestiens faisoit moult bele chiere	To Christian children he looked full fair
Avec eulz se jouoit et avant et arriere	And played with them 'both before and behind'
Sans le Juitel ne savoient riens fere . . . (59).	Without the Jew, they knew not what to do . . .

The little Jew plays, then, with Christian children, despite his father's disapproval. This father is a glassmaker, a resident of Bourges—clues that cast some light on the social condition of the Jews at the end of the twelfth century and on their relations with Christians.

Similarly, the wife of a rich Jew, who subsequently is converted, is described as *moult vaillante et charitable femme en sa loy* ("a most brave and charitable woman under her law") (60).

We find the same elements in the *Dialogus Miraculorum,* written by the German author Caesarius of Heisterbach in 1219. A little Jewish girl of Louvain is baptized and enters a convent. Through intrigue and corruption, her father extorts an order from the bishop of Liége obliging the mother superior to return his daughter because she is a minor. The duke also becomes involved, and papal intervention is required for the triumph of good principles. Certain points of the story are perhaps authentic. The reader cannot help being struck by a curious reflection that the author puts in the girl's mouth, when she is scarcely five years old. The child, in fact, is astonished: how is it that Jews and Christians have a different name, since they speak the same language and are dressed in the same way?[10] Here we have a further suggestion of the state of Jewish "assimilation" still persisting from the twelfth to the fourteenth centuries.

And so long as this is the case, the Jew seems readily "redeemable," which perhaps explains the popularity at this time of the "disputations" in dialogue, at the end of which the Jew is finally won over and converts to Christianity. Some of these verses are in the vernacular, and we hear the Jew proclaim:

Nos somes decéu par trop fole atendance	Our foolish hope was in vain,
Fole atente nos a empechiez, decéuz,	And expectation has deceived us,
Celui atendions qui pieca est venuz	Waiting for one who has not come,
Messias est venus; je me vos baptizier	But Messiah has come: I shall be baptized
Et ma mauvaise secte guerpir et renvier (61).	And renounce my wicked sect.

Others, in Latin, reach the same denouement:

Nos erroris paenitet, ad finem convertimur:
Quidquid nobis inferet persecutor, partimur (62).

And in a twelfth-century Latin drama there is a Christian saint to whom a Jew has recourse in order to protect his wealth. He appoints the image of Saint Nicholas to guard it. The money is stolen, but Saint Nicholas appears and restores the treasure, and the Jew is converted (63). In another Latin drama of the same period, apparently of Austrian origin, the advent of Antichrist is represented on the stage

---

[10] *Cur distinctio nominum fieret Judaeorum pariter et christianorum cum unius vultus atque loquelae homines essent utriusque gentis* (Caesar. Heisterbac. *Dial. Mirac.*, 2, 25; Aronius, *Reg.*, No. 414).

(64). When Antichrist has gained dominion over the whole world, only the Synagogue remains in opposition. But this kind of homage is unique.

All this literature was accessible to only a part of Christendom, a part that was still quite limited. Nonetheless, the great cathedrals were now being built, those works of faith and love that were simultaneously religious and social encyclopedias, intelligible to the mass of the faithful. On their pediments the story of the Crucifixion was represented, in increasingly realistic detail. Also shown was the opposition between the Synagogue, a ruined widow with veiled eyes, and the Church, a shining warrior maiden.

Such is the canvas upon which will appear, a half-century after the First Crusade, the first specific and concrete grievances against the Jews. We have seen how they were massacred; now we shall see how they were accused of murder.

Ritual murder

The accusation of murder committed for magical or evil ends occurs in all countries and latitudes. Doubtless this is a consequence of the once universal practice of human sacrifice: abandoned and regarded with horror, the bloody ritual is imputed to the heretic, the enemy. Perhaps even the legends of children with their hands cut off or poisoned by candy, periodically recurrent in the course of present-day wars, are merely a modern disguise of this age-old myth. Thus in nineteenth-century China, Christian missionaries were accused of kidnaping children and tearing out their hearts or eyes to use in charms and remedies (65). In Indochina, it was to the Chettys sect that the population attributed this heinous crime (66). In Madagascar, in the time of Gallieni, the same accusation was lodged against agents of the French government.[11] In ancient times, this complaint was

[11] Which led the Madagascar government to publish the following edict in 1891:

addressed by the Greeks to the Jews; by the Romans to the early Christians; by the Christians to the Gnostics, the Montanists, or to other adherents of heretical sects. Thus we are dealing with a virtually universal theme, a veritable archetype that reappears at the surface wherever a society is confronted with disturbing and detested foreigners.

It appears that Christian society initially cherished no such animus toward the Jews, since we find no trace of this charge before the twelfth century. It also seems that this animosity arose as a consequence of the passions unleashed by the Crusades. For, spontaneously, between 1141 and 1150, the accusation appears in three different places and in three different forms; these, combined and giving rise to infinite variations, henceforth characterize the history of anti-Jewish persecutions down to our own day.

The theme achieved its final form—that of the murder of a Christian child in order to incorporate its blood in the unleavened bread—only after a long evolution. Initially, it was related to a Christian ceremony—the Passion—and not the Jewish Passover, the blood thus obtained (or else the heart or the liver) being intended for magical ends as atrocious as they were varied. A notion of vengeance prevails here, mingled with visions of a satanic pharmacopoeia. Essentially it is a repetition of the murder of Christ (in the flesh or in effigy), and Canon Thomas of Cantimpré even expresses astonishment at the ignorance of the Jews: to end their torments, only the blood of the true Christ could be of any help, and thus it was futile for them to attack an unfortunate Christian every year (67). Elsewhere, this theme was rapidly

---

"1) No alien, whether French, English, or of any other nation, seeks to buy human hearts. If evil-minded persons spread this rumor and say that foreigners are buying human hearts, seize, bind, and bring them to Tananarive to be tried.

"2) If rumors are spread, whatever their nature, it is your duty, as members of the government, to gather the people together, to warn them and to prove the falsity of these rumors, which are solemnly forbidden in the realm; it is a crime to circulate them." (Cf. *Le Temps* for February 25 and March 1, 1892.)

combined with the belief in a secret and mysterious Jewish society, a conclave of sages holding its sessions somewhere in a remote country and choosing by lot the place where the sacrifice was to be performed, as well as its performer. Thus the myth of the Elders of Zion was foreshadowed as early as the twelfth century.

As we have seen, the first case of ritual murder is reported in 1144, in England. The body of a young apprentice having been discovered on Good Friday eve in a woods near Norwich, the rumor spread that the boy had been murdered by the Jews, in mockery of the Passion of the Saviour. The accusers specified that the murder had been planned far in advance: a meeting of rabbis, convening at Narbonne, supposedly had designated Norwich as the place for the annual sacrifice. The authorities put no faith in the accusation, and the sheriff of the city attempted to protect the Jews. There were riots, however, and one of the prominent Jews of the district was murdered by an impecunious knight who happened to be his debtor. The case gave rise to a local cult; for several centuries, the relics of this Saint William, the young apprentice, were a goal of pilgrimages (68).

Thus from the start there are certain essential elements that, down through the centuries, will be characteristic of ritual murder. To them may be added another that also constantly recurs: a renegade Jew, recently baptized, allegedly furnishes the fantastic information about the motives of the crime and its mode of execution. In the Norwich case one of the chief accusers was the newly baptized monk, Theobald of Cambridge.

The next case seems to have been much more elementary. In 1147, in Würzburg, during the preaching of the Second Crusade, the body of a Christian was found in the Main. Immediately the Jews of the city were accused of the murder, and several of them were hunted down and massacred (69).

But the charge that arose three years later was infinitely more subtle and involved the theme of the profanation of the Host. This was already an old theme—it is to be found in Gregory of Tours—but previously it had been treated as a legend set in some remote Oriental place: Beirut or Antioch. For the first time, the facts are now related as though taking place quite nearby, before the narrator's eyes, a kind of "news bulletin"; most important, the profaned Host is transformed into the corpse of a little child. But let us turn to the chronicler of Liége, Jean d'Outremeuse, who assures us that in 1150 the following miracle occurred.

"In this year, it happened at Cologne that the son of a converted Jew went on Easter day to church, in order to receive the body of God, along with the others; he took it into his mouth and quickly bore it to his house; but when he returned from the church, he grew afraid and in his distress made a hole in the earth and buried the Host within it; but a priest came along, opened the hole, and in it found the shape of a child, which he intended to bear to the church; but there came from the sky a great light, the child was raised out of the priest's hands and borne up to heaven" (70).

The chronicler does not tell us if the affair led to a trial or what the fate of the profaner was.[12] Here, too, the essential elements are found together: the sacrilegious act of the Jew (who is a double renegade!), the transformation of the Host

[12] Let us note that an analogous case, described by the Jewish historian Joseph Ha-Cohen in his famous chronicle *Vale of Tears* (sixteenth century) seems to refer to the First Crusade. This is how he relates the episode, after having described at length the massacres of 1096:

"In the days of the Emperor Henry [Henry IV of Germany, reigned 1056-1106], ten wicked men accused a Jew of France, saying, 'He has boiled the Host with oil and water in a cauldron, we have watched, and behold, we have seen a child appear out of it.' When they sought to kill him, he escaped from their hands, but they rose as though to devour him alive, and the judges caused him to be seized and tortured, without his making any confession. But when they tortured his wife and his children, these latter admitted that which he had not intended or conceived, and they put him to the fire, holding the Talmud in his hand. And his sons and his wife they estranged from the Lord God of Israel. The rumor of this event having spread, all the inhabitants of the country rose against the Jews in the cities far from the court of the king, put many of them to the sword, and laid hands on the spoils." (*Vallée des Pleurs*, Julien Sée ed., Paris, 1881, p. 28.)

into living flesh, and one of those miracles that suited the clergy so perfectly. Can we discover why the accusation, in its two chief variants, appears at this precise period? Had the ancient fable been brought back to Europe by Crusaders returning from the Orient? Had it risen to the surface as a convenient religious justification for a debtor's attack on his creditor? Was it born spontaneously in the minds of the low clergy or of the preaching monks whose impassioned sermons, describing with a bloody and refined precision the sufferings of Christ and the martyrology of the saints, sowed an agitation and a remorse that were "projected" by troubled consciences onto the Jews? Was there an inexpressible relationship between the paschal lamb and the scapegoat? A shadowy complex of sin, guilt, and redemption is involved here; but nothing is more obscure than the way in which myths are born.

At least the circulation of this myth, as well as its effects, are well known. Accusations of ritual murder seem to have been rare at first—doubtless a legend of this kind spreads only after a certain incubation period.[13] Chronicles indicate several cases in England at the end of the twelfth century (71), and at the same time the fable spreads to the Continent. In 1171, at Blois, after due trial, thirty-eight Jews were burned at the stake; in 1191, at Bray-sur-Seine, the number of victims reached one hundred (72). But it was notably in the next century that the calumny spread, this time throughout Germany in particular, where the year 1236 alone was made infamous by several bloody executions for this alleged crime (73). The disorder reached such proportions that Emperor Frederick II became alarmed and charged a commission of high dignitaries to establish once and for all whether the terrible accusation of using human blood rested on any basis of truth. Princes and prelates found the question so difficult that they could not reach an agreement. As an enlightened man, the emperor then turned to superior spe-

[13] Similarly, the fable of the Elders of Zion, launched about 1900, began to circulate widely only after 1920.

cialists, that is, to converted Jews who, "having been Jews and having then been baptized into the Christian faith, could conceal nothing, as enemies of the other Jews, of what they might have learned against them in the Mosaic books . . ." (74). He summoned these converts from all the cities of the empire and even asked "all the kings of the West" to send him such men. He retained these experts at his court "for some considerable time" in order to permit them "to seek out the truth most diligently" (75).

The findings of this learned committee were quite explicit: there was nothing in either the Old Testament or in the "Jewish statutes called the Talmud" from which it might be concluded that the Jews "thirsted for human blood" (76). On the contrary, their laws expressly forbade such usages. And by his Golden Bull, promulgated in July, 1236, the emperor attempted to acquit the Jews once and for all of the dreadful accusation.

He had no success; the fable had taken root too deeply. Ten years later, the Holy See itself took up the matter. In 1247, Innocent IV promulaged a first bull relative to the question, which was to be followed by many others down through the centuries. Here is an eloquent extract from the bull of 1247:

"Although the Holy Scriptures enjoin the Jews: 'Thou shalt not kill' and forbid them to touch any dead body at Passover, they are wrongly accused of partaking of the heart of a murdered child at the Passover, with the charge that this is prescribed by their laws, since the truth is completely the opposite. Whenever a corpse is found somewhere, it is to the Jews that the murder is wickedly imputed. They are persecuted on the pretext of such fables or of others quite similar; and contrary to the privileges that have been granted them by the apostolic Holy See, they are deprived of trial and of regular judgment; in mockery of all justice, they are stripped of their belongings, starved, imprisoned and tortured, so that their fate is perhaps worse than that of their fathers in Egypt . . ." (77).

All these efforts were fruitless, and henceforth accusations of ritual murder or of profanation of the Host gradually replaced the Crusades as a pretext for mass exterminations. A case in point is that of the bleeding Host of Röttingen, discussed on page 99. From another papal bull, dated 1273, it appears that an abominable practice originated at this period: blackmailers hid their children and accused the Jews of having kidnaped them. Thus they were able to enter Jewish houses and to pillage them by main force, or to employ other no less lucrative forms of extortion.[14] Events such as these sometimes had far-reaching repercussions. Certain of these incidents, deeply engraved in the popular imagination, gave rise to veritable cults, and thus propagated the bloody theme down through the ages. In the place where the heinous deed was supposed to have been committed, miracles were described. Canonizations took place, pilgrimages continued for centuries, giving ample cause to provoke the naïveté and credulity of the people. Thus, an accusation of profanation of the Host was made in Brussels in 1370, and some twenty Jews perished at the stake, while the rest were banished. Two commemorative chapels were built during the following century, and the celebration finally gave rise to the chief religious festival of the capital—still observed today with great pomp on the third Sunday of July—as well as to an abundant literature.[15] Similarly, a case of ritual murder was reported in 1473 at Trent in the Tyrol,

[14] "It happens sometimes that Christians lose their children and that the enemies of the Jews accuse them of having kidnaped and killed these children in order to offer sacrifices with their heart and blood, and it also happens that the parents themselves, or other Christians who are enemies to the Jews, hide the children and attack the Jews, demanding of them, as ransom, a certain sum of money, on the entirely false pretext that these children had been kidnaped and killed by the Jews . . . whereas their law clearly and expressly forbids them to sacrifice, eat, or drink blood. . . ." (Bull of Gregory X, October 7, 1272; cf. Stern, *Urkundliche Beiträge über die Stellung der Papste zu den Juden*, Kiel, 1893, p. 5.)

[15] Cf. J. Stengers, *Les Juifs dans les Pays-Bas au Moyen Age,* Brussels, 1950, pp. 24-27. The author's bibliography (pp. 134-37) includes over twenty works on the 1370 case.

and nine Jews were arrested, questioned, and after lengthy torture finally confessed to everything that was asked of them, in particular to the murder of a little boy named Simon. Papal intervention had no effect: the Jews were executed. Supported by the "spontaneous confessions" of the victims, the calumny spread like a trail of powder. Several similar cases appeared in Austria and in Italy during the same period, all followed by expulsions or autos-da-fé (78). The scene of the original deed became a pilgrimage site. A commemorative chapel was erected there, and the miracles and cures that were effected on the tomb of little Simon led to his beatification in 1582, although the Holy See still did not consent to attribute his murder to the Jews.

Sometimes cases of ritual murder gave rise to monuments of another kind. Thus the Endingen affair, in Bavaria—where, we must note, the murder occurred in 1462 and the accusation was not made until 1470—served as a basis for the *Endinger Judenspiel,* one of the most famous plays of the Renaissance popular theater in Germany (79). Still more tangible is the commemoration of a case in Bern. On the pretext of the disappearance of a little boy, the Jews were expelled from the city in 1294. The incident gave rise to a legend sufficiently tenacious for a monument to be erected in the center of the town two hundred years later, the Kinderfressenbrunnen (well of the child-eater), a local curiosity that today's tourist can still visit (80). Similar examples are legion. Diligent chroniclers have estimated more than one hundred cases of profanation of the Host (81), more than one hundred and fifty trials for "ritual murder" (82), and the number of cases we do not know about must be infinitely greater.

Hence, misdeeds attributed to the Jews are periodically evoked in an atmosphere of great religious fervor, and this very repetition roots the legend still deeper, nourished on these pathetic reminders. This alone suffices to explain the fact that a number of cases of ritual murder were to appear in the nineteenth century, and that even in our own day there are still serious Christian investigators who believe them.[16]

The *"rouelle"* and the trial of the Talmud

Whereas the grim legends just described emerged from the depths of popular imagination and were opposed by ecclesiastical authorities, those very authorities in the thirteenth century issued two directives that in turn gave rise to new legends, all quite as tenacious. These directives were the imposition of a distinctive sign to be worn by all Jews, and the express condemnation of their sacred books.

The first measure was decided by the Fourth Lateran Council that, in 1215, marked the pinnacle of pontifical power. For three weeks, nearly fifteen hundred prelates from all points of the Christian horizon met and endorsed the sovereign decisions taken by Innocent III. Some of these, adopted at the Council's final session, concern the Jews. Here is an extract:

"In the countries where Christians do not distinguish themselves from Jews and Saracens by their garments, relations are maintained between Christians and Jews or Saracens, or vice versa. In order that such wickedness in the future be not excused by error, it is decreed that henceforth Jews of both sexes will be distinguished from other peoples by their garments, as moreover has been prescribed unto them by Moses. They will not show themselves in public during Holy Week, for some among them on these days wear their finest garments and mock the Christians clad in mourning. Trespassers will be duly punished by the secular powers, in order that they no longer dare flout Christ in the presence of Christians" (83).

Thus we may observe that the decision was made necessary by the equality in which Jews and Christians still lived in the thirteenth century, "speaking the same language and

[16] Cf. p. 274, note 20.

wearing the same garments," as Caesarius of Heisterbach has already told us.[17] We may also note that the Lateran Council confined itself to posing the general principle of discrimination in clothing, leaving the details to the secular authorities, who were to decide how the difference was to be marked. And the decision did not aim at Jews alone; the text also mentions Saracens. To these were subsequently added heretics, followed by lepers, prostitutes, and other outcasts.

The enforcement of the measures varied considerably in method and degree, depending on the country. France, as the Church's eldest daughter, conformed most rapidly, especially since at this period the Albigensian Crusade strengthened vigilance over evildoers of every kind. It was in France, in particular, that the idea seems to have appeared of adopting an ancient Moslem rule[18] and of indicating differences by special insignia to be worn on the clothing. From the start, the circular form (whence the French term *rouelle*) and the color yellow were designated. We can only speculate about this form, which was that of a coin: a symbol of the Jews' eagerness for profit, or of Judas' thirty pieces of silver? As for the color yellow, which is even today pre-eminently the color of the wicked and the jealous, it was even more closely linked with these attributes in the Middle Ages. The color may also have been derived from the alliteration between Jew, Judas, Jonathan,[19] and *jaune* ("yellow" in French). In any case, we see from the outset the intention of making the discrimination afflictive and humiliating. It is quite understandable that the Jews made considerable ef-

---

[17] Cf. pp. 54 f.

[18] In A.D. 850, the Caliph of Baghdad Muttawakkil, had ordered all infidels—Christians, Jews, or others—to wear distinctive insignia on the sleeve and a yellow hat; but this order was soon ignored.

[19] As M. Bulard points out, a certain kind of lady apple with yellow skin was called "apple of Jonathan" in the Middle Ages; furthermore, Jonathan is the name that occurs most frequently in stories of Jewish profanations of the Host. (M. Bulard, *Le Scorpion, symbole du peuple juif dans l'art religieux des XIVe, XVe, et XVIe siècles*, Paris, 1935, p. 37, note 1.)

fort to avoid a measure that so marked them for the mockery and vindictiveness of the mob. Hence, between 1215 and 1370, in France alone, twelve councils and nine royal decrees[20] prescribed the strict observance of this law, on pain of heavy fines or corporal punishment. The industrious Philip the Fair even made the insignia a source of revenue: rouelles were sold and the franchise leased. In 1297 the proceeds were fifty *livres tournois* from the Jews of Paris, and a hundred from those of Champagne. When, in 1361, King John the Good recalled the Jews to France, he ordered that the color of the insignia should henceforth be half red, half white. Doubtless the Jews insisted on this change of color in stipulating the conditions of their return. Moreover, they were not obliged to wear the rouelle when they were traveling,[21] which indicates that the authorities were fully aware of the risks to which the wearers of the insignia were exposed.

In Germany, where a particular kind of hat rather than an insignia was first prescribed, the measure was adopted more slowly. The proceedings of the Council of Vienna in 1267 (84) deplore that the order enjoining the wearing of conical hats was not being obeyed by the Jews. And it is again a hat, this time red and yellow, that is mentioned in many texts of the fourteenth and fifteenth centuries; it was only in the following centuries that a rouelle was substituted for it.

Other regions had other requirements. The Jews of Poland had to wear a pointed green hat. Strips of cloth sewed across the chest, sometimes in the shape of the tables of the Law (*Tabula*) (85) were the rule for England; but again a rouelle

[20] Councils of Narbonne (1227), Arles (1234), Béziers (1246), Albi (1254), Arles (1260), Nîmes (1284), Vienne (1289), Avignon (1326 and 1337), Vabres (1368), and synodal statutes of Rodez (1336) and Nîmes (1365); decrees of Saint Louis (1269), Philip the Bold (1271, 1272, 1283), Philip the Fair (1288), Louis X (1315), Philip V (1317), John the Good (1363), Charles V (1372). (Cf. V. Robert, *Les Signes d'infamie au Moyen Age*, Paris, 1889, p. 7ff. It is also from this work that we have taken the other details about the rouelle.)

[21] By the Councils of Arles (1234), Avignon (1326), and by the decree of Charles V (1372). (*Ibid.*, p. 22.)

for the Jews of Italy and Spain, where, however, the measure was usually not enforced. On the other hand, it is curious to note that by an edict of 1435, King Alfonso ordered the Jews of Sicily to attach a rouelle not only to their clothing but also over their shops.

The importance of these defamatory insignia to the Christians is clearly apparent from the example of Christian heretics. Instead of the rouelle, the latter were obliged to wear two crosses sewed on their clothing, and this penalty was regarded by the inquisitors, as well as by the people, as the most humiliating punishment that could be inflicted. Together with flagellation, it was the third degree in the canonical scale of punishments, coming after pious works and fines, and exceeded only by *peines majeures:* prison or the stake. The delinquent, when reconciled with the Church, could take off the insignia, whereas the Jew could escape from them only by conversion. The stigma, rouelle or hat, became the accepted attribute of the unconverted Jew. In the fourteenth century, artists and illuminators rarely represented them otherwise, even when portraying Biblical Jews, patriarchs of the Old Testament. By a remarkable osmosis, these views took root even among the Jews themselves, certain of whose manuscripts of the fourteenth and fifteenth centuries represent Abraham, Jacob, and Moses in the same costume (86). This visible sign, which henceforth indicated the circumcised, impressed on men's minds the notion that the Jew was a man of another physical aspect, radically different from other men. This concept has certainly contributed to the birth of various legends that we shall discuss later, and from which the notion followed that the Jew was a being *corporeally* different from other men, that he belonged to some other species than that of the human race.

As we have seen, debates between Jews and Christians concerning the comparative merits of their religions enjoyed a great vogue during the first centuries of Christianity, and a copious patristic literature was devoted to them. They were revived in medieval Europe, often taking place in a climate of remarkable frankness and cordiality (87). But the propagation of a new kind of myth—that of a loathsome and criminal doctrine secretly taught by Jewish texts—put an end to them.

The struggle against the Albigenses and the Waldenses had brought about the creation of special institutions—the Inquisition, the Dominican order—expressly charged with eradicating all heresies. But if the function creates the organ, the organ in turn creates and perpetuates the function: an inquisitor's duty is to discover sacrilege everywhere. These Dominicans could not help showing interest in infidels in general, and in Jews and their doctrines in particular. Furthermore, the immediate occasion seems to have been furnished them by certain Jews themselves.

At the beginning of the thirteenth century, the guardians of Christian orthodoxy were greatly troubled by the influence of Aristotelian ideas that, through Arab and Jewish translators, were beginning to infiltrate Europe. In 1210 and in 1215 the Holy See forbade the teachings of Aristotle's *Physics* and *Metaphysics;* in 1228 Gregory IX expressly forbade "corrupting the divine Word by the contact of the fictions of the philosophers." The alarm of certain Jewish theologians over the new rationalist tendency (whose principal Jewish expositor was Maimonides) was still greater, and they covered the "Maimonists" with abuse. Possessing no central coercive authority, but maintaining excellent relations with the doctors of the Inquisition, it was to the latter that some French rabbis turned, asking them to become guardians of the purity of the Jewish faith. We are told that two of these rabbis, Solomon ben Abraham and Jonah Gerondi, made the following remarks to the Dominicans of Montpellier: "Why do you pay no attention to our heretics and our atheists, corrupted by the doctrine of Moses of Egypt [Moses Maimonides], author of impious works? Since you are uprooting your heresies, uproot ours as well, and order the burning of the wicked books." The inquisitors did not wait to be asked a second time. Searches were made and in 1234 Maimonides' works were burned with great solemnity in Montpellier as well as in Paris.

In this manner, apparently, the interest of the Inquisition was awakened to the content of the Talmud. This enormous and almost inaccessible treatise, written from the fourth to the sixth centuries in Babylonia, contains a little of everything. Paradoxically, while the orthodox studied each word and each comma of the sacred text with equal reverence, it was the disciples of Maimonides who recommended making a distinction between its two parts: the halakah, or the law proper, of dogmatic value; and the haggada, a miscellany of tales and parables, moral precepts, superstitions, and medical formulas. Some years later, at the very period when converted Jewish experts convened by Frederick II were clearing Judaism of the accusation of ritual murder, another converted Jew undertook an action in the opposite direction. A Dominican brother of la Rochelle, the apostate Nicholas Donin,[22] went to Rome and told Gregory IX that the Talmud was an immoral book offensive to Christians. The Pope addressed himself to the kings of France, England, Castile, and Aragon, as well as to various bishops, urging them to open an investigation to verify the truth of the accusation. Saint Louis (Louis IX) was the only one to act. Throughout France, copies of the Talmud were seized, and in

---

[22] Not much is known about Nicholas Donin; toward the end of his life he was reproved by Pope Nicholas III for having attacked the Franciscans. A letter from his contemporary, Jacob ben Elias, suggests that he was murdered: ". . . misfortune assailed him because he had spoken against certain wise and prudent men. He was struck down and died without anyone to avenge him. . . ." (Quoted in S. Grayzel, *The Church and the Jews in the Thirteenth Century*, Philadelphia, 1933, p. 339.)

The same letter also asserts that Donin took an active part in propagating the legend of ritual murder, together with that of the evil influence of the Talmud—which is not surprising. The role of renegade Jews, men uprooted and readily thrown off balance, men with "complexes," as we would say today, has always been of prime importance during the persecutions of the Jews. We shall have more than one occasion to return to this subject.

1240 a great public debate began in Paris, in which the most important participants were Eudes de Châteauroux, Chancellor of the Sorbonne, and Nicholas Donin on the Christian side; and Yehiel of Paris and Moses of Coucy on the Jewish side. We have the full account of the debate, in Latin as well as Hebrew (88). The themes treated were grouped into thirty-five articles, among them the following:

Was it true that in the first century, after the fall of Jerusalem, the Rabbi Simon ben Yohai proclaimed: "Seize the best of the *goyim* and kill them"? And precisely what did *goy* mean? Was it true that a *goy* who rests on Saturday or who concerns himself with the study of the Law deserves death, according to the Talmud? That Jesus was an illegitimate child? That he would be condemned in hell to the torment of boiling mud? That since the destruction of the Temple, God possesses no more than a space of four square cubits in the world? That in Paradise, Leviathan would be served at the table of the just? These were some of the questions on which the discussion turned. Stoical and honest, the rabbis faced them with great courage. To the quotations of their adversaries, they replied with other quotations (for, just as in every compilation that is a repository for the wisdom of nations, for any maxim of the haggada, one can be found that states precisely the contrary);[23] they set forth the many commandments prescribing an equal charity toward Jews and non-Jews, commandments to be scrupulously honest toward aliens—commandments much more characteristic of the spirit of the Talmud. But the result of the debate, in

[23] Furthermore, the style peculiar to the haggada must always be taken into account. At virtually the same period when Simon ben Yohai exclaimed: "Seize the best of the *goyim* and kill them!", Rabbi Eleazar, another doctor of the Law, raged against the ignorant Jews (*am haretz*) in terms that the haggada reports as follows:

"Rabbi Eleazar has said: 'One has the right to strike an *am haretz* even on the Day of Atonement, even if this day falls on a Saturday'; his pupils said to him: 'Master, say "kill" rather than "strike."' But he replied: 'To kill requires a blessing; to strike requires none'" (*Pesahim,* 49b).

which the accusers, like the judges, were champions of Christ victorious, was obviously determined in advance. The Talmud was condemned and all copies of it were solemnly burned—the same fate that the works of Maimonides had met eight years before. One of Maimonides' detractors, the Jonah Gerondi referred to, imposing cruel penances on himself, wandered from one community to the next and proclaimed in the synagogues: "Maimonides is right and his teaching is true. We lied!"

The Jews tried in vain to rehabilitate their sacred texts. A few years later, Innocent IV consented to a re-examination of the verdict, but in 1248 a second commission, presided over by the famous Dominican Albert the Great, merely reconfirmed the verdict of the first. The following year, Albert went to teach in Cologne, where he seems to have stirred up new and resounding judgments. This upheaval, going beyond the narrow limits of specialized theologians, roused public opinion against the Jews. We find its echo in various minnesingers of the period: for example, Konrad von Würzburg (1268):

We der veizen, touben	Woe to the cowardly Jews, deaf
argen Jüden kint, die nicht ruechen walten	and wicked, who have no care
des, das sie behalten	to save themselves
möchte wol vor arger helle pine	from the sufferings of hell.
Talamut hat si vil gar betoubet	The Talmud has corrupted them
und ir ere beroubet (89).	and made them lose their honor.

In Seifried Helbling:

Ez war wol der in verbut	It would be well to forbid
ir ketzerlichez Talamut	their heretical Talmud,
ein buch valsch une ungenaem (90).	a false and ignoble book.

In an anonymous poet of the same period:

Der da ist in abgründe	They have fallen so low
Gamaliel in künde	For Gamaliel has taught them
An Talamut de Vünde	The heretical Talmud
Die valschen vünde rouben	Whose false sayings
In sinne rehtes gelouben (91).	Conceal from them the true faith.

In France, the popular *Desputaison de la Sainte Église et de la Synagogue* by the jongleur Clopin, which dates from the same period, is apparently also a direct echo of the great controversy of 1240. Addressing a large public, Clopin created a particularly long-lived myth—which anti-Semitic agitators were to make abundant use of in the nineteenth and twentieth centuries. In it the Jews were represented not only as poisoners of the body, but as poisoners of the mind. Moreover, there is no distinct cleavage between these two concepts, just as, in the spirit of the age, there was no clear division between the salvation of bodies and the salvation of souls. The two themes are merged in the strange and considerable role played throughout the Middle Ages by Jewish physicians, revered and feared after the fashion of powerful magicians to whom the most atrocious crimes were imputed, yet whose services were solicited with great insistence. We shall return to them later.

We now come to the changes the period of the Crusades brought about in the structure and internal life of Jewish communities. These communities naturally reacted to the impact of both the persecutions of the Jews and of the strange ideas that were beginning to develop about them. They accommodated themselves by a kind of adaptive evolution which, in turn, through an inevitable reaction, gave rise to still more fantastic concepts to impress Christendom in the centuries to follow.

five

The Jewish Reactions

It is easy to imagine how shocked the Jews themselves were at the massacres of 1096. It is only natural that under such circumstances the victims should have sharper memories than the persecutors. In fact, the imprint left by the persecutions was henceforth to singularize Jewish destiny, leaving an indelible stamp upon the Jewish mentality. As the Jews' segregation grew more marked, they became confined to a special economic role. This role developed in the context of the great social transformations that characterize the age of the Crusades; and it is these social changes that we shall first describe.

From trade to usury

We have seen that the Jews were the tradesmen par excellence of Carolingian Europe and that they were noteworthy in being the only merchants to maintain contact with the Orient. Not all Jews were merchants; and if, in the rare texts of the period that have come down to us, they are represented chiefly as tradesmen, it is because the lower classes, the artisans and clerks, had no occasion to leave many traces in documents. But the Jews did not maintain their monopoly over international commerce for long, and from the tenth century, Venetians and Byzantines, followed by the Lombards, appeared in the market fairs of Champagne or Flanders. Furthermore, in the rudimentary economy of the period, which dealt almost entirely with goods, commercial exchange—and money—played only an insignificant role. (On the other hand, the role of the usurer was much greater than it is today, just because money was scarce and could be obtained, when needed, only from a professional.)

But by the twelfth century, trade routes to Asia were open to Europeans, and spices, rare foodstuffs, and luxury products were carried by Italian ships rather than over perilous land routes; thus these products became more accessible to both major and minor lords, and commerce received a great impetus. At the same time, after several centuries of stagnation, cities began to develop rapidly and an exchange economy to replace the economy of barter. A class of Christian merchants appeared, an urban elite that gradually ousted the Jewish tradesmen. Of course, this change was less a question of interdenominational rivalry, the deliberate eviction of one clan by another, than of an organic, long-term process linked to the general transformations of medieval society. A number of factors were to contribute to this process, which was to make the relegation of the Jews to usury almost inevitable.

The first medieval merchants were constant travelers; obliged to provision themselves, they were their own bankers and, on occasion, their own moneylenders. The developments that began with the First Crusade led many Jews to convert their property into possessions that could be concealed easily in case of danger—that is, into gold or silver. Since legal tender was extraordinarily scarce at the time, its possessor naturally turned into a moneylender: this was as true of the monasteries and other ecclesiastical establishments and of the first Christian merchants as it was of the Jews. At the same time, religious agitation made travel and commerce increasingly difficult for the Jews. Many texts dating from the years 1146-1148 show that during the Crusades the Jews might at any time be attacked on the highroads (92). Above all, their new rivals, the Italian and Hanseatic merchants, could count on the protection of their native cities and lobby for protective legislation in their favor. For example, access to ships sailing to the Orient was forbidden to Jewish merchants by an edict, the first of its kind, passed in Venice in 945 (93). Nonetheless, with regard to domestic trade by land routes, there are many examples of Jewish commercial activity until the beginning of the thirteenth century. But the tendency toward moneylending—that is, usury—as the Jews' sole occupation, where the financier waited for his client at home and had no need to venture forth into the world, was even more accentuated, since the Jew, at a disadvantage in all other domains, here possessed an advantage all his own. He was not exposed to the thunders of ecclesiastical censure, which, though it had never been able to halt Christian usury altogether, nonetheless trammeled it severely—a Christian usurer could be excommunicated and, from the fourteenth century, was answerable to the Inquisition.[1] It is true, though little known, that the Talmudic tradition, too, initially opposed usury. Even on the eve of the First Crusade the great Rashi proclaimed: "He who loans money at interest to a foreigner will be destroyed" (94). But a century later, the rabbis had already agreed that the community must adapt itself to circumstances: of course, "no loans at interest must be made to the gentiles, if a livelihood can be earned in another manner," but "at the present time, when a Jew may possess neither fields nor vines permitting him to live, the lending of money at interest to non-Jews is necessary and consequently authorized."

The authorities were quick to exploit this advantage for their own ends. In fact, the increasingly precarious situation of the Jews drove them to seek the protection of the princes, petitioning "charters" that, while affording a tem-

---

[1] From the thirteenth century, authors such as Mathieu Paris identified usury with heresy. This identification became official after the Council of Vienne in 1311, which authorized the courts of the Inquisition to prosecute Christians practicing usury. (Cf. Parkes, *The Jew in the Medieval Community*, London, 1938, pp. 288-99.)

porary security, made the Jews dependent on their protectors. Originally free men, the Jews became, within an increasingly stratified society, the serfs of their lords. *Servi camerae nostrae,* the German emperors were to call them, while in France it was said they "belonged to the barons" (95). They were the lords' men, or rather the lords' chattels: possessions all the more useful since money could be extracted from them under pressure, and they could be ignored otherwise. This was expressed by the celebrated British jurist Henry de Bracton in the following terms: "The Jew can have nothing of his own; all that he acquires becomes the property of the king and not his own; the Jews live not for themselves but for others: thus it is for others that they acquire, and not for themselves." [2] Ultimately, the Jew could live only by means of money—not in the sense in which this is understood in our modern capitalist society, but in a much more significant sense: the right to life, which Christian society granted the merest yokel, had to be *bought* by the Jew at regular intervals. Otherwise, regarded as useless, he would be driven out or implicated in some grim case of poisoning or ritual murder. Money became much more important to him than his daily bread—as necessary to him as the air he breathed. Under these circumstances, money finally acquired for the Jew a quasi-sacred significance.

However, the Jews were far from constituting the chief source of the princes' revenue; even in their new field of activity they constantly had to counter strong Christian competition. Despite all the efforts of the Church, Christian usurers did excellent business throughout the Middle Ages. In particular, the Italian brotherhoods of the Caorsins and the Lombards, often subject to a control analogous to that imposed on the Jews, and holders of the same kind of privileges, devoted themselves to even larger operations through-

---

[2] Ducange quotes this pertinent definition in his famous *Glossaire* (article "Judaei"); *Judaeus vero nihil proprium habere potest, quia quicquid acquirit, non sibi acquirit, sed regi: quia non vivunt sibi ipsis, sed aliis, et sic aliis acquirunt, et non sibi ipsis.*

out Europe and played a much more important role than the Jews in the development of capitalist techniques. But the Caorsins and Lombards were eventually assimilated into the general culture and disappeared: only a few place names or linguistic vestiges perpetuate their memory.[3] The Jewish usurer has survived. He has been promoted to the dignity of an archetype because behind him stood the silhouette of another archetype: that of Judas Iscariot, the man with the thirty pieces of silver. Ultimately the specter thus evoked, creating an unbearable tension between Christian society and the Jews, contributed significantly to the stereotype. Even in our own day we tend to attribute a virtual financial monopoly to the medieval Jewish usurer, whereas the few known statistics suggest how minor his role was in the movement of money. Thus, while the total taxes collected in 1241 by the imperial treasury of the Holy Roman Empire amounted to 7,127½ marks, the Jews' share in this figure was only 857 marks (96). Similarly, according to the *Livre de taille* for the year 1292—a record of taxes to which the population of Paris was subject—out of a total of more than 12,000 livres, the share of the 125 taxpaying Jews in the city was only 126 livres, whereas that of the Lombards was 1,511 livres (97). This is obviously an extreme example, for at the same time the royal treasury collected a much greater amount in taxes from all the Jews in France (98). The role of Jewish finance and usury varied according to time and place, but with the exception of England in the twelfth century, it was nowhere predominant.

We shall now briefly examine this role in the three principal nations we are considering.

England constitutes a special case. The Jews appeared here only after the Norman Conquest, and in the absence of any local rivalry they rapidly became a tightly knit class

---

[3] Thus the "Rue des Lombards" in Paris and in certain provincial cities. In Russian, "Lombard" designates a pawnshop even today; the same was true in England and Germany until the beginning of the nineteenth century. The word still has this meaning—remarkably enough—in Yiddish.

of financiers. From the start they managed to associate closely with the kings in their operations, turning over to the royalty the notes of defaulting debtors in return for a share of the sums due. They were the "king's men," vassals of a special kind, since they were the chief source of their suzerains' revenues. During a period of rapid national expansion in the twelfth century the Jews became rich by advancing money to the barons and to the clergy, whose needs for legal tender and appetites for luxury were considerable: the chroniclers enviously describe their splendid stone houses. They were subject not to regular taxes but to special contributions that the kings demanded in case of need—especially for the Crusades. At the end of the twelfth century the Jews' monopoly was strictly controlled by the creation of a central office, the Exchequer of the Jews. Here, in the presence of royal officials, was to be transacted every loan and financial operation.

The Jews' rapid rise during the twelfth century was followed in the thirteenth by an equally rapid decline. This decline was foreshadowed by the extortions of King John during his conflict with foreign enemies and rebellious barons at home. In 1210 he demanded so exorbitant a contribution from the Jews that the latter were unable to comply. He then arrested a great number of them, and one of the wealthiest, Abraham of Bristol, was jailed in a dungeon where one of his teeth was torn out every day: on the eighth day the unfortunate usurer committed suicide (99). Thereafter, expulsions of Jews were followed by readmissions; but in competition with the Lombards, their role rapidly became negligible. In this atmosphere, religious considerations became paramount, and in 1290 the Jews were officially expelled from England. The exact fate of the lost tribe of English Jews is unknown: doubtless the majority of the survivors merged with French and German Jews. But their memory remained sufficiently vivid to nourish many literary themes throughout the Middle Ages and to induce Shakespeare, three centuries later, to create the unforgettable prototype of the usurer, Shylock, whose origins have so often been debated. Perhaps in the tragic theme of the "pound of flesh" there is a transposition, with diametrically reversed roles, of the Abraham of Bristol episode. And, some twenty generations later, we find that the name of Fagin, the repulsive usurer in *Oliver Twist*, seemingly derived from Cok Hagin, last of the Arch Presbyters of the Jews on the eve of their expulsion.

The unusual case of the English Jews is in strong contrast to the history of those of France and Germany. In these countries the Jews never had a monopoly on finance.

In France, against a background of rapid economic development during the twelfth century, the Jews transacted their usual commercial and financial operations and grew rich. But the accession of Philip II was the first blow to their prosperity. Philip's biographers state that from childhood the young prince had been nurtured on anti-Jewish legends; in any case, upon his accession, he had all the Jews of the realm arrested, and released them only after they had paid a ransom of fifteen thousand silver marks (1180). He then annulled all their credits except for a fifth share, which he himself took over (1181). Lastly, he ordered their general expulsion (1182) (100). It is true that under the feudal parceling out of the territory the effect of these measures was limited to the possessions of the crown; therefore, when in 1198 Philip decided to recall the Jews, he concluded an agreement with Count Theobald of Champagne, demanding the return of "his" Jews, who belonged to him by rights (101). Subsequently, by an act that the scholar Petit-Dutaillis has regarded as the first serious attempt made by royalty to assert its legislative power over all the baronies of the kingdom (102), Louis VIII extended this concept of personal authority over the Jews to the entire country (1223). Consequently, the existence of Jewish communities, which could be expelled and recalled according to a prince's whim or the state of his treasury, became extremely precarious and unstable.

Expulsions and confiscations impoverished the Jews, who were increasingly in competition with Christian usurers, and led to a noticeable lessening of their economic role. This trend finds expression in the decree of Melun in 1230 (103), which, denying the validity of any debts owed to Jews, virtually relegated them to the lowest form of usury—henceforth they could lend only on pledges, that is, to peasants, artisans, or the poor. Big business and high finance became the province of the Caorsins and Lombards. However, humble as they were, the Jews continued to be essential for certain transactions, and Saint Louis (Louis IX), despite all his efforts, was unable to suppress Jewish usury. When, early in the thirteenth century, Philip IV ordered the mass expulsion of the Jews, they were sufficiently missed by the common people for a Geffroi de Paris to write:

Toute pauvre gent se plaint	All the poor complain
Car Juifs furent débonnaires	For the Jews were much milder
Beaucoup plus en faisant leurs affaires	In the conduct of their business
Que ne sont maintenant les chrétiens.	Than the Christians are now.
Garanties ils demandent et liens,	These demand guarantees and mortgages,
Gages demandent et tout extorquent	Pledges, too, and take everything
Que les gens plument et écorchent . . .	Until they have stripped men quite bare . . .
Mais si les Juifs demeurés	But had the Jews remained
Fussent au royame de France,	In the kingdom of France,
Chrétiens moult grande aidance	Christians would have had
Eussent eu, qu'ils n'ont plus (104).	Much succor that is theirs no longer.

It is hardly surprising that under these circumstances the decree of July 28, 1315, calling back the Jews, refers to the "common outcry of the people" (105) demanding their return.

We find similar developments on the other side of the Rhine, with this difference: that they took place more slowly, especially in the eastern districts, so that the Jews' state there remained better for a long time. This is attributable to a real culture lag. What applies to France in the twelfth century applies to the Rhine Valley in the thirteenth and to the eastern marches of the Holy Roman Empire in the centuries to follow. Thus there are unquestionable evidences of a lively commercial activity on the part of the Jews along the Rhine, continuing up to the fourteenth century (106); and imperial decrees of the fifteenth century attest to the presence in Austria of Jewish merchants trafficking in textiles, wine, and porcelain, as well as of Jewish artisans (107). Apparently the sumptuary laws were initially applied only in a very lax fashion within the Holy Roman Empire, and the very edicts designed to enforce them suggest the persistence of a Jewish proselytism that remained quite active (108), as is confirmed by various Jewish sources (109). The distinctive feature of the status of the German Jews was the general protection accorded them by the emperor. This relationship, beginning, as we have seen, during the period of the First Crusade, gradually found legal expression in the concept of "serfs of the imperial chamber," which one finds for the first time, applied to all Jews, in the Golden Bull promulgated in 1236 by Frederick II, clearing the Jews of the accusation of ritual murder.[4] Imperial jurists attempted to assign the origin of this tradition of protector of the Jews to the Roman emperors, and more precisely to Vespasian and the destruction of the Temple.[5] The effectiveness of this protection, con-

[4] Cf. pp. 60 f.

[5] This is the interpretation given by two German codices of the thirteenth century, the *Sachsenspiegel* and the *Schwabenspiegel*. According to the *Sachsenspiegel*, imperial protection was first granted by Vespasian to Flavius Josephus, who had cured his son Titus of gout; more realistic, the *Schwabenspiegel* saw in it the counterpart of the "Temple tax" Vespasian had begun to collect after the destruction of the Temple.

firmed at frequent intervals, evidently varied with time and place, but on occasion the emperor took his role seriously enough to intervene on behalf of the Jews of another country: for example, at the time of their expulsion from France by Philip IV (110).

Moreover, in contrast with the French and English customs, the German emperors levied taxes, the price of their protection, not on individual Jews but on their communities, thereby strengthening the communal organization of the German Jews and their sense of collective responsibility. This is important, since these German Jewish communities proved to be the only ones able to perpetuate themselves during the succeeding centuries.

Another custom, in force throughout Europe and over which Voltaire (in his *Dictionnaire philosophique*) later gloated (111), points up the relative importance of economic and religious factors in the functions allowed the Jews. The Talmudic tradition prescribed disinheriting children if they renounced the Jewish religion. The Christian princes not only authorized their Jewish serfs to observe this tenet of their own laws (as they were authorized to observe all the rest), but on their own initiative extended it to the converts themselves, forcing them, at the time of conversion, to hand over their property to the royal or imperial exchequer. This was a logical arrangement in a period when the Jewish usurer constituted a precious possession, whereas his conversion was costly to the prince. In effect, the arrangement was a kind of sinking fund. It also represents, on another level, a kind of homage paid to the faithful of a sect that still performed useful and sometimes eminent functions in the society of the time. Soon clerics were to be found who justified the practice canonically. The Holy See vainly opposed a practice that made the fate of the apostates, repudiated by the Jews and robbed by the Christians, impossibly wretched and that was obviously not likely to encourage conversions. It was only after the Jews' economic role had narrowed considerably that the Church was able to win this point, so that the baptism of a Jew did not spell his ruin. This occurred, as we shall see, much later, at a period when the degradation of the Jews, having reached its nadir, appeared complete in the eyes of Christian society and provoked an almost demonological concept of the detestable and disgraced Jew. From this example we see the complexity and multiplicity of the factors that controlled Jewish destinies, and which two centuries ago Montesquieu expressed in these chilling terms: "Their property was confiscated because they wished to be Christians, and they were burned when they had no such wish" (112).

Birth of a Jewish mentality

The massacres of the First Crusade were to leave an indelible imprint on Jewish memory, a kind of collective trauma. Contemporaries are usually not in a position to grasp the full significance of an event, and the Jewish authors of the twelfth century, when they expressed their anguish and their rage, did not suspect the use to which their writings would be put. Certain parts of their chronicles have been incorporated into the Jewish liturgy and are still today recited annually at the time of the commemoration of the destruction of the Temple.[6] Other elements, transposed, have furnished the fabric of countless religious chants, the *selihot* and the *kinot*.[7] In the *Memorbücher* in which it became customary to record the names of the victims of persecutions, many lists are preceded by the evocation of the "cities of blood," Speyer, Worms, and Mainz (113). Thus the memory of the first

[6] The day of 9 Ab, which generally falls within the month of August. This obviously concerns only the liturgy of the Ashkenazim; Sephardic liturgy contains nothing equivalent.

[7] These form chants that are also recited, by choice, the day of 9 Ab. The *selihot* generally end on a note of hope, while the *kinot* are pure lamentations.

martyrs was perpetuated and a tradition was created and strengthened, inspiring succeeding generations to follow the example of their ancestors.

Chronicles such as those of Solomon bar Simeon or Eliezer ben Nathan are of great importance to the historian (114). They indicate first of all the fury that seized the survivors. Terrible were their denunciations, in which they used a highly special semantic: the word "church" is regularly replaced by "place of impurity," the word "cross" by "evil sign," the word "baptize" by "pollute," and so on (115). "The pope of sinful Rome rose up and urged all the peoples of Edom to believe in the Christ crucified: to unite in order to go to Jerusalem and conquer the city so that the strayed might return to the site of their shame, to the tomb of him whom they have chosen as their God . . ."; thus begins Solomon bar Simeon. "Let the bones of Emicho, persecutor of the Jews, be ground in a mill of fire!" he continues. And subsequently: "O God of vengeance, O Lord God of vengeance, appear! It is for thee that we have let ourselves be slaughtered every day. Return sevenfold the wrongs of our neighbors, so that they may curse you! Before our very eyes let the nations be punished for the blood of thy servants that they have shed . . . then they shall know that it is in the name of a dead man, of the void, that they have shed the blood of virgins, of children, and infants, that their faith is meaningless and that they have taken an accursed path. . . ." Nor is Eliezer ben Nathan less violent: "Strike our wretched neighbors sevenfold, punish them, O Lord, as they have deserved! Cause them distress and suffering, send them thy curse, destroy them!"

But this fury remains impotent. It is not possible to take vengeance on the persecutors; the disproportion of strength is so obvious that the calamities that overwhelm the Jews represent to its spokesmen an upheaval of nature rather than a struggle between two camps. And since all the exhortations addressed to God remain without effect (though our chroniclers do not fail to perceive a divine punishment in the woes that befall the vanguard of the Crusaders), since it must be acknowledged that "sinful Rome" celebrates victory while the fate of the Jews merely grows worse, it must be concluded that this is a just retribution, that the sins of the chosen people have not yet been sufficiently expiated. "No prophet, no sage or wise man can conceive why the sins of the community were found so grave that death alone could expiate them, as if the community itself had shed blood. But in truth, He is an equitable judge, and the fault is ours!" "Our sins permitted the enemy to triumph; the hand of the Lord weighed heavily upon his people. . . ."

Thus, far from shaking the Jews' faith in divine justice, their ordeals inspired in them a sense of guilt that, cast in the ancient mold of the commandments and the Law, only strengthened their devotion to the Lord. And they continue to slake their thirst at the sources of an invincible hope: "May the blood of the reverent be our merit and our expiation for us, our children, and our grandchildren, for all eternity, even as the sacrifice of Abraham, who bound his son Isaac on the altar in order to sacrifice him. Let these just, these pure, these perfect men become our advocates before the Lord, and may He soon deliver us from our exile. *Amen!*"

We find the same accents of resignation, hope, and an unfailing faith on the occasion of many another calamity, as in the moving plaint that relates the martyrdom of Isaac, chatelain of Troyes, and his family, victims in 1288 of a trial for ritual murder. This little masterpiece of medieval poetry is written in the French of the period:

Prechor vinrent Içak le Cohen[8] *requerir.*	Sinners have come for Isaac Cohen.
Tornast vers lor créance o l'kevanroit perir.	He must abjure, or perish.
Il dit: "Que avez tant? Je vol por Gé morir.	He says: "What do you want of me? For God I will die.

[8] Priest, in Hebrew.

Je suis Cohen: ofrande de mon cors voil ofrir."	As priest, I will offer him the sacrifice of my body."
"A peine eschaperas, puis que nos te tenons.	"You cannot escape, we hold you fast.
Deviens chrestiens." Et il repondit tantost: "Non!	Become a Christian," but he swift replies: "No.
Por les chiens ne lerrai le Gé vil ne son nom."	For the dogs, I would not leave God nor his name!"
An l'apeloit Haim, le mestre de Brinon.	Then Haim was called, the master of Brinon,
Encore un kadosch[9] *fut amenez avant;*	And another *kadosh* was led forth;
An li fist perit feu e l'aloit an grevant;	Then they thrust him into a slow fire
Huchoit Gé de bon cor e menu e sovant	And with good heart he prayed to God often and low,
Docement sofrit poine por servir Gé vivant.	Gently suffering his pain in the name of the living God.
Gé vanchere, emprinére, vanche nos des felons!	God of vengeance, jealous God, avenge us on our foes!
D'atandre ta vanchance nos semble li jors long! (116)	From awaiting your vengeance, the day seems long to us.

Henceforth martyrdom becomes a kind of institution. Each new victim of Christian fury is a warrior fallen to hallow the Name; often he receives the title of *kadosh* (saint), a kind of canonization. (If the Christians, too, canonize their martyrs, we must note that what is for them a generally legendary event, a reminder of Roman persecutions, acquires for the Jews a tragic and virtually everyday reality.) In particular, the sacrifice of the children, massacred by their own parents, is identified with the sacrifice offered by Abraham, and the story of the patriarch and his son becomes, under the title of Akeda (the sacrifice of Isaac), the very symbol of Jewish martyrology. One of the most tragic passages in the chronicle of Solomon bar Simeon relates how Isaac the Pious, Jew of Worms, baptized by force, leads his two children by night to the synagogue, slaughters them upon the altar,

[9] Saint, in Hebrew.

returns to his house and sets it on fire, and finally ignites the synagogue and perishes in the flames (117).

While each Jewish victim was regarded as a warrior fallen on the field of honor, the battle waged by the Jews was not like other battles. Making a virtue out of necessity, the Jews of Europe resolutely took the path of a purely passive resistance to evil (evil is equated with Christian society) and revealed a tenacity of which history offers no other examples —a passive resistance coming all the more easily in view of their nonparticipation in professions requiring physical effort and the direct struggle against nature.

The Jews replied to Christian animosity by a hatred just as intense but necessarily restrained or repressed. Whereas the aggressive potential of the Christians could be expressed at will and discharged directly, Jewish aggression was obliged to seek other channels and to become in some way transmuted. The psychic energies thus accumulated had ample opportunity to function in the realm of the struggle for existence—in the pursuit of negotiable currency. But this precious substance, without which it was impossible for the Jews to assert themselves in a hostile and detestable world, remained indissolubly linked to that world. In a sense, money was its permanent symbol.

To escape this outer world, the inner world of study constituted an indispensable complement. At all times the rabbis had placed the study of the Law above earthly possessions, above all other things, but never had these precepts been followed so fervently. It was with real frenzy that the Jews of Germany and northern France plunged into the Talmud and pored over it day and night in the synagogues; it is good, one text reminds us, to ruin one's life in study. Thus appears that famous Jewish ambivalence: money is overvalued because without it death or expulsion threatens; and precisely because it is overvalued, it becomes the object of contempt, while other facets of life become more highly regarded.

But learning was pursued in circumstances hardly favorable for its free development. Everything—the growing weight of the persecutions as well as the very spirit with which the persecutors were imbued—combined to make the mentality of the Jews timorous and narrow, for at this period the Jewish community was still remarkably open to external influences. Thus the belief in evil spirits sent down ever deeper roots in northern Europe; Jewish folklore was infiltrated with Christian superstitions, fairy tales, legends of devils or elves. Similarly, tales and fables, the moralities so popular at the time, were translated into Hebrew by the rabbis for the edification of their flocks. But among the moral precepts, it is chiefly those that praise modesty and humility that take precedence (here, too, we glimpse a reflection of the Jews' specialized profession: it is improper for a usurer to be arrogant). "God has given the human soul a bestial envelope, in order that man may not become proud!" exclaimed Rabbi Moses of Coucy (118). "God alone may be proud, man must be humble. Be respectful of your kind, keep your head bowed, your eyes lowered, raise only your heart toward the heavens . . ." instructed Rabbi Moses of Évreux (119). Still more importance is attributed to the scrupulous observance of the Law, and the greater part of Jewish wisdom henceforth consists in the elaboration of increasingly strict rules. Gone are the days of a Rashi's bold sallies; the rabbis confine themselves to a timorous acceptance of the traditional learning, without fundamentally changing anything, and complain of the inadequacy of their own insight. Prohibitions are added to prohibitions, which Rabbi Isaac of Vienne explains thus: ". . . there was a time when there were great doctors, wise and enlightened, in whom the faithful could trust, but in our time the knowledge of the Torah has fallen away and wisdom has vanished. Let us then praise the timid who doubt their own knowledge and abstain from making the observance of the Law easier: they will be better rewarded for their circumspection than those who pride themselves on their innovations in their studies . . ." (120). This humility, this lack of intellectual assurance, is characteristic of a school edict of the thirteenth century, and we note, in reading it, that its author was quite aware of the reasons for this sterility.

"Let a master not instruct more than ten students at a time. For although our sages had fixed the number of students at twenty-five to a master, this was valid only for Palestine, whose climate is favorable to the flowering of minds, and at a time when the Jewish people were independent— for the free man is strong, lucid, and bold, and learns more easily than the oppressed man. The latter's mind is weak and barren, subject to cruel and insolent princes; ceaselessly at strife, he is fearful and timid, and his rancor limits his energy. This is the reason why we must advise masters not to accept more than ten students at a time . . ." (121)

Jewish hostility toward the outside world is also characteristic of certain maxims of the *Book of the Pious* (*Sepher Hasidim*), a famous anthology of precepts collected by Judah the Hasid at the end of the thirteenth century. "Deliver me from the hand of strange children, whose mouth speaketh vanity, and their right hand is a right hand of falsehood"—these words from the One Hundred and Forty-fourth Psalm found abundant commentaries. The *Book of the Pious* counsels: "The sages have said: a Jew must not be found alone with a non-Jew. . . . The songs of the churches must not be translated into Hebrew or sung in the synagogues. . . . Young children must not be sung to sleep to the sound of Christian melodies. . . . The walls of a house that have been covered with the blood of martyrs must never be covered over or painted, in order that the blood may cry to heaven." Some of the adages in the *Book of the Pious* deserve to be read and remembered even today: "You may regret your speech, you can never regret your silence: before speaking, you are the master of your words, but thereafter your words become your master." "If you fear you may regret a promise, say no rather than yes, for nothing is so base as a yes followed by a no." Others, directly concerned with relationships between Jews and Christians, are no less instructive: "The conduct of the Jews corresponds in most places to that of the Christians; when the Christians of a city are depraved, the Jews are depraved as well." "Excommunication must not be cast upon a city whose lord has persecuted the Jews or constrained them to baptism, for the excommunication will remain in force even if the city changes its lord." "Poor as he is, a Jew must beg rather than steal Christian money and run away, for thereby he profanes the name of God, and the Christians will say that all Jews are thieves and liars." The practical wisdom of such precepts is evident.

What Jewish studies and culture lost in depth at this period, they gained in breadth. Previously the rabbis had elaborated learned treatises; what they now wrote was within the reach of every believer. In order to warn against weakness, they composed for these troubled times simple manuals (such as the *Little Book of Commandments* by Rabbi Isaac of Corbeil), so that each Jew could instruct himself concerning his obligations and rights. Study, that supreme value, was put within the reach of all, and the popularization of Jewish culture was from now on to be one of its distinctive features.

Thus, in reaction to persecutions, the very special Jewish mentality emerged; this, together with the nature of the Jews' professions, was to invite even greater Christian animosity. A really vicious circle—merely suggested at the period we are concerned with—was to develop amid the complex interplay between the passions of the men of the Middle Ages and their real interests. For the moment, the practical interests still predominate: the Jews play a useful and even indispensable economic role, and consequently they are neither sufficiently segregated nor sufficiently degraded to be universally detested.

Conclusion

Our history is approaching a disturbed and decisive period during which, while the Jews were disappearing, or nearly so, from the medieval scene, their image increasingly obsessed Christian souls. (Without doubt we shall find some correlation between these two series of apparently contradictory events.) Let us survey briefly their status in the thirteenth century, which in so many respects marks the peak of medieval civilization.

We have frequently noted the degree to which the Jews were integrated into the surrounding society. We have seen that apart from the liturgy and sacred texts, they spoke the same language as the Christians and that beneath the rouelle they wore the same clothing. Furthermore, it appears from various legislative documents that they still possessed the right to bear arms (122) and that, like able-bodied and free Christians, they were subject to trial by ordeal (123); it was only later that (by a privilege they shared with children and the aged) they were exempted from these rights. Thus they were considered to be men like other men, though miscreants or even (as the historian Cecil Roth has subtly observed) hardened sinners who, while quite aware of the truth of Christianity, pretended not to believe in it, out of pure malice (124); far from being hermetically isolated from the world around them, they continued to participate in its activities. As we have seen, even in the world of thought, certain Jewish thinkers were affected by Christian influences. As a counterpart to the German mysticism of the thirteenth century, a Jewish mysticism appeared in the Rhineland, finding its expression in the writings of Judah the Hasid. His students, and pre-eminently Eleazar of Worms, developed the method of attributing esoteric meaning to the numbering of the sacred texts (practical cabala). This was the period when Jews and Christians devoted equal zeal (but with quite divergent results) to symbolic and allegorical interpretations of the Old Testament. Reciprocally, Jewish learning strongly influenced Christian thought. While the first Aristotelians fed on Maimonides, Nicholas of Lyra studied Rashi. Yet, *si Lyranus non lyrasset, Lutherus non saltasset,* and these contacts between Christians and Jews in the twelfth and thirteenth centuries made an essential contribution to the movement of ideas that, three centuries later, culminated in the Reformation. In fact, one might say that despite the tension that prevailed between them and which was to increase, Jews and Christians were still members of one and the same society, one and the same civilization.

This state of affairs is reflected in many revealing texts. Thus the good trouvère Rutebeuf, who in his major works (such as the *Miracle de Théophile*) already portrays the conventional type of wicked Jew—a willing instrument of the Devil—offers in his minor plays his friend Charlot the Jew, a jongleur and Bohemian like himself. Of course, in Rutebeuf's eyes, being a Jew constitutes a grave defect, even worse than being syphilitic, and "Charlot has neither belief nor faith, any more than a dog that gnaws at carrion" (125); but defective as he is, this Charlot is accepted by our poet as an equal. Although he differs from Christians by his vice (which is that of being a Jew), he does not differ from them in essence. Of this Charlot, who certainly existed, we know only what Rutebeuf has told us; but at the same period there was in Flanders a Jewish trouvère, Mahieu of Ghent (called the Jew), who had embraced the Christian religion for the same reason that the majority of conversions take place in our own day: he was eager to please a lady with whom he was passionately in love. He explains his case quite frankly in his verses:

De sa biauté et délis	Yea, her beauty and delight
Et del mont est la meillor	Is in all the world greatest
Or n'en aist Jesu Cris	More than that of Jesus Christ
Dont j'ai fait novel seynor	Whom I have made my new
(126).	Lord.

A Jewish minnesinger, Süsskind von Trimberg, flourished at the same period in Germany. Together with Walther von der Vogelweide and Hartmann von Aue, he sang at the courts of barons and princes. Doubtless he was less favored by the nobles than his Christian confreres, and probably he suffered from this discrimination—a parallel between the thirteenth and nineteenth centuries would perhaps be appropriate here. Like Heine six hundred years later, he complains of the harshness of the great and proposes to "turn back into a Jew," to let his beard grow and wear the long cloak and hat of the Jews (127). Indeed, an illuminated text of the period (128) shows the poet in this garb at a bishop's court; but though he wears the conical hat and a beard, the features of his face are in no way different from those of the others' persons. In general, pictures of Jews in the twelfth and thirteenth centuries afford another revealing clue: apart from some English documents (129) (and England, as we have seen, constituted a special case), the Jews, while they sometimes differed from the Christians by their clothing, were distinguishable from them neither by their features nor by their actions or gestures. We see them on horseback; we find them swearing oaths in the company of Christians. The majority of the charters delivered to them by the German cities of the thirteenth century expressly grant them the status of citizens (*Bürger*[10]). The splendid illuminations embellishing the famous manuscript of the Dresden *Sachsenspiegel* confirm the tenor of this codex: the Jew is still a free man, authorized to bear arms, which gives him the right to defend himself if attacked and also the duty to defend his city, if need be, together with his Christian fellow citizens.

[10] Here is an especially characteristic passage from one charter: "A Jew will be accepted as a citizen in the following manner: he will first appear before the bishop of the Jews and the Jewish elders, and they will accept him according to their custom; this done, the bishop of the Jews, accompanied by the elders and the other Jews, will lead the man they have accepted before our lord the bishop of Worms and the magistrates, and will say that for their part they have accepted him as a citizen, then they too will accept him as a citizen, and he will swear loyalty to the bishop, to the magistrates, and to the city. He is then accepted as citizen, and he will give a cask of wine to the bishop and a half a cask to each judge and to the clerk of the city, and gratuities to the servitors." Worms charter (exact date unknown). (Cf. W. Roscher, *Volkswirtschaft,* Vol. 2, 3rd ed., p. 336.)

The *Sachsenspiegel* dates from about 1225. The *Schwaben-spiegel*, written nearly fifty years later, already reveals the strong influence of the canonical legislation, with its theory of the "perpetual serfdom" of the Jews, which this codex mentions expressly. Apparently canonical ideas were gradually penetrating secular legislation; it was at the same period, furthermore, that they found official expression in the *De-cretales* of Gregory IX (1234) and above all in the writings of Saint Thomas Aquinas. In this period we are concerned with a still quite moderate doctrine that, while positing the principle that the Jews' property belongs to the princes, specifies "not depriving them of those things necessary to life" or demanding of them "unaccustomed things." Here is how Saint Thomas puts it:

"It would be licit, according to law, to hold the Jews, on account of their crime, in perpetual servitude, and thereby the princes might regard the possessions of the Jews as belonging to the state; nonetheless, they should use them with a certain moderation and not deprive the Jews of those things necessary to life . . . let no service be demanded of them by force that they were not accustomed to performing previously, for unaccustomed things ordinarily cause more disturbance in men's minds."

However:

"I consider that the punishment must be greater for a Jew and for any usurer than for another culprit, particularly since it is known that the money taken from him does not belong to him. One can also add to the fine another penalty, lest it not appear to suffice for his punishment that he be deprived of the money owed by him to another.

"It would be best to force the Jews to labor in order to gain their livelihood, as is done in certain parts of Italy, instead of letting them live in idleness, enriching themselves by usury alone . . ." (130).

It is on the whole the problem of the usurer, that nightmare of the Church, rather than the problem of the Jew, that is settled in this way. The penalties imposed upon the Jew are merely those of the usurer. Even for the "angelic doctor," the Jew is more important for his economic role than for his symbolic significance, which, for the moment, is barely perceived.

PART THREE
THE CENTURY OF THE DEVIL

The second half of the thirteenth century in Germany was a period of political chaos. While the pretenders to the imperial crown waged endless and senseless wars, the great and petty lords gained increasing freedom, and the cities constituted leagues or made themselves into principalities. There were many small private wars; there were urban and feudal insurrections. There was also the following incident, which, on the threshold of the century to come, was a kind of foreshadowing of the grave events that would mark it.

In the town of Röttingen, in Franconia, in the spring of 1298, the Jews were charged with profanation of the Host. An inhabitant of the town named Rindfleisch, a gentleman, according to some, though others called him a butcher (for *Rindfleisch* means "beef flesh"), aroused the populace, exhorting them to vengeance. Under his leadership, an armed band fell upon the Jews of Röttingen, who were massacred and burned down to the last one. There was nothing new about this—we have already seen that there had previously been a great number of such cases, but what followed is more unusual. Rindfleisch's band did not stop there: far from dispersing, his *Judenschächter* (Jew killers) wandered from city to city, looting and burning Jewish neighborhoods and slaughtering the inhabitants, except for those who accepted baptism. Invading most of the cities of Franconia and Bavaria, except for Regensburg and Augsburg, Rindfleisch's campaigns lasted several months (April-September, 1298). One contemporary Christian chronicler declares that nearly one hundred thousand Jews were massacred at this time; such a figure cannot be greatly exaggerated, for we have lists of several thousand victims (131).

What is new about the incident is that for the first time *all* the Jews of the country were held responsible for a crime imputed to one or at most several Jews. It is quite likely that as usual the accusation was a pretext for large-scale pillaging. But heretofore incidents of this nature, numerous as they were, had remained in a sense localized. This one spread, and we may say in modern terms that apart from the excesses of the Crusaders it was the first case of Jewish "genocide" in Christian Europe. Henceforth, the fourteenth century was to be studded with countless tragedies of this kind. Ultimately only a few handfuls of impecunious and vagabond Jews remained in northern Europe, while, at the same time, anti-Semitism in the strict sense of the term was established among the gentile populations. But first let us look at the broad outlines of this tormented century.

six

Background:
The Fourteenth Century

We have reached that very important period when the imposing and monolithic structure of medieval Christendom slowly
begins to crumble and when new groupings, ultimately to
become the modern nations and already displaying national characteristics, first suggest themselves, when the old
social framework weakens and there is felt the rumbling force
of the people—urban artisans and humble agricultural laborers—seeking to assert their rights. Such gigantic transformations do not take place without great upheaval, and it was
at the cost of countless ordeals and suffering that the birth of
a new society was begun. For Europeans, the fourteenth century was undoubtedly the century most teeming with crises
and catastrophes of all kinds. Perhaps some day it will be
compared to our own.

Politically, the Hundred Years' War had exhausted France
and England, while Germany remained in a state of permanent anarchy. Socially, there were the Jacqueries of France,
the peasant revolts of the Low Countries and England, and
above all that bloody urban agitation, those "democratic rev-
olutions" which in most German cities, in Italy, and in Flanders set the ambitious professional guilds against the patri-
cians, exhausted by power. In these uprisings, as we shall
see, many massacres and expulsions of Jews occurred. Even
the natural calamities of this century were worse than previous ones: there was the great famine of 1315-1317 and, most
important, the plague of the Black Death of 1347-1349. And
lastly, another epidemic, no less formidable—the witch hunt

—broke out in the second half of this accursed century; but this will be discussed in another part of this section.

The countless anti-Jewish excesses of the preceding centuries, even though sporadic, had already prepared the ground sufficiently so that in a grave crisis, a collective disaster, the Jews were immediately designated as responsible. To see in detail how this functioned and with what speed it led both to the aggravation of the Jews' fate and to a redoubling of hatred and fear of them, we shall examine more closely a singularly instructive example. The scene is France, and the drama, in two acts, lasts from 1315 to 1322.

In 1315 a terrible famine, perhaps the worst in its history, swept Europe. The summer of 1314 had been rainy and that of 1315 saw a veritable deluge: the harvest was a catastrophe, and where, as in Flanders, vast regions were flooded, it was virtually nonexistent. It was in vain, Geffroi de Paris tells us, that prayers were addressed to Heaven: "Canons and collegians . . . all prayed to God, that he might send good weather unto earth—but for a long while all that was in store . . . was great famine and great hunger. And dearth of bread and wine . . ." (132). The famine was so great that in Paris and Antwerp people died by the hundreds in the streets, and the desolation must have been equally great in the villages. Cases of cannibalism were frequent. Lacking flour, bakers made their bread "with the dregs of wine and the droppings of pigs," and the price of wheat rose from twelve sous per septier to sixty. The harvests of 1316 and 1317 were also bad, and though there was some improvement in 1318, in certain regions the consequences of the famine—epidemics and social upheavals—made themselves felt for a long time to come (133).

Thus it was that in 1320 the peasants of northern France, exhausted by poverty, left their isolated homes and set off together, in the hope of improving their lot. Set off for where? They were not certain themselves; ultimately they headed south, milder in every season, and their numbers swelled as they proceeded. Preaching friars, as starved as the peasants, added certain mystical touches, an ideological significance. One young shepherd had visions: a miraculous bird perched on his shoulder and exhorted him to fight the infidels. It was to be a Crusade, then, and thus was born the "Shepherds' Crusade." On their way, the hordes lived off the land, pillaging as they went, and since it was a Crusade, they chose Jews by preference as victims. Without our knowing just how, the "shepherds" reached Aquitaine, where the story of their undertaking becomes clearer: the chroniclers have left us circumstantial accounts of their crimes in this province. The blood of Jews flowed at Auch, at Gimont, at Castelsarrasin, Rabastens, Gaillac, Albi, Verdun-sur-Garonne, Toulouse, and other places, unopposed by royal officials and apparently with the silent approval of the people. (There is still today near Moissac a place called "Trou-aux-Juifs"—Jew hole.[1]) Here is the vivid account of one Christian chronicler:

"The shepherds laid siege to all the Jews who had come from all sides to take refuge in whatever strongholds the kingdom of France afforded, fearful at seeing the approach of the mob. At Verdun-sur-Garonne, the Jews defended themselves heroically and in a superhuman manner against their besiegers by hurling many stones, beams, and even their own children from the top of a tower. But their resistance served to no purpose, for the shepherds slaughtered a great number of the besieged Jews by smoke and by fire, burning the doors of the stronghold. The Jews, realizing that they would not escape alive, preferred to kill themselves rather than be massacred by the uncircumcised. They then chose one of their number, who seemed the strongest, so that he might kill them. This man put some five hundred of them to death, with their consent. He then descended from the castle tower with the few Jewish children who still remained alive. He sought a parley with the shepherds and told them what he had done, asking to be baptized with the children who re-

---

[1] Compare many German or Alsatian suburbs called "Judenloch" or "Judenbühl" (Jew hill) designating places where the Jews were massacred during the Black Death epidemic of 1347-1349.

mained. The shepherds answered him: 'Have you then committed such a crime upon your own race, and thereby seek to escape among us the death you deserve?' They killed him by quartering. They spared the children, whom they made Catholics by baptism. They continued even unto Carcassonne in the same wise, and upon the way multiplied their crimes . . ." (134).

We recognize, in this account, the accents of the age of the Crusades. According to one Jewish source, one hundred and forty Jewish communities were exterminated by the shepherds (135). (Of course, the statistics provided by medieval authors are subject to question; nonetheless, they give a suggestion of numbers as well as a glimpse of the impression these events made upon contemporaries.) Finally, the authorities decided to act against the shepherds, who, after having attacked the Jews, began to turn against the clerics. At Avignon, Pope John XXII preached against them; in Paris, King Philip V sent troops against the horde and easily dispersed their unorganized ranks. By the end of 1320, no more was heard of the shepherds; all we know is that several groups, crossing the Pyrenees, reached Spain, where for some time they indulged themselves in further massacres.

This was the first act. It appears that such massacres provoked among the people who witnessed them, even if they did not participate in them, a certain alarm, some superstitious feeling, a sense of malediction, and the fear that the Jews would seek revenge. These very apprehensions gave rise to a new legend, one that was to justify retroactively the crimes committed. The coincidence in the dates is in fact so striking that it is impossible not to infer a relationship between the massacres of 1320 and the new accusation lodged against the Jews some months later, on the very sites of their martyrdom. In the course of the summer of 1321 a rumor arose in Aquitaine alleging that a dreadful conspiracy had been plotted by the lepers and the Jews—the former as executors, the latter as conceivers of the plan—to put all Christians to death by poisoning their wells and springs.

There was no dearth of horrible details: a drug consisting of human blood, urine, and three secret herbs, to which the powder of the consecrated Host was added, was tied in small bags and thrown into the wells of the region. Who could doubt this, since a huge leper, captured on the lands of the Lord of Parthenai, had confessed everything? [2] He had stated that the poison had been given him by a rich Jew who had offered him ten livres for his trouble, and that a much larger sum had been promised him should he manage to recruit other lepers for this sinister task. According to another version, the powder consisted of a mixture of frogs' legs, snakes' heads, and women's hair, the mixture impregnated with a "very black and stinking" liquid, horrible not only to smell but to see. Here, too, there could be no doubt as to the magic virtues of the concoction, since it did not burn when put into a roaring fire. Moreover, the Jews were not the only instigators of the plot: seeking further, it was possible for the investigators to establish, thanks to certain "Arab letters" intercepted and duly translated by the learned "physician," Pierre of Acre, that in fact it was the kings of Granada and of Tunis who were at its source. In still another version, it was no longer a question of Mohammedan princes but purely and simply of the Devil.

Thus for the first time we are dealing with concrete charges that Jewry is plotting the destruction of all Christendom, with the help of a very learned and very precise method. This, we repeat, followed upon an extermination of Jews that was not at all legendary, but quite real. We can, with some authors, consider that certain council decisions of the previous century—such as those of Breslau and Vienna (1267), forbidding Christians to buy victuals from the Jews for fear that the latter, "who regard the Christians as their enemies, might per-

---

[2] "And when they asked him as to the composition of these poisons, he said that they were of men's blood and urine and of three manners of herbs, the which he could not or would not name, and that with them was put of the body of Jesu Christ, the whole of which was dried and made into a powder." (*Chronique de Saint-Denis*, in Bouquet, *Recueil des historiens des Gaules et de la France*, Vol. 20, p. 704.)

fidiously poison them"—formed the basis for this new myth
(136). We can even seek other precedents for it (137); but
what was in earlier instances only a rhetorical exhortation,
spoken from the pulpit, here shows an altogether different
aspect. The conspiracy formed by Jews and lepers, those
pariahs par excellence, is in itself sufficiently significant.

Although the legend of the Jews as professional poisoners
was to enjoy a considerable vogue several decades later, it
had, for the moment, only a limited impact. Public terror and
anger were expressed in several lynchings: "The common
people wrought this justice without calling upon either bailiff
or provost," says one chronicle (138). Royal power (without
our being able to ascertain whether King Philip V himself
believed in the legend) skillfully made use of these events as
a pretext for satisfying the people and at the same time enriching the royal treasury. To satisfy the people, detailed instructions were sent to all seneschals and bailiffs, informing
them of the criminal enterprises of the lepers and Jews, "so
notorious that in no manner can they be hidden," and enjoining them to investigate the Jews within their provinces. Many
arrests and trials occurred throughout France, in Aquitaine
as in Champagne, where forty Jews, we are told, committed
suicide in the prison of Vitry-le-François, and in Touraine,
where one hundred and sixty were burned in Chinon. The
confiscations that followed—to enrich the royal treasury—
apparently constituted the main purpose. They were extended, in fact, even to those Jews acknowledged to be innocent: those of Paris had to pay a fine of 5,300 livres, while
the total fine for the entire country was 150,000 livres (139).
As a fiscal maneuver, the incident assumes its place in the
context of the policy followed in the fourteenth century in
France by the royal power regarding the Jews, true *eponges
à phynances* (financial sponges): expelled, recalled, and
subject to mass arrest many times over. But seen in the harsh
light cast on the growth of popular superstitions, the policy
goes infinitely beyond this context. To massacre first, and
then, from fear of revenge, to accuse afterward; to attribute

to the victims one's own aggressive intentions; to impute to them one's own cruelty: from country to country and from century to century, under various disguises, this is the device we find. (Thus the Nazi killers, to justify themselves for having massacred Jewish children, were known to speak of "potential avengers"; thus a municipal council of Bonn, Germany, dismissed a Jewish doctor for fear that he might take revenge on his German patients.)

We find the same sequence of events in Germany fifteen years later. Against the background of permanent anarchy then prevalent there, two gentlemen, the Armleders, have visions and repeat Rindfleisch's exploits in an effort to avenge Christ. In 1336, Jews are massacred in Alsace and Swabia (140), and it is only *after* these first massacres that the accusations are made. Cases of profanation are reported in Deggendorf, Bavaria (141), and in Pulka, Austria (142), serving as a pretext for new massacres. The emperors and princes, even had they been moved to protect the Jews, did not have the necessary authority to oppose these riots; on the contrary, in 1345, inaugurating a new custom, King John authorized his subjects in Liegnitz and Breslau to destroy the Jewish cemeteries in order to use the tombstones to repair the city walls: *sepulchra hostium religiosa nobis non sunt,* it would be said later on (143). But we are now on the eve of crucial events that were no less important for the Jews than those of 1096, and which were to weigh heavily upon the destiny of all Europe.

The Black Plague

Let us recall the description that Boccaccio has left us of the plague:

"In the cities, men fell sick by thousands, and lacking care and aid, almost all died. In the morning, their bodies were found at the doors of the houses where they had expired during the night. . . . It reached the point where no further account was taken of a dying man than is today taken of the merest cattle.

"Nor were the villages spared. Lacking the succor of a physician, without the aid of any servant, the poor and wretched farmers perished with their families by day, by night, on their farms, in their isolated houses, on the roads, and even in their fields.

"Then they abandoned their customs, even as the city dwellers: they no longer took any concern for their affairs nor for themselves; all, expecting to die from one day to the next, thought neither of working nor of putting by the fruits of their past labors, but sought rather to consume what they had before them. The cattle, the flocks, the beasts of burden and of the barnyard, the very dogs, those faithful companions of man, wandered unheeded about the countryside, in the fields where the harvests had been abandoned, without being gathered or even cut. . . . To return to the city,[3] here the cruelty of the scourge was such that in the course of four or five months, more than one hundred thousand persons perished, a number greater than that estimated to be its population before this dreadful malady."

Such was the Black Plague, a catastrophe that in the space of three years, from 1347 to 1350, annihilated a third and perhaps more[4] of the population of Europe, and beside which our century's wars and threats of "atomic extinction" may seem to be child's play. Many authors have claimed that it was at this very period that the knell of medieval civilization sounded, or even that the plague constituted "the most marked schism in the continuity of history that humanity has

[3] The city: Florence, where Boccaccio was living at the time of the Black Plague.

[4] As we have said, all statistics relating to the Middle Ages are subject to question. But in this case, certain authors have managed to achieve partial results that are quite precise, based for instance on the mortality of priests in a given diocese or on the replacement of professors in a university. The figures thus obtained (cf. A. Campbell, *The Black Death and Men of Learning*, New York, 1931) indicate a mortality of from one-third to one-half of the population.

ever known" (144). The question may be evaluated differently, depending on the point of view from which it is examined and on one's concept of history. In the problem that
concerns us, which is primarily one of a collective obliteration
and its social repercussions, the consequences of the great
panic of the years 1347-1350 were tremendous. We must
also note that the epidemic, attacking elite groups and clerics
as well as the masses, had in consequence a marked lowering
of the intellectual level [5] and a general corruption of manners; that it unhinged men's minds, aroused the expectation of
the Apocalypse, and spread popular obsession with the Devil.
Moreover, even as late as the end of the century, there were
constant new outbreaks of the terrible scourge.

It is not at all surprising, under these conditions, that the
Black Plague, climaxing the chain of events we have discussed in the foregoing pages, should have sealed the fate of
the Jews of Europe: their image, in the eyes of Christians, was
henceforth to be seen through a cloud of sulfur and ashes.
In a sense, the year 1347 can be compared to the year 1096,
for the repercussions of the epidemic were of two kinds: the
immediate effect—the destruction of the Jews throughout
Europe; and the remote effect—the coming-of-age of the
specific phenomenon which is Christian anti-Semitism.

Throughout Europe, men wondered anxiously: Why this
scourge? What was the reason for it? Cultivated people, particularly doctors, composed learned treatises, from which it
appeared, according to the best rules of scholastic philosophy, that there were two kinds of causes for the epidemic:
primary causes, of cosmic origin (unfavorable conjunction
of the planets; earthquakes) and secondary or terrestrial
causes (pollution of the air, poisoning of the waters). Even
the hypothesis of contagion was mentioned by some enlightened thinkers. Simpler minds did not bother with such subtle-

[5] Thus, following the dearth of teachers, "popular" English was substituted for French in the schools of England. Such is the origin of modern
English.

ties: for them the plague was either a divine punishment or the evil-doing of Satan or both at once, God having given free rein to His antagonist to chastise Christendom. Satan, in these circumstances, operated as usual with the help of agents who polluted the waters and poisoned the air. And where could he recruit them if not from among the dregs of humanity, among the outcasts of all types, the lepers—and above all from among the Jews, the people of both God and the Devil? Thus the Jews were promoted on a grand scale to their role of scapegoat.

These rumors appeared first, it would seem, in Savoy, sometimes preceding the scourge, sometimes following it. A man with the suggestive name of "Jacob Pascal" (Jacob a Pasche or Jacob à Pascate: the link with the legend of ritual murder is evident), of Toledo,[6] allegedly distributed doses of deadly drugs to his coreligionists in Chambéry. It is noteworthy that the technique attributed to the poisoners, as well as the composition of the poison, was in every respect identical to that described thirty years before, during the "shepherds" incident. On the orders of Duke Amadeus of Savoy, the Jews were arrested at Thonon, Chillon, Le Châtelard, and, after being tortured, confessed. One of them, Aquet of Ville-Neuve, acknowledged that he had operated all over Europe: in Venice, Calabria, Apulia, and Toulouse . . . (145). From Savoy, the legend spread to Switzerland, where trials followed by executions took place in Bern, Zurich, and around Lake Constance. The consuls of the good city of Bern were even moved to write to German cities— Basel, Strasbourg, and Cologne—in order to warn them of the dreadful Jewish conspiracy. In Germany, events rapidly took a different turn. In many cities the princes and magistrates attempted to protect the Jews. In September, 1348, Pope Clement VI published a bull in which he pointed out

6 Why Toledo? Perhaps this is a confusion between Toledo and the *Toldoth Yeshu,* a sacrilegious biography of Jesus written in the East during the first millennium of the Christian era, and which Agobard of Lyons already knew.

explicitly that Jews died of the plague just as frequently as Christians, that the epidemic also broke out in regions where there were no Jews, and that there was thus no reason to incriminate them (146). But such efforts were usually ineffectual, for in the German cities it was the people who took the initiative in these massacres, followed by looting, which also represented for them a rebellion against the established order. Thus in Strasbourg, where the memory of the Armleder brothers' exploits was still vivid, these internal struggles lasted nearly three months. The municipality proceeded to hold an investigation and concluded that the Jews were not guilty. It was thereupon overthrown and the new municipality found nothing more pressing to do than to imprison all the Jews, numbering some two thousand, and to burn them the next day in their own cemetery (February 14, 1349), while their property was distributed among the city residents. "Such was the poison that caused the Jews to perish," one chronicler wrote as their epilogue (147). These massacres and lootings took place in the great majority of German cities: in Colmar, where a "Jew hole" (*Judenloch*) still perpetuates its memory; in Worms and Oppenheim, where the Jews themselves set fire to their district and perished in the flames; in Frankfurt and Erfurt, where they were put to the sword; in Cologne and Hanover, where some were massacred and the rest exiled.

Other fanatics persecuted the Jews solely from religious motives. As a result of an outburst of fanaticism aroused by the scourge, bands of penitents, the "flagellants," wandered from city to city, mortifying themselves in order to appease and avert divine wrath; thirty-four days of flagellation sufficed, apparently, to obtain from Jesus the remission of all sins. Leading an austere life and singing hymns, the "flagellants" traveled throughout Germany and even into France, and their public exhibitions, acclaimed by the populace, generally terminated in a massacre of the Jews. The pope undertook an investigation of the "flagellants" and received from his legate, Jean de Feyt, a very unfavorable report (148). In

France, royal justice quickly put an end to their activities, but in Germany and the Low Countries, the results of their wanderings were much more serious. Here is a vivid description of them as recorded by the chronicler Jean d'Outremeuse:

"The good cities were full of these 'Flagellants,' and the streets as well; and they all called each other 'brother' as a token of alliance . . . and they began to forget the service and the ritual of the Holy Church, and maintained in their folly and their presumption that their rites and their songs were finer and more worthy than the ceremonies of the priests and clerics, and thereby it was feared that even as they multiplied, these people, in their heresy, would end by destroying the Holy Church and by killing priests, canons, and clerics, lusting to have their wealth and power. In the time when these 'Flagellants' went among the countries, there came to pass a great wonder that must not be forgotten, for when it was seen that this mortality and this pestilence did not cease after the penitences which these beaters [the 'Flagellants'] caused, a general rumor spread; and it was commonly said and certainly believed that this epidemic came from the Jews, and that the Jews had cast great poisons in the wells and springs throughout the world, in order to sow the plague and to poison Christendom; which was why great and small alike had great choler against the Jews, who were everywhere taken where they could be held, and put to death and burned in all the regions where the 'Flagellants' came and went, by the lords and by the magistrates . . ." (149).

In Germany, the extermination of the Jews, whether inspired by greed or piety, reached such a point that in the regions where there were few or no Jews (as in the territories of the Teutonic Order), Christians allegedly of Jewish origin were apparently massacred in their stead (150). Certain of the accusers, in order to establish the Jews' responsibilities more definitely, declared that the Jews were immune to the plague—they did not die of it or died in smaller numbers—and this legend took root so deeply that it was still believed by certain nineteenth-century historians, who tried to explain it as the result of better hygienic conditions in Jewish homes.[7] However, even at the time, the chronicler Conrad von Megenberg noted:

"In many wells, bags filled with poison were found, and a countless number of Jews were massacred in the Rhineland, in Franconia, and in all the German countries. In truth, I do not know whether certain Jews had done this. Had it been thus, assuredly the evil would have been worse. But I know, on the other hand, that no German city had so many Jews as Vienna, and so many of them there succumbed to the plague that they were obliged to enlarge their cemetery greatly and to buy two more buildings. They would have been very stupid to poison themselves . . ." (151).

No major Jewish community in Germany, with perhaps the exception of those of Vienna and Regensburg, was exempted from massacres during the fateful year 1348. These became so prevalent that Emperor Charles IV took the precaution of ceding in advance to certain municipalities, against a specified sum, the property of "his" Jews, in anticipation of their ultimate extermination. "May God forbid!" added the prince (152): merely a stylistic flourish, for the massacre followed at once. This is what happened, especially in Frankfurt, Nürnberg, and Augsburg.

Though there are no reliable statistics about the number of victims, we can gain some idea of the extent of the destruction from the fact that during the years following the plague, the Jews became for some time a rare and valued commodity. Thus the city of Speyer, in 1352, invited the Jews to return, with strong promises of protection and total security (153); the archbishop of Mainz did the same (154); and a codex published at this period, the *Meissener Rechtsbuch,* contains stipulations exceptionally favorably to the Jews: their synagogues and cemeteries are to be well protected, the Christians must aid them in case of attack, and so on (155). Similarly, in France, where expulsions and recalls had

---

[7] This is the express opinion of Jewish historians such as Graetz, Dubnow, etc.

alternated from the beginning of the century, the Jews were recalled by John the Good (John II) in 1361, under much more favorable conditions then they had enjoyed previously. Slowly, several Jewish communities were reconstituted; again they took up usury, generally on a small scale, and added another specialty: trade in old clothes. But soon the expulsions began again, and the status of the Jews no longer resembled in any respect what it had been in the preceding century. Let us consider this briefly.

The condition of the Jews in Europe after the Black Plague

The tragedy of the Black Plague dizzily hastened the process that had been in operation for more than two centuries: hereafter, the history of the Jews was to follow a fantastic and capricious course. As we survey their social position during the second half of the fourteenth century, the most important thing to note is that the economic "foundation" becomes insignificant in their history. In modern terminology, it is the "superstructure" that swells in importance (which is indeed what constitutes, from this angle, its considerable interest, since the exceptions help us to understand the rule).

According to the terms of one charter, a legal document designed to bring about the return of the Jews to France in 1361, "They have neither nation nor territory of their own in all of Christendom where they may remain, frequent, or reside. . . ." [8] The text is explicit: Whereas in the preceding centuries the Jews usually had a specific legal status and legal guarantees, and massacres or expulsions were the exception, henceforth an outlaw life becomes, so to speak, their

[8] "They have neither nation nor territory of their own in all of Christendom, where they may remain, frequent, or reside, if it be not by the strict and pure will and permission of the lord or lords under whom they agree to remain as their subjects and who consent to receive and accept them." (Laurière, *Ordonnances des rois de France*, Vol. 3, p. 471.)

normal condition, and if they manage to live somewhere in security for a time, it is because the local potentate tolerates them; because this is his interest—or his whim.

Take the case of France. We have seen that neither Philip II nor Saint Louis (Louis IX) had managed to expel the Jews (though the former tried, and the latter often thought of doing so), nor had they even brought about important changes in their status. In 1306, Philip the Fair (Philip IV) was more successful. He expelled almost all of them, though he retained the richest for several months, in order to collect the sums that were owed them down to the last .sou, for in the mind of this eminently practical prince, the chief consideration was to benefit the royal treasury. In response to the "common outcry of the people," as we have seen, the Jews were recalled by Louis X in 1315, but six years later, after the "shepherds" incident, they were expelled again, and it would seem that for some forty years there were no Jews in France: at least, there is no mention of them in any reference or chronicle. But in 1361 the financial plight of the kingdom had become so acute that the treasury was unable to raise the money to ransom John II, taken prisoner by the English. The Dauphin Charles decided to appeal to the Jews, among other measures. They were readmitted to France under entirely new conditions. They were subjected to a heavy individual tax of seven Florentine florins per year per adult, plus one florin per child; but on the other hand, they were permitted to acquire houses and land, and a special "guardian of the Jews" (Louis d'Étampes, a distant cousin of the king) was appointed to safeguard their interests. Above all, they were authorized to charge the exorbitant interest of 87 percent; and finally—a significant detail—the Jewish community was authorized to expel a member without seeking the authorization of the "guardian of the Jews," but, in this event, must pay the treasury the enormous sum of one hundred florins in compensation for the taxpaying citizen who thus disappeared . . . (156). In such ways everything was set up to extract, via the Jews, as much money as possible.

For twenty years they enjoyed relative tranquillity, but they were no longer the convenient and familiar moneylenders whose return the people had once demanded. They had become hated and despicable financial agents. Disturbances in their own organization and internal cohesion also increased at this time, and apostasies seem to have been frequent. As usual, the renegade Jews immediately became the principal enemies of their former coreligionists, as one decree of 1378 indicates:

"Several of their law, who have recently become Christians, envious and spiteful because they no longer derive any advantage from having done so,[9] have sought and do seek from day to day to accuse the Jews, making many denunciations . . . on account of which accusations and denunciations they have been and are oftentimes seized, molested, belabored, and injured . . ." (157).

Under these circumstances, when, upon the accession of Charles VI in 1380, upheavals and riots broke out, popular resentment turned against the Jews, who were murdered and pillaged throughout France. This "notorious and enormous commotion made against them in the said city of Paris as well as in several other places" (158) continued without any pretext of avenging religious offenses; and now the clergy added its own weight, and the archbishop of Paris himself sided with the rioters. Royal power managed to protect the Jews, but this state of affairs could not last; because the contributions demanded of the Jews grew increasingly heavy, the privileges granted to them so that they could meet these contributions often grew in proportion. (Thus one decree of February, 1389, orders that all disputes between Christians and Jews be settled by the "guardians of the Jews," that is, by officials appointed to protect them, and paid by them. Furthermore, Jews are authorized to have their defaulting debtors imprisoned) (159). Such advantages raised popular resentment to the bursting point, while

[9] That is because they can no longer enjoy the profits they made when they were Jews.

inciting the government to put increasing pressure on the Jewish financiers, who were rapidly becoming paupers. For a few more years, against the background of the desperate struggle of Burgundians against Armagnacs, various reversals took place, and finally the anti-Jewish faction triumphed. In 1392 a decree abrogated the old custom by which Jews who accepted baptism forfeited their property (160). This indicates that the Jews had already become a negligible factor as a source of revenue; henceforth, their fate was sealed. In September, 1394, "moved by piety and fearing the evil influence of the Jews upon the Christians" (161), the king ordered the Jews' expulsion, this time putting a definite end to the age-old history of French Judaism.[10] The edict was promulgated on the Jewish Day of Atonement; this is one of the first manifestations of the contemptuous concern for the Jewish calendar that we shall find repeated many times down through the centuries.

But France, which even in the fourteenth century was a nation ruled by a central authority, is much less suitable for our inquiry than Germany, particularly since it was the Jews within the area of the Holy Roman Empire who were henceforth to constitute Judaism's chief branch. The course of their debasement was to be, in broad outline, much the same as it was in France, and their expulsion soon followed. Yet there was this difference: that in a minutely partitioned territory, the process crumbled into a dust of individual destinies. This very breakdown was ultimately to permit the Jews in Germany to exist there, for it made a general and simultaneous expulsion of the Jews from Germany impossible.

The definitive loss of the German Jews' rights of citizenship dates from 1343. In that year, Emperor Louis IV, carrying the theory of the Jews' "serfdom" to its logical conclusion,

---

[10] The historian Robert Anchel has formulated the hypothesis according to which a certain number of Jews, concealing their identity, continued to live in France after the expulsion of 1394. His arguments, though not entirely convincing, are often extremely provocative. They are to be found in his book *Les Juifs de France*, Paris, 1946, p. 125.

instituted a poll tax of one florin, to be paid to the imperial treasury by every Jew over twelve years of age. And, according to medieval concepts, a man who pays tribute on his body can no longer be considered a citizen.

We have already noted that the general economic disintegration following the Black Plague caused certain German cities and principalities to locate and recall the Jews and to treat them for a decade or two as a kind of precious item. But the stipulations on their residence were quite different from what they had been. The protection of the "imperial chamber," whose serfs they continued to be in theory, no longer existed except on paper, like the power of the emperors themselves. The latter, impelled by their need for money, ceded to the cities "their" Jews or the credits of their Jews. Thus Louis IV stated in 1343 to the Jews of Nürnberg: "You belong to us, body and belongings, and we can dispose of them and do with you as we please" (162). After the Black Plague, it was usually the cities or the local princes who granted new charters of residence. These were now distinctive in being granted only on uncertain terms and for a limited time. The expulsion of the Jews upon the expiration of this time limit therefore does not constitute a persecution—it is a normal and legitimate operation. Thus it was quite legally, in a sense, that the Jews became eternal wanderers. There were also "irregular" expulsions, in violation of provisions of the charter; and some occurred under circumstances so chaotic that we cannot say whether or not they were legal. Certain charters even expressly provided that the Jews be expelled before the end of their term in the event of disorder occasioned by their presence: as, for example, the charter granted by the city of Trier in 1362 (163).

As in France, the Jews at first enjoyed, for a generation or two, a period of relative peace. But in 1384 a new development occurred in southern Germany: in Augsburg, in Nürnberg, and in neighboring small towns, Jews were rounded up and released only after payment of a sizable ransom. The following year, the delegates of thirty-eight cities, meeting in

Ulm, proclaimed a general cancellation of debts owed to Jews. Two years later, in 1388, the first general expulsion from Strasbourg was ordered, followed by expulsions from the Palatinate in 1394. Throughout the fifteenth century, expulsions continued. Here are some of the most important: in 1420, from Austria; in 1424, from Fribourg and Zurich, "because of their usuries" (164); in 1426, from Cologne, "in honor of God and the Holy Virgin" (165); in 1432, from Saxony; in 1439, from Augsburg; in 1453, from Würzburg; in 1454, from Breslau. The list, which snowballs at the end of the century, could be extended indefinitely. Some of these expulsions became permanent, while others were followed by readmissions, which explains how it was possible for the Jews of Mainz to be expelled on four different occasions within fifty years: in 1420, by the archbishop; in 1438, by the town councilors; in 1462, following a conflict between two candidates for the archepiscopal seat; and in 1471, again by the archbishop.

The reasons given for expulsion were sometimes of a temporal nature, such as to protect the people from Jewish usuries; sometimes religious, such as to procure divine forgiveness. Sometimes the reasons were stated with precision and in detail. Thus, in demanding Duke Leopold's authorization to expel the Jews in 1401, the magistrates of the city of Fribourg invoked the well-known fact that "all Jews thirst for the Christian blood that permits them to prolong their existence" (166). More simply, the cities of Alsace complained in 1477 of disturbances resulting from the presence of Jews: Swiss confederates going into France pillaged the Jews regularly, and this caused disorder; thus the Jews must be expelled (167). In reality, disputes over the Jews generally pitted their "owners"—princes or municipalities who derived a certain profit from their presence—against the mass of citizens, who derived no profit and who hoped to benefit from the Jews' disappearance. Most often, the citizens finally succeeded in forcing the hand of the authorities—or resorted to force without seeking permission to do so. Thus the townspeople of Riquevihr, in Alsace, without even bothering to ask their seigneur, decided one fine day in 1420 to expel the Jews, tracking them down in the streets and killing those who in their opinion were not fleeing quickly enough (168). On the other hand, when the municipality of Regensburg, supported by its bishop, attempted in 1476 to expel the Jews, on the classic pretext of ritual murder, it met with failure. The Jewish community of the city was supposed to enjoy the favor of Emperor Frederick III. Its emissaries presented themselves at his court with the plea that since the Jews of Regensburg had been living in the ancient city even before the birth of Jesus Christ, they could in no way be held responsible for his crucifixion; doubtless, too, they used arguments of a more practical nature, so that Frederick III, by a judgment worthy of Solomon, settled the conflict by imposing a fine of 8,000 guilders on the municipality, another of 10,000 guilders on the Jews, and ordered the maintenance of the status quo. The citizens who, let us recall, had protected the Jews during the period of Rindfleisch's excesses in 1298, as well as during the Black Plague, then resorted to other measures: bakers no longer sold bread to the Jews, millers refused to grind their flour, the markets were open to them only after four in the afternoon, when the Christians had finished making their purchases. . . . Finally, the Regensburg Jews were expelled in 1519 (169).

Vale of Tears it was called in the next century by a famous Jewish chronicler,[11] and with the aid of such records written against a background of local slanders, cases of profanation of the Host or ritual murder, or merely spontaneous pogroms, of which we have seen many examples, Jewish history was to be written in later ages. To quote a German historian of the nineteenth century: "Thus it happened that they [the Jews] no longer had any place of fixed abode in the major part of

11 The work that the learned doctor Joseph Ha-Cohen wrote under this title in Italy around 1575 may be considered as the first attempt to produce a history of the Jews. The author was the first to utilize Jewish and Christian sources simultaneously.

Germany, being authorized only to stop for a few days, in return for payment of a toll charge. Whereas, following the Crusades, their status in the German countries had become precarious, by the end of the Middle Ages they were veritable wandering Jews, traveling from city to city without having any settled home in any land" (170).

Indeed, one can count on the fingers of one hand the German cities that, at the end of the fifteenth century, granted the Jews an assured right of residence. In a continuous tide, sometimes by whole communities, the German Jews emigrated to the more hospitable regions of Poland and Lithuania. Others camped near the city gates, settling in some outlying suburb: the Jews of Nürnberg in Furth, those of Augsburg in Pfersee, and so on.

It would seem that the less numerous they became, the more attention was paid to them. Where they were not expelled, they were the object of countless new persecutions. And where the legal documents of the preceding centuries reflect a generally satisfactory condition, those of the end of the Middle Ages are filled with degrading decrees.

In cases of capital punishment, it was an established custom by the end of the fourteenth century to hang a Jew by the feet and sometimes to hang beside him a fierce wolf-dog as well (171). In questions of civil litigation, the oath of a Jew was often no longer acceptable (172); even when it was, the ceremony, which by the end of the thirteenth century often assumed a humiliating aspect (according to the *Schwabenspiegel,* a Jew had to take his oath standing on a pigskin), now turned into farce or sacrilege. According to a Silesian law of 1422, a Jew had to stand on a three-legged stool and stare at the sun, speaking the traditional formula; if he fell, he paid a fine (173). In 1455 the municipality of Breslau decreed that a Jew must swear bareheaded, spelling aloud the sacred Tetragram . . . (174). As for the ecclesiastical authorities, they decreed at the Council of Basel, in 1434, that Jews would not be admitted to university studies; on the other hand, it was important that they be obliged to attend Christian sermons for their edification (175). The ceremonial procedure, as it was to be practiced in Prague, Vienna, or Rome during the following centuries, shows however that this was much more a matter of persecution than of true missionary zeal. Old charges of a religious nature were revived or reinvented. Jews were accused of vilifying Jesus daily in their prayers, and a pogrom took place in Prague in 1399 (176). In Spain, early in the fifteenth century, a malicious report was circulated that on the Day of Atonement Jews are released from all their solemn oaths (177); this slander spread throughout all Europe. With secular and ecclesiastical authorities rivaling one another in fervor, a Jew's every act, every step in his relationships with Christians, was marked by degradation.

seven

The Image of the Jew

What feelings were inspired in the mass of Christians—clerics, bourgeois, or simple laborers—as witnesses of the Jews' tribulations and degradation? As we have already discovered, animosity toward the Jews fed on the very massacres it provoked: one killed Jews first and hated them afterward. This sequence (whatever its psychological explanation) is quite regularly verified by experience. During the second half of the fourteenth century, anti-Jewish hatred reached such a peak that we can confidently date from this period the crystallization of anti-Semitism in its classic form, the form that later led Erasmus to observe: "If it is the part of a good Christian to detest the Jews, then we are all good Christians." [1]

What is most important to note is that henceforth this antagonism seems to feed on itself, irrespective of whether or not Jews inhabited a given territory. If the Jew no longer dwelt there, he was invented; and if the Christian population came into less and less conflict with Jews in daily life, it was increasingly obsessed by their image, which it found in reading, saw on monuments, and contemplated at plays and spectacles. These fictitious Jews were obviously and specifically those who were supposed to have put Jesus to death, but the men of the Middle Ages ultimately failed to distinguish between the mythical Jew and the contemporary Jew, and anti-Jewish feeling derived additional nourishment from this confusion. The Jews came to be detested in France

[1] Si christianum est odisse judaeos, hic abunde omnes christiani sumus.

and England, just as they were in Germany and Italy; and the intensity of feeling toward them, if we try to grade it according to country, seems to depend more on the substratum on which the national culture rested and to be more accentuated in the Germanic than in the Latin countries. Hence, everything contributes to make Germany pre-eminently the country for anti-Semitism.

Countless literary and artistic documents attest to this state of affairs. One might almost say that anti-Semitism increases in proportion to the development of art and literature and of their diffusion among the masses. There is virtually no genre—fabliau, satire, legend, or ballad—in which Jews are not present or are not described with ridicule or hatred, often with the help of that scatological touch so popular at the period. These themes mingle and develop from country to country. Here is an early sample, which calls in Saint Louis (Louis IX), that model of all Christian virtues, for enlightenment on how to handle Jews.

A French satire of the fourteenth century, written in the vernacular, presents a Parisian Jew, famous among his coreligionists, who fell into the public latrine. The other Jews came to his aid. "I beg you," he cried, "not to pull me out now, for today is the Sabbath. Wait till tomorrow, so as not to violate our law." They agreed and left. Some Christians who were present hastened to report the incident to King Louis. The king then ordered his men to keep the Jews from removing their coreligionist from the latrine on the Lord's Day. "He has observed the Sabbath," he said; "he will observe our Lord's day as well." So it came to pass, and when they came on Monday to rescue the unfortunate creature from his miserable predicament, he was dead (178).

This same narrative exists in a German version, in a form perhaps still more characteristic, since the pope, the spiritual guide of Christendom, is substituted for Saint Louis. We do not have the exact text of this second version, but it is mentioned in the Jewish chronicle *Vale of Tears,* which alludes to "a German book written in the Latin tongue" and states in conclusion that "the Jews at this period had great distaste for life" (179).

There were virtually no Jews left in the Low Countries after the Black Plague (180), but many literary works were devoted to them. Certain poems referred to the famous case of the profaned Hosts of Sainte-Gudule in 1370; others described ritual murders:

Les juifs . . .	The Jews . . .
Mauvais et cruels comme des chiens	Wicked and cruel as dogs
Saisirent brutalement l'enfant	Brutally seized the child
Le jetèrent par terre et le piétinèrent . . .	Threw him down and trampled him . . .
Le déshabillèrent rapidement	Swiftly stripped him bare
Et lorsqu'ils l'eurent mis nu	And once he was naked
Les sales Juifs, les chiens puants	The filthy Jews, stinking dogs,
Ils lui firent plusieurs blessures	Inflicted several wounds
Avec des poignards et des couteaux (181).	With daggers and knives . . .

There were no Jews left in England after they were expelled in 1290; but here, too, the anti-Semitic theme was to enjoy great favor. A story of ritual murder appeared about 1255. During the following century it gave rise to some twenty-one different versions of a ballad entitled "Sir Hugh or the Jew's Daughter" (182), and Geoffrey Chaucer, in his "Prioress' Tale," written about 1386, was clearly inspired by it:

Ther was in Asye, in a greet citee,
Amonges Christene folk, a Jewerye . . .
And as the child gan forby for to pace,
This cursed Jew hym hente, and heeld hym faste,
And kitte his throte, and in a pit hym caste.
I seye that in a wardrobe they hym threwe
Where as thise Jewes purgen hire entraille.

O cursed folk of Herodes al newe! . . .
O yonge Hugh of Lyncoln, slayn also
With cursed Jewes, as it is notable,
For it is but a litel while ago,
Praye eke for us . . . (183).

At this period, Italy was the only European country where
the theme of the Jew occasionally enjoyed favorable literary treatment. Even in religious drama, types of honest
and good Jews were occasionally included (184). And yet
it was in Italy, shortly after the Black Plague, that there re-
appeared one of the legends whose origin is lost in the night
of time. Whether borrowed from the East or inspired by the
cruel Roman laws of the twelve tables, the theme of the
"pound of flesh" had hitherto presented, in its various forms,
a pitiless creditor who was either a resentful slave or the obvious incarnation of the Devil (Diabolus). Then, about
1378, the Florentine author Ser Giovanni Fiorentino, in his
tale *Il Pecorone,* decided to transform the character into a
Jew (185). We know the singular fortune of this adaptation: after many other metamorphoses, it was to inspire
Shakespeare two centuries later to write the immortal *Merchant of Venice.*

But it is in religious drama, the incomparable vehicle for
propaganda in that period, that anti-Jewish sentiment is
cultivated most assiduously. Incidents taken from the New
Testament, presented in the vernacular, still constituted
the chief repertory of the theater of the Middle Ages. But the
theater, as it emancipated itself from the tutelage of the
Church, took ever greater license with religious history. In
order to indulge the spectator's primitive and violent taste,
while at the same time edifying him (for moralizing was still
the purpose of this theater), the incidents and stage business
that were meant to emphasize the greatness and sanctity of
the Saviour and of the Holy Virgin were set off against the
background of the fathomless perfidy of the Jews. The choice
of epithets coupled with each mention of the latter readily
gives a notion of this tendency: "false Jews," "false thieves,"

"false miscreants," "wicked and felonious Jews," "perverse Jews," "disloyal Jews," "traitorous Jews," "false and perverse nation," "false swine," "false and cursed race" (186); thus the very word "Jew" was charged with that pejorative sense which the dictionaries of the various European nations still reveal.[2] We need hardly add that only the adversaries of Jesus are Jews, his apostles and believers being obviously Christians.

In a general sense, the theater of the Middle Ages was extremely violent. One of its chief resources was an appeal to the most obvious forms of sadism. It swarmed with "play" of a brutal crudity, acts of torture, crucifixions, and rapes. Certain scenes are difficult to describe in decent terms in our own day. As the director of one of these performances moralizes at the close:

> "You have seen virgins deflowered
> And married women violated."

In fact, this was well within the limits of the truth.[3] Superimposed on the manners of the Middle Ages, the theater added certain recurrent features. In particular, where the argument did not include scenes of anti-Jewish violence, every effort was made to introduce them artificially (as the action of a popular "Western" today is defined in terms of the tremendous fight at the end in which the good are rewarded, the wicked are punished, and the spectator is left with a clear conscience). The realism was intensified by the fact that in its naïveté, the medieval theater, unconcerned with anachronisms, represented the Jews (and the other characters) in the accoutrements, names, etc., by which they were known at the time.

Thus certain German miracles concerning the Assumption

---

[2] See, for example, pp. 179, 204, 239 f.

[3] In fact, the action of the play involved a scabrous surgical operation that Nero performed upon his mother "in order to learn how he had been born." (Cf. G. Cohen, *L'Histoire de la mise en scène,* Paris, 1926.)

of the Virgin included a final scene added later, called "Entertainment on the Destruction of Jerusalem," which had no organic link with the action and in which Titus, having become a Christian knight, put the city of the Jews to fire and sword in order to avenge the Divine Mother (187). In other plays the action was contemporary. Thus, in the *Mistère de la saincte hostie* (188), a Jewish usurer suborns his Christian debtor and forces her to give him a piece of the consecrated Host. He immediately turns against the Host —"Desire seized me to crucify it, cast it into the Fire and persecute it, and against the ground to trample, boil, beat, and stone it"—and whatever he does, the Host bleeds but remains intact. Witnesses of this miracle, the Jew's wife and children, are touched by grace and denounce him. They request baptism at once. When the provost comes for him, the Jew immediately offers to accept baptism:

Volontiers me baptiserai	I shall be baptized gladly
Parce que sentence aurai	Since thus I shall have pardon
Qui point ne me fera mourir.	To keep me from dying.

The provost is not taken in: *Ce n'est qu'une échappatoire* ("It is merely an excuse"), and the Jew is condemned to be burned. He dies calling for "his book" (the Talmud, doubtless), and uttering horrible imprecations:

O diable, il me semble que iarde	O Devil, I feel I am burning
Diables, diables brusle et ars	Devils, devils burn and flame
Ie ars je brusle de toute pars	I flare and flame in every limb
Je depars en feu et en flamme	I perish now in fire and flame
Mon corps mon esprit et mon ame	My body, mind and soul
Bruslent et ardent trop en ardamment	Burn now and fiercely consume
Dyables venez hastivement	Devils come speedily
Et m'emportez à ce besoing.	And carry me off from this ordeal.

As for his accomplice, the Christian debtor, she is burned too, but she dies in sanctity, after repenting.

Many miracles of the Holy Virgin are preserved that evoke the theme of the profaning Jew; it is not known whether they were staged or not. Some date from an earlier period, going back to Gautier de Coincy: for example, those collected around 1450 by Jehan Miélot, and in which we see the Virgin haranguing the people against "that damned folk the Jews, who prosper now a second time and seek to make my only son, who is the light and salvation of all loyal Christians, die by the torment of the Cross a second time . . ." (189). This is evidently a reference to the theme of the profanation of the Host; in it the distinction between the age of Christ and the present time is entirely erased. But what matters here is the popularization of the stereotype of the Jew by means of theatrical performance.

This was primarily accomplished by the mystery plays of the Passion, which, appearing in the fourteenth century, were to enjoy an enormous vogue in the next century. Quite characteristically for the grim atmosphere of the late Middle Ages, they emphasize the most painful and bloody incidents in the life of Jesus, more or less ignoring the story of his birth, teaching, and Resurrection. Taking place in a climate of complete faith and communion, the performance of a mystery had nothing in common with the production of a play in our own time. To give an idea of the astonishing vigor of the feelings it provoked, a very remote comparison might be drawn with contemporary boxing matches, or better still with the political celebrations favored by the monolithic parties. The life of the city stopped; shops and workshops were closed; convents, monasteries, and courts were deserted. For several days at a time, the entire population left its homes and gathered "for the shows," so that guards had to be assigned to watch the deserted streets and houses—and sometimes, too (as we know in the case of Frankfurt, Freiburg, and Rome), to protect the local ghetto.[4]

[4] In 1338, the councilors of Freiburg forbade the performance of anti-

Let us try, then, to imagine ourselves in the main square of a Bavarian city where one of the most popular German mysteries, the *Alsfelder Passionspiel*, is being performed before the populace massed in front of the stage on trestles (190). The first day, immediately following a brief prologue, the devils come on stage, plotting the betrayal of Jesus. They are twenty in number, and except for Lucifer and Satan, bear Germanic names of a typically medieval truculence: Natyr, Hellekrugk, Bone, Spiegelglantz, Rosenkranz, Raffenzann, Binckenbangk. The devils decide to assign the carrying out of the unnameable crime to the Jews. After some diversions, the latter, fourteen in number, gather in turn (at the end of the first day of the performance), and their names, except for Caiaphas and Ananias, also have the same grotesque resonance: Natey, Holderlin, Borey, Snoppenkeile, Lendekile, Effikax, Gugulus.

Their plans are laid and, the following day, the spectacle continues with the scene of the revolting dealings between the Jews and Judas. The payment of the thirty pieces of silver will be stipulated, each party to the bargain seeking to cheat the other, thus parodying, in general, the usurers of the period. The culminating action, the Crucifixion of Jesus, reads as follows:

CAIAPHAS
Jesus, take off your clothes.
They shall go to the soldiers.
Lie down on the Cross
And stretch out your feet and arms!

(He is stretched on the Cross and the second executioner says:)

Jewish scenes; in 1469, those of Frankfurt ordered special measures for the protection of the ghetto during the performance; in 1539, the show was stopped in Rome, for it had been regularly followed by the sacking of the ghetto. (Cf. H. Pflaum, "Les Scènes de Juifs dans la Littérature Dramatique," *R.E.J.*, Vol. 89, 1930, pp. 111-34; and M. Vatasso, *Per la Storia della Dramma sacro in Italia*, Rome, 1903.)

SECOND EXECUTIONER
Give me three heavy nails
And a hammer and tongs!

Bind his hands and feet fast
And lay him out along the Cross
To the notch that is marked.
Let his legs and feet go so far,
And let the nails pass through.
Thus he cannot escape.
This nail I shall drive through your right hand.
You shall suffer pain and grief!

FIRST EXECUTIONER
Helper, the hands and the feet
Do not reach to the notches!

THIRD EXECUTIONER
I shall give good counsel:
Bring a rope;
We shall stretch his arms;
We shall draw out his body
So as to pull it to pieces!

Let us stop there. The scene of the Crucifixion continues for over seven hundred lines: the executioners, anonymous flagellators, invent ever-new sufferings (performed in incredibly realistic fashion, a red liquid representing blood, and the binding so convincingly done that the actor playing Christ would often succumb, apparently, during the performance), while the Jews present rejoice and mock Jesus in every conceivable fashion.

In the *Alsfelder Passionspiel*, the Jews are merely *provocateurs*; in the famous French mystery attributed to Jehan Michel (191), they take over the tortures as well. This begins in Pilate's palace (Pilate, of course, is given a noble role), and the manuscript reads:

Here they strike him upon the shoulders and head with reeds.

ROULLART

Regardez le sang ruisseler
Qui le museau loy ensen-
glante.

MALCHUS

He faulce personne et sen-
glante
Je n'ay pitié de ta douleur
Non plus que d'un vil frivo-
leur
Qui rien ne peut et si rebarbe.

BRUYANT

Juons-nous à plumer sa barbe

Elle est par trop saillant.

DENTART

Celue sera le plus vaillant
Qui en aura plus grant poig-
née.

Here they tear out his beard.

GRIFFON

Je lui ay si roide empoignée
Que la chair est venue après.

DILLART

Je m'en vueil doncques tirer
près
Pour en avoir ma part aussy.

DRAGON

Regardez quel lopin cecy
J'en tire gros comme de
bourre.

BRUYANT

Mais voyez comme je m'y
fourre
Tenez il n'en a pas ung peu.

ROULLART

See the blood streaming
And how his whole face is
covered.

MALCHUS

Here, false and bloody man,

I pity not your pain
More than that of a vile trick-
ster
That nothing avails, he is so
low.

BRUYANT

Let us play at pulling out his
beard
That is too long anyway.

DENTART

He will be the bravest
Who gets the biggest handful.

GRIFFON

I have torn at him so hard
That the flesh has come away
too.

DILLART

I would take my turn at tearing

So as to have my share as well.

DRAGON

See what a clump this is
That I pull away as if it were
lard.

BRUYANT

But see how I go about it now.

Behold he has not one left.

Here Pilate's indignant intervention puts an end to the bloody scene.

PILATE	PILATE
Son martire tant me desplait	His martyrdom so displeases me
Que a peine regarder le puis	That I can scarcely endure to see it.
Or regardes seigneurs juifz	Yet regard these Jewish lords
Regardes que cest homme endure;	Watching what this man endures;
Voyez la douleur qui l'assomme	See the pain that overcomes him
Il porte de tous les maulx la somme	He bears the worst of all evils
Ecce homo *vecy l'homme.* . . .	*Ecce homo,* this is the man. . . .

The scene of the Crucifixion is even more intense. The Jews draw lots for the parts of Christ's body that each will torment. They spit upon him, and one of them exclaims:

| *Il est tout gasté* | He is all covered |
| *De crachas amont et aval.* | With spittle high and low. |

The violence of these remarks (and we must remember that they are being spoken on a stage!) remains painful and difficult to accept in our own day. Imagine the effect they must have had on the childlike and unsophisticated mentality of the men of the medieval period! In a total identification, the crowds lived Christ's agony intensely, transferring all their rage to his tormentors, with a real massacre often following the depicted one. This may have been a necessary compromise, a release for the sufferings with which these crowds identified themselves; or a camouflage, masking the unspeakable pleasure of having dared crucify one's own God and Saviour!

The interdependence between the scenic and the plastic arts during the Middle Ages is one of the most interesting of historical studies. It is generally supposed that iconography was the dutiful daughter of religious drama and gradually incarnated its chief motifs. However it came about, it is certain that with regard to our subject iconography developed in the same direction as literature and the theater.

As we have shown, in the high Middle Ages Christians were presented with the edifying contrast of the Church as a resplendent virgin and the Synagogue as a fallen widow. These motifs were depicted on the tympanums and stained-glass windows of the cathedrals, sometimes framing Christ on the Cross. In early versions these symbolic personifications, so charged with meaning, obeyed the rules of a certain symmetry. The two rivals remained closely balanced; they assumed the same postures; they were dressed in the same costumes; they bore the same equipment. As a result, certain figures of the Synagogue are characterized by elegance and an incomparable charm (for instance, the admirable head with bandaged eyes on the tympanum of the Cathedral of Strasbourg, which dates from the end of the thirteenth century) (192)—just as most of the heads of the prophets have great nobility. But later artists increasingly resorted to another symbolic contrast from which this inner symmetry is absent. On one side the Saviour is flanked by a Roman centurion, Longinus, who, at the foot of the Cross, was blinded by the true faith (sometimes the blind centurion has regained his sight); on the other side is a "sponge bearer," the Synagogue—her sponge is soaked in vinegar and she is trying to poison Christ's wounds. This figuration was in line with the increasing trend of embroidering the sober narrative of the Gospels in order to remove from the gentiles any particle of responsibility for the deicide and to transfer the entire opprobrium to the Jews. (We have seen the virtuous indignation attributed to Pilate in Jehan Michel's mystery). In a more general way—just as in mysteries, treatises, and sermons—the representation of the Crucifixion, depicted in bloody and often overpowering detail, becomes in the fourteenth century the chief subject of artists. Obsession with human suffering; obsession, too, with its various sequels—death, the kingdom of the Devil, hell and its thousand torments (themes that before this period were virtually unknown or were at most suggested with great discretion)—these are the dominant motifs in the art of the period, and the fervent imagination of painters and sculptors is given free rein.[5]

There is also a link between these grim obsessions and the ravages of the Black Plague. After 1400, there appears in Europe the theme of the "dance of death," or "danse macabre." There is a close relationship between these hellish entertainments and the theme of the "banquet during the plague," wild feasts during which the guests seek to drown their anguish as the death carts in the street roll the corpses to a communal grave.

Against this apocalyptic background the portrayal of the Jews is enriched with ever-new inventions.

In Italy, at the end of the fourteenth century, artists venture to identify Jews with scorpions. In paintings and frescoes, this odious creature often appears on the standards, shields, and tunics of the Jews: a figuration found again in the next century in Savoy, in Germany, and even in Flanders (193). As a corollary to this subtle allegory, the product of Mediterranean genius, a cruder image, broader and in fact more scurrilous, appears in Germany: that of the sow in association with Jews, giving them suck and fornicating with them, on countless stone monuments in Magdeburg, Freising, Regensburg, Kehlheim, Salzburg, Frankfurt, and on churches in the Low Countries (194). One of these reliefs—most of which have disappeared—is described by Martin Luther in his famous pamphlet *Vom Schem Hamephoras:*

"Here in Wittenberg, on our church, a sow is carved in stone. Some young piglets and some Jews are suckling her; behind the sow is a rabbi. He raises the sow's right leg, with his left hand he pulls out his member, leans over and diligently contemplates, behind the member, the Talmud, as

[5] We recommend the splendid studies by Emile Mâle on this subject.

if he desired to learn something very subtle and special from it. . . ." [6]

It is in Germany, too, that in the second half of the fifteenth century there appeared the caricature of the Jew with a long nose and misshapen figure, which was to constitute the delight of anti-Semites for centuries to come.[7] In this case, the contrast between the pink-and-blond coloring of the Germans and the darker complexion and shorter body of the Jews must have played a decisive part. Apparently Germany is also responsible for another attribute attached to the Jews, one that was also to enjoy unique success: the horns. Actually, their origin seems to have been a double one. From the most remote times, Moses, and Moses alone, was represented with horns, apparently the result of an erroneous interpretation of a passage in the Old Testament,[8] and without any pejorative connotation. Until the thirteenth century, these horns are not seen on the forehead of other patriarchs, nor even on that of an Ananias or a Caiaphas. The pointed hat of the Jews, the *pileum cornutum,* as worn in Germany from the end of the thirteenth century, seems to have been a second source of inspiration. Hence, on the monuments and in the paintings of later centuries, we frequently find Jews with horned heads: for example, on the stained-glass windows of the Cathedral of Auch and in Veronese's "Calvary," now in the Louvre.

Horns: the most significant attribute of the Devil. We have already been much concerned with the Devil in preceding pages, just as we have involuntarily been led to observe the linking of the obscene with the sacred. Perhaps this will help us understand the image of the Jews during the waning Middle Ages and to explore its nethermost depths.

[6] See p. 219.

[7] The oldest known caricature of this kind is found in Schedel's *Weltchronik* (1493); it represents the murder of little Simon of Trent.

[8] Exodus 34: 29: ". . . the skin of his face shone while he talked with him"; the Vulgate gives the erroneous translation: ". . . the skin of his face had horns . . ."

Horns
,
Devil

But for this we must halt our inquiry for a moment, abandoning the Jews and turning instead to the Devil. For this is the period when the Christian imagination pictured the Prince of Darkness residing on earth, engaging in varied and sustained activities, and likely to appear anywhere.

Devils, witches, and Jews

Was the Prince of Darkness created wicked, or was he a fallen angel who became wicked by his own will? And if he was a fallen angel, from what rank had he fallen: the supreme order, high rank, or low? What was his chief sin, the one that had caused his eternal damnation: pride? envy? As for the legion of other devils he commanded, were some of them born as men? Did they have bodies? Such questions had preoccupied the Fathers of the Church since the first centuries of Christianity. But while teachings relating to the devils were being woven into a body of doctrine, the ecclesiastical authorities of the high Middle Ages showed a remarkable skepticism about their manifestations on earth. At this time the accounts of their misdeeds generally corresponded to no more than pagan superstitions, still easily recognizable as such. Thus, in 466, the Council of Ireland anathematized those who claimed to be wizards. In 563 the Council of Braza spoke in the same terms. Three centuries later, Bishop Agobard, that great oppressor of the Jews, thundered with great good sense against the superstitions of his age, against belief in invisible demons that throw stones and inflict blows, or in *tempestari* that can cause storms. In short, the Devil, in the eyes of the Church at this period, constituted a problem chiefly of a moral order because his presence was seldom manifested on earth. Exception was taken to magicians, whose evil spells were not doubted. Some were even condemned to death, but stories of witches' sabbaths, of werewolves, of sexual relations with the Devil, were rejected as idle tales. This was without doubt the best way of thwarting the propagation of such absurdities.

The same was true in the next centuries, when the struggle against heresies mobilized most of the energies of the clergy. In 1310 the Council of Trier proclaimed that "no woman may claim to have ridden during the night with Diana or Herodias, for that is an illusion of the demon." In short, if a woman who called herself a witch was punished (the punishment being excommunication, at worst), it was not for having consorted with the Devil but for having committed —under his moral control—the sin of an odious lie.

The people, however, were not of this belief. They were in the grip of ancestral supersititions, and they often executed a summary and brutal justice against alleged wizards, witches, and casters of evil spells. There were lynchings without any form of trial. But these incidents were sporadic and isolated, as were the anti-Jewish excesses of this period.

Meanwhile, the scholastics were constructing their imposing edifice of interpretation of the terrestrial and celestial worlds. The Devil occupied a considerable place within them. Starting from fundamental dogmatic axioms, his attributes and powers were defined by means of a subtle dialectic, some of which methods are curiously analogous to the most acrobatic reasonings of the Talmud. Thus Saint Thomas Aquinas argued that demons could assume carnal form, could eat—that is, seem to eat—but could not indulge in the reality of digestion or that of procreation. Nonetheless, successively assuming the form of a succubus (female) and an incubus (male), they could, thanks to their astonishing speed, introduce into a woman the seed of man which they had just received. Even so, the children thus procreated were not the seed of the Devil, since his role had been limited to that of a simple intermediary.[9] Yet, going further, Saint Thomas declared that the Huns were truly the spawn

[9] *Summa theologica*, 1, Quaest. 51, art, 3, 6.

of demons. Thereby he took a great step forward toward belief in the corporeality of the Devil.

All this makes it easier to grasp how, in the next century, in the short space of fifty years, a complete reversal of the prevailing attitude took place. The chief authors of the scholastic doctrines were Dominicans—those same Dominicans who, since the beginning of the fourteenth century, had been charged with uprooting heresies and who had created the fearful and effective apparatus of the Inquisition, one of those organizations functionally intended to uncover crime everywhere. Now the chief heresy of the period was Catharism, a doctrine that taught that Satan, and not the God of mercy, rules the earth: consequently, the crime par excellence that the inquisitors had to ferret out was commerce with the Devil. Now confusion was sowed in men's minds. The number of pathological cases continued to rise. On the one hand, an increasing number of believers, weary of beseeching God, despaired of Him and invoked the Devil; on the other, the Church granted its official *imprimatur* to the very phantasms it had opposed down through the ages. The reversal began around 1320, when the new demonological doctrines received the first official consecration of the Holy See. Pope John XXII, suffering apparently from a delusion of persecution—he saw enemies and poisoners everywhere—published the bull *Super illius specula* against false Christians who "sacrifice to demons and worship them, produce or procure images, rings, flasks, mirrors, and still other things to which they attach the demons by their magic arts, gaining answers from them, seeking their aid in order to carry out their wicked designs, submitting to the most shameful servitude for the most shameful things. . . ."

The popes lived in Avignon during this period, and it is possible that the rumors circulating in France concerning the poisoning of wells by lepers and Jews added to the anxieties of John XXII. His successor, Benedict XII, confirmed his directives. The first known trial for witchcraft occurred in

1335 in Toulouse. In 1337 the inquisitor Nidder published the first detailed description we have of wizards, their misdeeds, and the means of recognizing them. After the great plague, the search for the Devil's auxiliaries proceeded with great speed. Each highly spectacular witch-burning produced a covey of new witches; each auto-da-fé (act of faith!) spread the belief in sorcery and its supernatural powers. Some gave themselves up to the black arts, others smelled witches everywhere. Thus the inquisitors who received the charge to stamp out witchcraft became its most active missionaries. Inquisitorial procedure insisted on the victim's confession. Torture,[10] euphemistically called "the question,"—continued sometimes for weeks and months, sometimes for several days in a row, sometimes with long interruptions—infallibly obtained these confessions, as precise and detailed as the inquisitor insisted they be, and afforded a complete description of the Devil's appearance, habits, and behavior. Thus the Devil became a living reality. While the ashes of burned witches served to sow new witchcraft, the repeated triumphs of the professional Devil-hunters could only reinforce their own faith in the importance and salubrity of their practices. As one of them, Paramo, observed proudly in 1404, the Holy Office had already burned over thirty thousand witches, who, had they enjoyed impunity, would have led the entire world to its utter ruin (195).

The witch-hunting mania increased in the fifteenth century. It flourished in the mountainous regions of Savoy and Switzerland, but above all in Germany, where, no doubt, vestiges of paganism were especially tenacious. In 1484, Pope Innocent VIII observed regretfully, in his bull *Summis Desiderantes*, that the Teutonic territories were filled with agents of the Devil (196). The German inquisitors Sprenger

---

[10] According to the inquisitorial doctrine, "the question" could be applied only once. Practice found an easy loophole: in case of reluctance on the part of the presumed witch, "the question" was not "repeated" but was "continued" as long as necessary to elicit confession.

and Institoris, theoreticians and men of action, wrote in this year the *Malleus Maleficarum* (Mallet of Sorcerers), a treatise that retained a position of authority until the dawn of modern times. Strengthened by pontifical support, the inquisitors held assizes from city to city, leaving behind a wake of fire and blood. The pyres grew more numerous as every misdeed, every accident, was imputed to witches. Terrified Christians suspected one another of being Satan's slaves. His hand was seen everywhere. No one can say how many witches were burned in Europe between the fourteenth and seventeenth centuries, but the number must be extremely high. During this period the Devil evolved from a moral principle of Evil into a strongly individualized personality, horned and hairy, who infested the earth. This transformation took place precisely at the time the powerful concept of the evil-doing Jew was being crystallized and spread throughout Christendom.

What were the Devil's chief attributes? He had horns, talons, a tail, wore a goat's beard, and he was black. He gave off a strong odor. All these were symbols of lewdness and extreme virility. Such is the description of him given by the witches, such is the portrait that the inquisitors record in their investigations and circulate in their manuals: a portrait created in fact chiefly by them, for during the "questioning" the victims merely yielded to the demands of their persecutors' imaginations. "These severe, harsh, and chaste men did not shrink from the description of any infamy and of any lust. They created the horrible in order the more to worship the holy, and it was by the pyres that they illuminated their symbols in suffering and in death." [11] Thus the Devil, God's double and antagonist, assumes opposition to Him in all things. "Baptism erases original sin, the Devil erases baptism; the man of God works good deeds and charity, the demoniac works evil and sows hatred. God sheds grace on His subjects, the Devil affords them evil spells; the

[11] Maurice Garçon and Jean Vinchon, *Le Diable, étude historique, critique et médicale*, Paris, 1926.

great mystic knows ecstasy, the Devil possesses men; the good Christian makes an alliance with God, the wizard a pact with the Devil; the Mass is the sacrifice agreeable to the Divinity, the Demon demands an identical and mocking sacrifice in which everything is done in hatred of the Divinity; and whereas God effects miracles, Lucifer works magic" (197).

The Devil's chief agent on earth is the witch (and not the wizard, who is only burned in exceptional circumstances), that is, a woman, symbol of impurity, weakness, temptation. Of course, some wretched women may have imagined a carnal union with the Prince of Evil; but here, too, the assignment of roles remains consistent with the spirit of the age. The contempt for woman, the fear and horror of temptation and the blandishments of the sex, contrast with the adoration of the Virgin and the cult of chastity.

If we examine the legends that circulate about the Jews in the same period, legends that cropped up sporadically during the preceding centuries but which now are accepted throughout Europe, we observe that the Jews are believed to unite in their persons the new attributes of the Devil and those of the witch. The Jews are horned. They are tricked out with a tail and the beard of a goat (that disturbing quadruped which serves as the perfect transmitting agent for all sins); the mephitic odors attributed to them are so violent that they have persisted down through the ages and even in our own time incited German scholars to investigate the nature and origins of the *foetor judaïcus*.[12] From this point of view, the Jews are hypervirile. They are veritable supermen, magicians secretly feared and revered. But at the same time they are weak and sickly, suffering from a thousand malignant afflictions that only Christian blood can cure (here we return to the theme of ritual murder).

---

[12] Thus the famous anthropologist Hans F. K. Günther believed in the existence of an hereditary *odor judaeus*, which he proposed to study with the help of chemical analyses. (Hans Günther, *Rassenkunde des judischen Volkes*, Munich, 1930, pp. 260-68, Chap. "Geruchliche Eigenart.")

They are born misshapen, they are hemorrhoidal and, men as well as women, afflicted with menses.[13] From this point of view, they are women, that is, inframen, scorned, loathed, and mocked. Sometimes the description is even more circumstantial, and the ills the Jews suffer are differentiated according to their tribes. The descendants of Simeon bleed four days every year, those of Zebulun spit blood yearly, those of Asher have their right arm shorter than their left, those of Benjamin have worms in their mouths, and so on.[14] Elsewhere, the laws against witchcraft constitute part of the statutes regulating the condition of the Jews, so obvious does it appear that the latter are also magicians (198). "To the masses, the Jew was a master of the occult sciences"

[13] A characteristic example of the combination of these various themes is afforded by the accusations made against the Jews on the occasion of the case of ritual murder in Trnava (Tyrnau) (1494):

"Firstly, the traditions of their ancestors tell them that the blood of a Christian is an excellent means to cure the wound produced by circumcision.

"Secondly, they see that this blood permits them to prepare a dish that wakens mutual love.

"Thirdly, suffering from menstruation, both men and women alike, they have noted that the blood of a Christian constitutes an excellent remedy.

"Fourthly, they are obliged, by virtue of an ancient and secret commandment, to offer yearly sacrifice with Christian blood. . . ." (Anton Bonfin, *Rerum Hungaricum Decades*, Dec. 5, Book 4.)

[14] The first known detailed description of the "Jewish maladies" occurs in a small work published in 1630 by the converted Jew, Franco da Piacenza. Once again we find the name of a renegade Jew at its origin. This description enjoyed great success; it was reprinted in Germany in 1634 (*Gründliche und wahrhafte Relation von einem Juden, Namens Ahasveros, mit einem Berichte von den 12 Stämmen, was ein jedweder Stamm dem Herrn Christo zur Schmach gethan, und was sie bis auf heutigen Tag dafür leyden müssen,* by Chrysostomus Dudulaeus, Reval, 1634) and in Spain at the beginning of the eighteenth century (*Centinela contra Judios,* a work attributable to the knowledge and vigilance of the Franciscan father Francisco de Torrejoncillo, 1728). The pamphleteer J. G. Schudt (*Jüdische Merckwürdigkeiten,* Frankfurt and Leipzig, 1714-1718) adopts the theme, though seasoning it with a grain of skepticism; thus, better informed than his future Nazi emulators, he admits that the *foetor judaïcus* might well derive from the Jews' immoderate use of garlic, as well as from their uncleanliness. Let us note further that there must have been, at the origin of this belief, a kind of association between Jewish impiety and infidelity and stench, to which were opposed the celestial aromas of the true piety (we still say today "the odor of sanctity").

(199). Furthermore, did the Jews not celebrate the *Sabbath,* even as the witches and devils?

In short, combining in their persons the entire gamut of the attributes of evil, the Jews lose their humanity in the eyes of Christians and are relegated to the realm of the occult. Even when they are not assigned strictly diabolical attributes, they are associated with the devils that are often pictured in the background of engravings and paintings representing Jews (thus the devils appear to be of Jewish essence). Elsewhere, Jews are given pigs' ears in place of horns (200). Popular superstitions abound in the same associations. The Jewish school is a "black" school; the Jew is the intermediary between the Devil and those who want to sell their souls to him; the cursed pact is sealed with his blood, and if a sick man wants to die, he need only ask a Jew to pray for him (201). In countless ghost stories, a Jew appears either in human form or as a will-o'-the-wisp (202). Many of these beliefs and others like them have persisted in the popular imagination down to our own day.

We may illuminate this identification between the Jew and the Devil in still another manner. It is indeed remarkable to note that certain illustrious theologians and preachers, certain duly canonized saints of the late Middle Ages who reveal an immoderate and persistent interest in the Devil, specialized in the persecution of the Jews. If we consider their actions and their writings, we find they have in common a prophetic and reforming zeal, characteristic of this period, the most complete model of which is Martin Luther himself.

A typical example is Saint Vincent Ferrer, the most famous of the preaching friars. He traveled through Spain and France, and his preaching "inspired enthusiasm and effected such considerable changes in the moral life of individuals and of groups that his oratory was regarded as practically a new gospel of Christianity" (*Dictionnaire de Theologie catholique*) (203). This powerful rabble-rouser, whom Catholics in our own day revere as an authentic miracle worker, remains in the popular imagination as the "preacher of the end of the world" (total Hiroshima—what work can be more agreeable to the Devil?). He preached so vehemently on this burning subject that "his countless listeners, supposing from the saint's thundering voice that the end had come, either cast themselves down groaning or struggled up again resuscitated. Such events were not to disappear from the memory of the people . . ." (204). Ferrer was obviously a saint of somewhat gloomy disposition, and, believing that the Last Judgment was at hand, he dedicated himself especially to the conversion of the Jews. At the head of a band of "flagellants," he would burst into synagogues and demand of the worshipers that they immediately reject the Torah and accept the Cross. It is not surprising that the Jews have remembered him with loathing. "He caused the Jews such sufferings that the years 1412 and 1413 may be counted as among the most grievous in all Jewish history" (Graetz) (205). "The Jews fell victim to the terror. . . . In Toledo, Ferrer entered the synagogue, drove out the worshipers, and renamed the place the Church of the Immaculate Virgin (Santa Maria Blanca). By the same terrorist methods, he persecuted the Jews of Saragossa, Valencia, Tortosa, and other places . . ." (Dubnow) (206). Thus Saint Vincent Ferrer is described in Jewish chronicles as the "scourge of the Jews." Yet this saint denounced the murder of Jews: "Christians must not kill Jews with knives, but with words." He even uttered rather flattering remarks about them,[15] providing they accepted conversion. When they did

---

[15] "Do you feel a consolation when a Jew converts? There are many Christians mad enough not to do so. They should embrace, honor, and love them; instead, they scorn them because they once were Jews. But they must not do so, for Jesus Christ was a Jew, and the Virgin Mary a Jewess, before becoming a Christian. It is a great sin to revile them. This circumcised God is our God, and you shall be damned even as he who dies a Jew. For they must be taught Doctrine so that they may be in the service of God. . . ." (S. Mitrani-Samarian, "A Valencian Sermon of Saint Vincent Ferrer," *R.E.J.*, Vol. 54, p. 241.)

not, he prescribed hermetic isolation. It was upon his instigation that the first Spanish ghettos, the *juderías*, were created in 1412 and that a series of anti-Jewish laws were promulgated.

Another "scourge of the Jews" was the energetic inquisitor Saint John of Capistrano. A fiery and grim prophet, he is regarded by his biographer as "that one among our saints who exerted the most marked and most decisive influence upon the men and affairs of his time" (207). He carried out his apostolate in Italy and Germany, where whole cities came to hear him. He chose death, judgment, and hell as favorite themes for his sermons. His chief writings are concerned with Antichrist, the Last Judgment, and the Apocalypse (208). It is reported that while preaching in the city of Aquila before one hundred thousand people, he evoked a legion of horrible demons whom he forced to fall prostrate, shrieking and roaring, before his banner (209). This ardent ascetic rarely lost an opportunity to attack Judaism. Princes who protected Jews were threatened with the wrath of God, and he boasted of abolishing "the diabolic privileges" of many Jewish communities. In Silesia, in 1453-1454, he brought about a series of trials for ritual murder, with subsequent autos-da-fé, and managed to abrogate the privileges of the Jews of Poland for some time (210).

The tormented souls of these great men of action were apparently obsessed with the world's end, punishment, and anti-Jewish passion. The story of the famous demagogue Savonarola, for several years the uncontested master of Florence, suggests that the revolutionary aspect of this agitation was an echo of the social aspirations of the discontented masses. Savonarola had visions and heard devils whispering in his ear: *Fratello Girolamo, fratello girellaio, padre confessione, padre confusione* ("Brother Jerome, brother weathercock, father confessor, father confusion"). It must be said in all fairness that far from keeping him in the odor of sanctity, the Church excommunicated him and burned him at the stake. At the peak of his power, however, after driving the Medicis from Florence, he established a form of theocratic democracy in which the private life of the people was subject to a quasi-totalitarian scrutiny, with children prodded to spy on their parents. Savonarola expelled the Jews from the city and established a municipal pawn office. In addition, he reformed the courts, revised taxes, and enacted a new constitution.

Other famous holy men of the period were of gentler disposition. But this did not prevent them from hating the Jews with equal virulence. It was as if they expended upon the Jews all the aggression their souls contained. The founder of the sect of the Holy Name of Jesus, Saint Bernardino of Siena, argued that the Jews were conspiring against Christians in two ways: Jewish usurers "extort from the Christians their worldly goods by public usuries," while Jewish physicians "seek to deprive them of health and life." He quoted the confession of one Jewish doctor of Avignon who "at his last hour declared he died a happy man because he had had the pleasure, throughout his life, of killing thousands of Christians with so-called remedies that were actually poisons" (211).

The successor and pupil of Saint Bernardino of Siena, the Blessed Bernardino of Feltre, seems to have been one of those great mystics whose powerful religious temperament was matched by remarkable organizational gifts. The poetic and delicate charity of this Franciscan recalls the great founder of his order. But in other aspects—the mortifications, fasts, and flagellations that he practiced as well as preached—he was indeed the child of his times. To him is attributed the charming apologia that follows, which he recited to the patients and attendants of a hospital:

"In the book of sufferers should be written: patience, patience, patience; and in the book of those who minister to them: charity, charity, charity. But each must be content to read his own book and not seek to see what the other's contains, for among a thousand small accidents caused by human weakness, if one asks of the other: 'Where is your charity?' he compromises his patience, and if the other replies: 'Where is your patience?' he compromises his charity. Let us not be like the schoolboy who, instead of learning his own lesson, peeks into the book of his neighbor; this schoolboy cannot answer the master's question, and will be punished" (212).

But all charity departed from Blessed Bernardino of Feltre when he dealt with the Jews. Then, according to his own expression, he changed into "a barking dog"; "Jewish usurers bleed the poor to death and grow fat on their substance, and I who live on alms, who feed on the bread of the poor, shall I then be mute as a dog before outraged charity? Dogs bark to protect those who feed them, and I, who am fed by the poor, shall I see them robbed of what belongs to them and keep silent? Dogs bark for their masters; shall I not bark for Christ?" (213).

His biographers praise him for not having fallen into the characteristic failings of the preachers of his day and for not having given himself up to apocalyptic prophecies of wars, scourges, and other bloody calamities. He abstained, it is true, from prophesying, save with regard to the Jews. Preaching at Trent, in the Tyrol, he warned the faithful of the Jewish peril and specified that "the feast of Easter will not pass without your knowing something of this" (214). Some days later the famous ritual murder of little Simon of Trent was committed.[16] (It is, of course, impossible to say whether it occurred impulsively, following the Blessed Bernardino's preaching, or if the latter was directly involved in some way.) At the same time that he was propagating the legend of ritual murder, Blessed Bernardino of Feltre effectively opposed usury. Under his energetic leadership, the Franciscan order opened pawn offices in the chief cities of Italy, thus permitting the poor to avoid resorting to Jewish or Christian usurers. Later, his example was imitated in Germany and France.

We see, then, that the problem is not a simple one. The exorciser of the Devil often corrected real evils at the same

[16] Cf. pp. 62 f.

time and was in part a genuine social reformer. Similarly, the imaginary Jew whom he persecuted and who tormented him was sometimes paralleled by a real usurer, whether Jew or Christian. This is only to be expected. In an age when the distinction between sacred and profane was never very clear, when every social activity was simultaneously a charitable deed and one pleasing to God, the two images were super-imposed: the Devil's hand was seen behind all evil, which is why it is impossible to distinguish between the Jew-Devil (who haunted all Europe) and the Jewish usurer (present at this period in only certain regions). But on the whole the illusion does not merely mask certain social realities: it deflects and dominates them.

Another illustration of the disquieting role that the Jews assumed in the Christian imagination—particularly eloquent because in direct contradiction to the social reality—is afforded by the Jewish physicians, who so deeply concerned Saint Bernardino of Siena and who played such a prominent part throughout the Middle Ages. What, then, is a physician? He was once a sorcerer, and even in our own day and age, in the special relationship between patient and doctor, he is still a character possessing an august and essential power. A physician remains more or less a magician. Thus the question for the Middle Ages was to know if his mysterious art of curing was granted him by God or by the Devil. By the Devil, answered many canonical texts, apropos of Jewish physicians. First apparently in date, the Council of Béziers in 1246 forbade Christians, on pain of excommunication, to resort to the care of Jews, "for it is better to die than to owe one's life to a Jew." This prohibition was reiterated by the councils of Albi (1254), Vienne (1267), by a decree of the University of Paris (1301), and by numerous councils of the fourteenth and fifteenth centuries. Thus, even at the risk of one's life, one must not have recourse to Jewish medicine. Furthermore, according to another version, such abstinence was not only an act of piety but also one of salutary prudence, since the Jewish physician, far from curing his Christian patient, sought only to worsen his condition. He deliberately poisoned him, in fact, for, according to obscure and very old legends, Charles the Bald (Charles II), Hugh Capet, and even the Emperor Charlemagne were among the victims of Jewish doctors (215). In time there were more precise accusations; statistics were quoted. Doubtless professional jealousy was involved to some extent, but we also find instances here of the themes of ritual murder and large-scale poisoning. The Vienna Faculty of Medicine reported that the private code of Jewish physicians required them to murder one patient in ten (216). According to a version common in Spain, the figure was one in five (217). This entire matter is necessarily obscure. It seems that no one really knew what the Devil wanted and how he operated. Did he seek to destroy the Christian's soul when, by means of the Jewish physician, he assured the cure of his body; or, since the salvation of the body is inseparable from that of the soul, was he seeking to destroy both at the same time?

Each version had its supporters. Despite this, or perhaps because of it, Jewish practitioners enjoyed extreme popularity among the princes, as among the common people. The popes of Christendom, especially, from Alexander III in the twelfth century to Paul III in the sixteenth, were traditionally cared for by Jewish doctors and granted them exceptional privileges. Physicians were exempted from wearing the rouelle or the Jewish hat, and sometimes exerted considerable political influence behind the scenes.

We may grant that the sovereign pontiffs, more enlightened than the mass of Christendom, did not share the common superstitions and simply preferred to entrust their lives to obliging, skillful, and dependable practitioners. But what of the inconsistent attitude of Count Alfonse of Poitiers, brother of Saint Louis and equally hostile to the Jews, who, after having been the protector of the Council of Béziers in 1254, summoned a Jewish physician from Spain to cure his failing eyesight (218)? Or of the rule established by the

kings of Castile early in the fifteenth century, according to
which "there will be no physicians among the Jews, with the
exception of the physician to the king" (219)? Of course,
humans are weak when faced with sickness; royalty consulted Jewish doctors even though their power might be
that of the Devil, but the common people were forbidden to
engage Jewish doctors: this was a weakness permitted only
to the great. Even when one succumbed to sin oneself, one
repressed it severely among one's subjects. Thus interpreted,
the problem here is ethical, not medical. Practically speaking, one would say that medical science is either good for all
or bad for all; it is only with medicine as an effect of the
Tempter's blandishments that an attitude so powerfully ambivalent is possible.

All these prohibitions had little effect. The bourgeois, in
the wake of the princes, preferred to be cared for by Jewish
physicians. Medieval chronicles swarm with examples of
privileges, favors, and subsidies provided for them. In 1369,
a Dr. Isaac, who lived in Mainz, was authorized to reside in
the palace of the prince-elector (220). In 1394, Solomon
Pletsch was appointed municipal physician of Frankfurt,
with an annual salary of thirty-six guilders and six cubits of
cloth (221). Still more highly remunerated was Baruch, physician to the prince-elector of Saxony, who received in 1464
thirty bushels of wheat, one cask of wine, six quarts of beer,
twenty ewes, and one ox every year, along with free lodgings
(222). When, in 1519, the Jews were expelled from Rothenburg, Dr. Isaac Oeringer was invited to remain (which he
refused to do) (223). It is also recorded that Jacob Loans,
personal physician to Emperor Frederick III, was the vener-
ated master of the humanist Reuchlin, and that Elijah Montalto, physician to Marie de Médicis, followed her to Paris
and became the personal physician of Louis XIII at a time
when France was strictly closed to the Jews. Similarly, according to the sharp-tongued Sauval, Francis I would entrust himself only to a Jewish physician, insisting further
that he be a pure Jew—that is, not adulterated by the waters

of baptism.[17] Other examples, collected by meticulous scholars, can be cited in great numbers. There were even highly reputed Jewish women doctors, such as Sarah of Würzburg and Zerlin of Frankfurt. All these practitioners were usually exempt from a poll tax and were often remunerated by the municipality. Meanwhile, the diligent enemies of the Devil tirelessly continued their work. "Rather be sick, if such is the will of God, than be cured with the Devil's help, by forbidden means. To appeal to Jewish physicians is to hatch serpents among us, to raise wolves in our house!" exclaimed a Frankfurt clergyman in 1652 (224). Similarly, the clergymen of Hall in Swabia (1657): "Rather die in Christ than be cured by a Jewish doctor and Satan!" (225). None of the great persecutors of the Jews, from Luther and Pfefferkorn in the sixteenth century to Eisenmenger and Schudt in the eighteenth, has failed to refer to this theme. To strengthen the argument, the Jewish physician is paired with the usurer, and together they are accused of waging war on two fronts: the fortune and the health of Christians. This notion, already fostered by Saint Bernardino of Siena, was developed by Du Cange in his famous *Glossarium* and summarized as follows by a nineteenth-century author: "Every man is weak in the face of disease and poverty: the Jews became physicians and usurers" (226).

The extraordinary persistence of the myth that Jewish physicians were poisoners is clearly indicated by the famous rumor that, early in 1953, startled the world when the rulers of a powerful empire announced that Jewish doctors, at the instigation of a Jewish organization, had made an attempt on

[17] According to this ancestor of "subhistory," "Francis sent to Spain to ask of Charles V a Jewish physician, for a malady of which the court physicians could not cure him; but [Charles V] finding none, and having sent him a newly converted Jewish physician, he no sooner learned that he was a Christian than he dismissed him without even allowing the man to take his pulse, nor even speaking to him of his sickness, and sent for another from Constantinople who restored him to health with the milk of she-asses. . . ." (H. Sauval, *Histoire et recherche des antiquités de la ville de Paris,* Paris, 1724, Vol. 2, p. 526.)

the precious lives of the supreme leaders of this empire and its army. A few months later, the case was reconsidered and dismissed; but its symbolic significance persists.

It would be interesting to know if the skill of the medieval Jewish physicians, who were nourished on Talmudic traditions and were familiar with the accomplishments of Arabic medicine, was superior to that of their Christian colleagues. This question is obviously beyond the scope of our inquiry. Nonetheless, it seems relevant to point out that many illustrious Jewish physicians were concerned with ministering to both body and soul, beginning with Maimonides, that great philosopher who was also a great doctor, and ending with Freud, that great physician who has so powerfully influenced the philosophy of our time.

As we have indicated, the shadow of the Jews continued to cause many a Christian heart to tremble, even long after the Jews' expulsion. Pierre de Lancre, who early in the seventeenth century diligently burned a great number of witches in the south of France, and who in his old age drew up a manual of witchcraft, devoted a section to the Jews, "more perfidious and faithless than demons." In a long chapter, he explains how they seek advice from the Devil, in order to protect their pernicious books and doctrines. He enumerates in detail the "stinking maladies" by which they are afflicted and then concludes: "The Jews deserve every execration, and as destroyers of all divine and human majesty, they merit punishment and indeed the greatest tortures. Slow fire, melted lead, boiling oil, pitch, wax, and sulfur fused together would not make torments fitting, sharp, and cruel enough for the punishment of such great and horrible crimes as these people commonly commit . . ." (227).

Witch-hunters were Jew-hunters; Jews were regarded as part of a kind of impious family: Devil, Jew, witch. More precisely, the role of the Jews in this scabrous mythology might be called a demonic counterpart of that of the saints, intercessors with God, but more accessible, more familiar, more human than the Almighty. Adopting what one of the most subtle medievalists has written of the cult of the saints, we might say that the hatred of the Jews, "by draining off the overflow of religious effusion and of holy fear, acted on the exuberant religiosity of the Middle Ages as a salutary sedative" (228). Or, again, if the Jew had not existed, it would have been necessary to invent him.

The final crystallization: the ghetto

Let us return to solid ground—to the real Jews, expelled from England and France and after the end of the fourteenth century tolerated nowhere in Europe except on the territory of what had been the Holy Roman Empire. The reason for this, as we have seen, was entirely political: only in a country subject to a single central authority could their simultaneous and total expulsion be brought about.

Where they persisted, the Jews were described in most of the chronicles of the time as predators who stripped great and small of their wealth and whose wicked activities marred the whole social life of the period. We have seen what Bernardino of Feltre thought of them in Italy. In Germany, according to Erasmus of Erbach, it was even worse:

"The Jews rob and flay the poor man. The situation is becoming truly unbearable; may God have mercy on us! The Jews are now established permanently in the smallest villages. They lend five florins on pledges that represent six times the value of the money loaned; then they demand interest on interest, and still more interest on that, so that the poor man eventually finds himself stripped of all he possessed" (229).

Various nineteenth-century German historians, especially Werner Sombart, have sought to prove by such quotations that the Jews played a primary role in the gestation of the capitalist system, and have thus contributed to an interpretation of history that has played its part in the genesis of the

Nazi *Weltanschauung*. Today, the best economic historians[18] doubt that the Jews did have any special influence on the great economic upheavals of the fifteenth and sixteenth centuries. In truth, the subject has not yet been adequately studied. It would be very difficult to assemble authentic documents, though the effort would surely be worth while. Lacking such documentation, a simple line of reasoning suggests that the Jews' role could scarcely have been a determining factor.

It is impossible to claim, in fact, that the economic structures of France and England at this period differed from, or were more backward than, those of Germany or Italy. Thus the presence or absence of Jews had no influence on the processes by which, throughout Europe, cities were developing, trade was becoming increasingly important, and wealth was beginning to take precedence over birth. It is apparent that in the chronicles in question the term "Jews" must be taken in its broader or imaginary sense, so as to include what some of these texts naïvely call "Christian Jews," referring to Christian usurers or to the founders of great commercial companies that were the forerunners of modern corporations. As for the German Jews in particular, the Ashkenazim, they were excluded not only from the social world but also from that of finance. We have seen that in the fourteenth century, the annual community tax they once paid the emperor or the prince was replaced by an individual "capitation"; the latter, in turn, gave rise to a corporal levy that classified Jews with domestic animals: "On each ox and hog and on each Jew, one sou," reads one contemporary text (230). Occasionally some individuals became noteworthy. At the end of the fourteenth century there were still a few Jews, such as Moses Nurnberg in Heidelberg and Joseph Walch in Vienna, who were official tax collectors. At the beginning of the sixteenth century, the German Jews found a

---

[18] Cf. H. Pirenne, *Histoire économique de l'Occident mediéval;* H. Heaton, *Economic History of Europe;* H. Tawney, *Religion and the Rise of Capitalism,* etc.

skillful and energetic protector in the person of Yosel of Rosheim, appointed by Charles V "supreme leader and regent of the Jews." But the great majority, small moneylenders or old-clothes dealers, earned their livelihood as and when they could, living in perpetual poverty and insecurity. Given the instability of their kind of life, their frequent changes of residence and the necessity for concealment, it is not improbable, as Sombart asserts, that they played a part in the elaboration of that convenient instrument of "mobilization and dissimulation of property," the letter of exchange. Here, too, lacking adequate documentation, we must confine ourselves to suppositions.

All of which is of secondary importance compared with the final withdrawal of the Jews into themselves, leading to the formation of a hermetically closed society within which the complex of manners and customs that we have considered in earlier chapters finds its definitive expression. Of prime importance is the reverence for money, source of all life. Increasingly, each action in the Jew's daily life was subjected to the payment of a tax. He must pay to come and go, to buy and sell, pay for the right to pray with his coreligionists, pay to marry, pay for the birth of his child, even pay for taking a corpse to the cemetery. Without money, Jewry was inevitably doomed to extinction. Thus, the rabbis henceforth view financial oppressions (for example, the moratorium on repayment of debts to Jews, ordered by one prince) as on a par with massacres and expulsions, seeing in them a divine curse, a merited punishment from on high (231).

In this sense, and this sense only, it might appear to a superficial observer that the Jews were the prime agents of the "capitalist mentality." But this money, so coveted and so precious, was given up without reluctance when moral duty called: a duty of solidarity, of ransoming prisoners or coming to the aid of coreligionists accused of ritual murder. In fact, one famous Talmudist even orders the communities of neighboring cities to pay their quotas in order to avoid a danger that he compares, be it noted, to a flood, a natural calamity; and his advice constitutes a precedent. (The text, given in the footnote, is an excellent example of the juridical finesse of reasoning based on the Talmud.)[19]

[19] This was the advice (*responsum*) given by the rabbi of Pavia, Joseph Kolon (Maharik), to the Jewish communities of Germany during the case of ritual murder of Regensburg (1476): "From all sides has come the news of the danger that hangs over the heads of our brothers imprisoned in Regensburg—may the Lord protect them!—and which also threatens the neighboring communities. The most celebrated rabbis have been summoned by the holy community of Nürnberg in order to discuss the ways and means of saving the accused, innocent of any crime, who are nonetheless condemned to death. But it is to be feared that certain coreligionists, certain whole communities or even relatives, deluding themselves with their imagined security and supposing they are exempt from all danger, will refuse their co-operation in the work of salvation, though in truth—may the Lord preserve us!—the wicked clouds may break over their heads if our unfortunate brothers of Regensburg are not saved. This is why I willingly supply an answer to my masters, who ask me to show them the way of light, so that the disaster not fall upon them.

"First of all, it is entirely justifiable that the neighboring communities should contribute to the expenses, for they too will drink from the cup of distress if the evil to which our brothers of Regensburg are exposed is not averted. The safety of these latter also concerns them; the catastrophe, if it occurs, will strike them as well. This is why, whatever their present situation, our decision must be taken in relation to what we may consider as certain for the future, and we must impose upon them the obligation to participate in the expenses made necessary by the work of salvation. We find an analogy for this case in the *Baba Mezia*. Rabbi Judah says: 'If a stream descending from the heights is lost in the sands or is deflected by stones, the farmers of the valley must contribute to its restoration, for they have need of it for their fields. But if the loss or the damming-up occurs in the valley, the farmers on the heights need not contribute to its restoration, for the latter will cause them more damage than advantage: the stream will flow faster and yield less moisture to the fields situated on the heights. It is quite different with respect to the contribution to the ditch which serves to evacuate the rain water that has accumulated in the city. In this case, the house owners of the upper parts of the city must contribute to the drainage labor when the lower parts are flooded. For even if these lower parts are the only ones threatened for the moment, the flooding of the upper parts is inevitable as well, if the struggle against the danger is not undertaken in time.' Similarly, in our case, the danger is inevitable for the neighboring communities if Regensburg is not saved, and they must contribute to that very rescue, even if they seem in security for the moment. Yes, the danger is inevitable, for our enemies labor ceaselessly for our perdition—may God protect us from them!—and these communities must keep in mind the verses: 'Happy is the man that feareth alway!' (Proverbs 28: 14.) And even if they object that

Skill, adaptability, cunning, solidarity in every circumstance, have always been characteristics of every minority group within a hostile society. In general, these groups sooner or later abandon their own values, the particular features, customs, and manners that constitute their ancestral heritage, and dissolve into the surrounding society. That the Jews have been an exception to the rule is doubtless due to the extraordinarily complex attitude of the Christians toward them, putting them in a situation that was virtually unique.

We have seen, in the preceding chapter, to what degree Jews were detested. But at the same time the Christians, far from ignoring or disdaining the Jews' heritage, fiercely claimed it for themselves. A whole system of interpretation, based on certain passages of the New Testament and still

the lying rumors that have done so much harm to the Jews of Regensburg have not reached their cities and that there can be no question of a certain danger, but of the fear of danger, I declare that even in this case they must contribute their quota. For our sages explain that when it is a question of a struggle against a danger not yet present, there is reason for contribution (*Baba Bathra, 8a*): when it is a question of reinforcing the city walls, defending the arsenal, or sending horsemen to see if enemy troops are approaching. And the fear of danger certainly exists in our case. Similarly, all the inhabitants of a city may be constrained to work upon its fortifications, and the owner of a house, even if he does not live in it, may be obliged to repair its door and supply it with a lock, in order to avoid all danger. How much more the neighboring communities of Regensburg need protection, not only for their bodies but also for their souls! And how much more, then, have they the duty to contribute to this protection, even if their members must sell the clothes that cover their bodies and the hair that grows on their heads! It is for the purposes of this protection that the pious rabbis have met in Nürnberg—may our Father in Heaven bring success to their endeavor! Each member and each community must meet the assessment and pay the tax, even if one is taxed more heavily than the other. Since they dare not, for fear of the princes and potentates, ask the communities for the payment of their contributions, I ask all the Jews of Germany, under threat of excommunication, not to oppose the decision of the rabbis and to pay their respective quotas, in order that our accused and wrongly persecuted brothers be freed. As for him who gives proof of ill will and chooses not to obey, let him be excluded from his community, let him be accursed, let water penetrate his body and oil, his bones, and let his name be anathema. As for him who obeys, a sure blessing awaits him. . . . Thus speaks a man incapable of ruling and who writes in humility, the insignificant Joseph Kolon." (*Responsa,* No. 4.)

honored today, was elaborated to show that the Church was the true chosen Israel.[20] The patriarchs were called to witness and were quoted as evidence. The Jews, it was specified in one interpretation, were indeed of the race of Abraham, but "elder sons," children of the servant Hagar, whence their "perpetual servitude." The Christians, however, descended (spiritually, of course) from Sarah in a direct line.[21] In another interpretation, two generations later, the Jews are the sons of Esau, the Christians those of Jacob;[22] two generations later, the Jews represent Manasseh, the elder brother, and the Christians Ephraim, the younger, who nonetheless received the patriarchal blessing.[23] This interplay of symbols, which derives principally from the Epistles of Saint Paul, assuredly constitutes a rich source for the psychoanalyst, who has a splendid opportunity to show the archetypal quadrille in which the younger brother, preferably aided by the mother, supplants the elder brother in the father's affection, or rather seizes his power. The psychoanalyst will add that

[20] Cf. the *Dictionnaire de théologie catholique:* "The theologian . . . knows that the Church has succeeded the Synagogue, that it is the heir to all its books; that the Jewish people, rejected by its infidelity, has been replaced by the Christian people, which has become the people of God. The Church ceaselessly repeats this in its prayers: *plebs tua, populus tuus, familia tua, gens tua;* these terms, part of the oldest liturgical terminology, are intended to insist upon this fact of the substitution of the Christian race for the Jewish one" (article "Liturgy," Paris, 1932, Vol. 9[1], p. 790).

[21] Galatians 4: 22-31: "For it is written, that Abraham had two sons, the one by a bondmaid, the other by a freewoman. . . . Which things are an allegory: . . . for [the one which gendereth to bondage is Hagar] . . . and answereth to Jerusalem which now is, and is in bondage with her children. But Jerusalem which is above is free, which is the mother of us all. . . . So then, brethren, we are not children of the bondwoman, but of the free."

[22] Romans 9: 6-13: "For they are not all Israel, which are of Israel: Neither, because they are the seed of Abraham, are they all children. . . . The elder shall serve the younger. As it is written, Jacob have I loved, but Esau have I hated."

[23] Hebrews 11: 21: "By faith Jacob when he was dying, blessed both the sons of Joseph; and worshipped, leaning upon the top of his staff." This verse refers to Genesis 48: Joseph takes his two sons Manasseh and Ephraim to Jacob's deathbed to receive his blessing. Jacob, against Joseph's will, blesses Ephraim, the younger, with his right hand, and Manasseh, the elder, with his left.

the elder brother is present only to screen the father and that in reality we are concerned with a direct and successful aggression against the father. Thus Judaism would be the supplanted father, inspiring extraordinarily violent and mixed feelings: hatred, fear, remorse. There is doubtless much that is true in this analysis, but we need not go to such lengths to understand not only the astonishing overevaluation of the Jewish heritage on the part of the Christians, and consequently of the Jews themselves, but also the way in which the value of so coveted a heritage was thereby enhanced and heightened for the Jews.

Similarly, the persistent efforts to convert the Jews served only to reinforce their notion of their own importance. In 1236, had not the Holy See announced that if the conversion of any pagan was a salutary work, the conversion of a Jew was especially precious? [24] Eschatological considerations were involved here. If, as we read in Saint Paul and in Saint Augustine, the general conversion of the Jews was to signify the end of time,[25] the Jews' acquiescence had the power to accelerate or retard Christ's final judgment and the renewal of the world. "The salvation of all peoples was, by

[24] "Though we open the heart of our paternal compassion to all those who come to the Christian faith, since the salvation of each is precious to us, nonetheless we bear to the converts from Judaism a still greater affection, hoping that if a branch of wild olive, grafted upon a good olive tree, gives delicious fruits, branches torn from a sacred root will afford even better, for they are naturally finer. . . ." (Bull of Gregory IX, May 5, 1236; L. Auvray, *Les Registres de Grégoire IX*, Paris, 1899, No. 3144.)

[25] Romans 11: 25-26: "For I would not, brethren, that ye should be ignorant of this mystery, lest ye should be wise in your own conceits; that blindness in part is happened to Israel, until the fulness of the Gentiles be come in. And so all Israel shall be saved. . . ." Saint Augustine is much more explicit: "And at or in connection with that judgment the following events shall come to pass, as we have learned: Elias the Tishbite shall come; the Jews shall believe; Antichrist shall persecute; Christ shall judge; the dead shall rise; the good and the wicked shall be separated; the world shall be burned and renewed. All these things, we believe, shall come to pass, but how or in what order, human understanding cannot directly teach us, but only the experience of the events themselves. My opinion, however, is that they will happen in the order in which I have related them. . . ." (*The City of God*, Book 20, Chapter 30.)

their malice, diabolically suspended" (Leon Bloy) (232).
What a terrible power they held! (We have seen the conclusion that Saint Vincent Ferrer drew from this situation. It
could be just as easy to conclude that the Jew is omnipotent!)
In this sense, one might say, the Church did everything to
propagate among the Jews the concept of their uniqueness
and their being the chosen people.

This was especially true of the period in which Jews and
Christians had a common language and broadly participated in the same culture. They confronted one another in
"disputations" that were sometimes amicable. They dis-
cerned and acknowledged human qualities in one another.
When the abyss separating them became uncrossable, the attempts at forced conversion continued but the dialogue was
broken off. The attitude of the Jews in the face of Christian
attacks became like that adopted toward wild animals or
the calamities of nature; the attitude of Christians toward
them no longer mattered. To invectives and insults, the Jews
replied with icy silence. The tradition of apologetical writings, characteristic of the life in the Dispersion and going
back to Flavius Josephus' *Against Apion,* breaks off with the
German Jews (233). Once an adversary is no longer considered properly human, no effort is made to persuade or con-
found him. The limitless scorn in which that adversary is held
affords a better understanding of how the Jews, without
abandoning one iota of their inner pride, could endure the
affronts and humiliations that had become the prevailing tex-
ture of their everyday existence.

They could endure every harassment except forced conversion. They invested all their dignity as men, all their virility, in their fidelity to the Law, in their total readiness for
martyrdom. To give in to apostasy, the renunciation of their
faith, would be for the Jews an acknowledgment of inferi-
ority and impotence. They faced the ordeal, when obliged to,
with a kind of enthusiasm, as a veritable consecration. At
the period of the Black Plague, in 1348, they ". . . went to
die dancing and singing, as gaily as if they were on their

way to a wedding: and would not convert, neither father nor mother for their children . . . and when they saw the burning fire, women and children leapt into it singing the while . . ." (234). There were cases of collective suicide acts: ". . . and they decided they might die the more swiftly, if they planned among themselves in such wise that one among them would kill all the rest, so that they would not be put to death by the hand of the uncircumcised. Then all would consent to this, that one who was old and of good life according to their law would put them all to death . . ." (235).

Thus the teaching of the famous Rabbi Meir of Rothenburg: "Whosoever has taken the firm decision to remain loyal to his faith and to die, if he must, a martyr, does not feel the sufferings of torture. Whether he be stoned or burnt, buried alive or hanged, he remains without feeling, no moan escapes from his lips" (236). The cult of the martyrs, the Akeda, was sustained in every way. It is one of the principal themes of Jewish literature; the first, and for a long time the only, subject of Jewish religious drama (yes, the Jews, too, had their Mystery of the Passion!), and its influence is noted in the details of their customs. According to certain rabbis, the widow of a martyr must not remarry (237); according to others, the blood he had shed must not be removed from the walls of the house, and he was to be buried in the clothes in which he had been killed (238). The cult of suffering, its systematic and reasoned promotion to the highest status, and its classification as divine punishment, but also as the expression of the love of God, gave it a profound meaning and thus made suffering endurable. Of course, such concepts were already implicit in the Talmud: "Precious are sufferings!" exclaimed Rabbi Akiba; but these ideals were characteristic of isolated thinkers until such time as Jewish suffering became an intensely and collectively experienced reality. Henceforth each individual Jew lived and participated in the drama. In this sense, we can say that the Ashkenazim of the end of the Middle Ages were the first authentic Jews. Not that they accepted their fate lightheartedly but they regarded it as enviable. They consciously applied to themselves the famous Talmudic maxim: "The Jewish people is not in a position to rejoice like other peoples." Consulted around 1450 as to whether severe penalties should be imposed upon an apostate seeking to return to Judaism, Israel Isserlein, the greatest Talmudist of the fifteenth century, replied: "We must remember that he who returns to Judaism imposes upon himself a continual penitence, for he turns his back upon the advantages and felicities from which he benefited as a Christian, and assumes the sufferings and persecutions which the Jew needs must endure. He did not have to bear this burden while he was a Christian, and in truth his fault is expiated when he assumes it of his own free will, with the sole purpose of again becoming a member of the Jewish community" (239).

Every aspect of Jewish community life reflects this climate of penitence and austerity. Only once a year, at Purim, was it permitted and even recommended to give oneself up to an open carnival gaiety, to wear costumes and get drunk and at last take revenge on one's persecutors by burning in the public square a wooden effigy of Haman, that prototype of all anti-Semites. But even this sole annual respite was later forbidden by the Christian authorities, and the ceremony was limited to a symbolic stamping accompanied by various noises during the reading of the Book of Esther in the synagogue. On other days, amusements were infrequent and were regulated severely. The secular theater, identified with debauchery, was strictly forbidden, as was dancing of boys with girls, even on the occasion of a wedding. Card games were authorized only on exception. Ultimately chess and social games such as charades on Biblical themes were the only diversions that did not provoke the censure of the rabbis. All ornamentation, all attempt at gaiety in clothing, was proscribed: men and women wore black or gray garments at a period when color and sumptuary extravagance prevailed. Here, as in many other ways, a "Jewish" costume, chosen by the Jews, corresponded to what the world at large, after having imposed the wearing of the rouelle, seemed to expect. Christians came to believe that a religious proscription forbade the Jews to wear bright colors, which was not at all the case. This inverse mimicry went so far that in the miniatures embellishing certain Jewish manuscripts, the characters of the Old Testament, dressed in dark robes and wearing the *pileum cornutum,* seem to be copied from contemporary German caricatures.

There was virtually no difference between rich and poor —all dressed in the same fashion, all were exposed to the same dangers and persecutions, all were distinguished by their very speech from the Christian population.[26] The close community of misfortune, the intensive practice of charity, blunted all class distinctions, as did the primacy accorded to study and erudition. But the intellectual life of the German Jews was limited to critical interpretation of the sacred texts. Though they sought to maintain the heritage of their ancestors, they did not venture into new fields. There was no autonomous research, and as for philosophy and science, these studies, except for medicine, were strictly forbidden. This prohibition is sometimes attributed to certain secret instructions given to the German Jews at the time of the destruction of the Temple, and not communicated to the Jews of other nations (240). Certain Ashkenazim regarded themselves then as the only possessors of the true Jewish tradition. This arrogant exclusivism is illustrated by the attitude of Rabbi Asher ben Yehiel, a student of Rabbi Meir of Rothenburg, who fled Germany after the Rindfleisch massacres and proceeded to Spain, where he became the rabbi of the Toledo community and undertook to take his new flock in hand. He mocked the Talmudic learning of the Span-

[26] About the end of the thirteenth century, the habitual language of the German Jews began to be differentiated from medieval German. This tendency was to increase until in the sixteenth century "Yiddish" was constituted as a separate dialect. (Cf. M. Waxman, "The Rise of Judaeo-German Literature," in *A History of Jewish Literature,* New York, 1953, Vol. 2, p. 613.)

ish Jews and thanked the Lord for having "preserved him from the poison of philosophy and the profane sciences." A severe censor of manners, he observed with horror that sexual relations between Jews and Christians were still frequent and insisted that the Jewish offenders' noses be cut off. Such was the communicative power of fanaticism that Asher was able to impose his will upon his new community for a time. Doubtless the wind of intolerance that had already risen in Christian Spain was of some support to him.

The end of the Middle Ages is the period when the old Jewish quarter was transformed into a ghetto, its gates locked at night and its inhabitants permitted to use Christian streets only by day. Behind the ghetto wall, the Jewish community withdrew into itself for good. Its members led frugal and pious lives, scrupulously regulated in the smallest details. This ordered monotony formed a striking contrast to the blows of fate the Jews risked daily in their dealings with Christians. Constant watchfulness on the one hand was contrasted with a way of life completely circumscribed from the cradle onwards.

As soon as he was four years old, on the last day of Shabuoth (anniversary of the Sinaitic revelation), the little Jew was taken to school, where he was taught the rudiments of the alphabet. So that study would always be sweet to him, the first Hebrew characters, which were in relief, were covered with honey. The first phrases he was given to read were molded out of cookies or written on eggs, which the children shared after their lessons. The rabbis taught that nothing was more admirable than study, that to provide instruction for the children of the poor was the most pious of works, even superior to the building of a synagogue. All little boys had to learn the Torah and the Prophets, Hebrew and Aramaic, and they were taught the rudiments of the Talmud (Mishnah). Then, as they progressed into the domain of the higher intellectual acrobatics of the Gemara, a winnowing took place. Only the most gifted students were sent on to the "high school" (*midrash gadol*): these, even if they did not become rabbis, would continue their studies throughout their lives.

At thirteen occurred the bar mitzvah, the ceremony of religious and civil coming of age. From this moment, the young Jew was considered marriageable, but the arrangements were carefully expurgated of any element likely to give rise to a romantic attraction between the sexes. Boys and girls lived separately and were not allowed to play or dance together. The betrothal was concluded through the intermediation of a professional matchmaker (often a rabbi), who was greatly respected, and usually the fiancés met only on the day the wedding contract was signed. The girl was rated primarily on the extent of her dowry; the boy, on his erudition. These businesslike marriages were also very fruitful ones, since nothing hindered the natural tendency to reproduce: the sexual act was also a commandment, conjugal fidelity the rule, and adultery an extremely rare exception that was punished severely. (We shall see later how certain Christian princes were to try to impose on the Jews the first "birth control" in European history.) Once married and a father, the life of a Jew, whether he was a *talmid hakham,* a sage in Israel, or a simple usurer, followed a set pattern. He was occupied with satisfying the needs of his family and with serving God through the three daily prayers, the various benedictions, and the six hundred and thirteen commandments to be followed throughout life and which could be transgressed only if his life was in danger. Usury and study were not regarded as incompatible—quite the contrary. One text even specifies that usury offers the advantage of affording plenty of leisure for study.

The little girl was compelled to learn to read and write but was rarely instructed in the Talmud. Her knowledge of Hebrew was quite limited. This is the reason that the first writings in Yiddish were books for women, giving rise to a literature in the vernacular that was not exclusively sacred literature. Thus it was chiefly through women that "profane" interests and amusements were introduced into the Jewish community.

In many respects, ghetto life at the end of the Middle Ages resembled the monastic life of religious orders. It was a closed community, separated from the surrounding world. It was a life consecrated to the service of God, one steeped in piety and sacrifice, filled with intellectual and spiritual exercises, and the renunciation of physical effort—its pleasures as well as its pains. Similarities of every type were apparent, and it is significant that in many German codices Jews and clerics were classified under the same heading (241). One might say that Christendom saw a mirror image between the clerics, who chose service to God, and the Jews, who had Lucifer for their master. However, clerics chose the sacerdotal life and made their vows by free choice and at adulthood, whereas the Jew's vocation had become almost uniquely hereditary. But at any moment the former (by being defrocked) and the latter (by conversion) were free to leave their condition. We have seen, with respect to the Jews, that this was uncommon.

All the more striking are the imprints left by apostates on Jewish history. Though Jews preoccupied men's imaginations at all periods and played an historical role disproportionate to their numbers, this disproportion is even more disconcerting in the case of that tiny minority of Jewish renegades, so many of whom are illustrious. It has been remarked that, from Saint Paul to Karl Marx, these renegades were the chief artisans of Western history. But most often, by making the conversion of Jews and the denunciation of Jews their chief vocation, they constituted a true scourge for the Jewish communities. From Theobald of Cambridge to Nicholas Donin, we have already encountered several names; from Johannes Pfefferkorn to Michael the Neophyte, we shall meet many more. More than the calamities that likely gave rise to the desertions, it was the simple fact of defection, sapping the foundation of the most holy tradition, that struck the Jews to the very heart. It is not surprising, therefore, that the apostates should have been the object of unparalleled revulsion and hatred, some traces of which we still find today in the most "assimilated" Jews, those most detached from religious matters. Nor is it surprising that honest conversions were impossible at a period when, in practical as well as emotional terms, privately as well as publicly, the line between Jews and Christians could no longer be crossed. Where, when, how, could human contact between catechist and catechumen be established? And if by chance this was possible, reason—that simple, commonplace reason of the Jews, which makes all discussion of the Christian mystery of the Revelation so difficult for minds not taught from earliest childhood—served as a final impediment. This is perfectly illustrated by the following Jewish apologia:

"A prince friendly to arts and letters had in his service a Jewish physician with whom he delighted to engage in theological discussions. One day, taking him by the arm, he led him into his library and said: 'Behold! All these learned volumes have been written to demonstrate the truth of the Christian dogmas. What do you possess that sustains your own?' 'Assuredly, the thirteen dogmas of Maimonides may be written on a single sheet of paper,' replied the Jew, 'but whatever the number and value of the volumes you show me, Sire, I shall never understand why God, in order to comfort humanity, should have found nothing better than to pass into the body of a virgin, to become a man, to suffer a thousand tortures and death—and all without any appreciable result!' "

(For the reader who may be shocked or offended by the foregoing lines, I suggest the recent work of Father P. Browe, *Die Judenmission in Mittelalter und die Päpste*, Rome, 1942, in which the author with scrupulous honesty summarizes various Jewish arguments of this kind.[27] That in so

[27] Here is the most characteristic passage of the work: "The great majority of the Jews remained faithful to their ancient faith and believed in a personal Messiah. They awaited him as a prophet and a prince of peace,

doing he should be amazed by the incredible blindness shown by the Jews down through the centuries merely emphasizes the difficulty of dialogue in these matters.)

---

not as God. Since they had separated from the Christians, they violently denied that God could become a man. That God could enter into the body of a woman, grow there, live afterward as a man among men, and finally die an outrageous death, signified for them the abandonment of their monotheism; as Saint Paul had already said, this was an incomprehensible stumbling block. 'Why, then'—thus Gislebert Crispin makes his Jewish adversary say on behalf of all—'does God, who suffices unto himself, who is greater than anything one can imagine, accept the misery of human nature and participate in its evils? What necessity incites him to act thus? . . .'

"The Jews drew one of their most valued proofs from Isaiah (2:4), where the kingdom of the Messiah is described as a kingdom of peace, in which 'they shall beat their swords into plowshares, and their spears into pruninghooks: nation shall not lift up sword against nation, neither shall they learn war any more.' 'From Jesus to our own day,' said Moses ben Nachman at the disputation of Barcelona, 'the whole world has been filled with violence and pillage, and the Christians shed more blood than all the other peoples taken together. Wherever one looks, war reigns supreme; there are scarcely enough smiths to furnish weapons to the warriors. Neighbors fight each other, oppress and slay each other, one nation wars against the next, all strive from childhood to wage war.' 'So, then,' says the Jew in the dialogue of Gislebert Crispin, 'you are in the wrong, you Christians, when you believe that the Messiah has already come. . . .'

"Since Saint Paul, Christians have always reproached the Jews, as men of flesh, for abiding by the letter and not raising themselves to the higher, spiritual meaning, not perceiving the mine of gold hidden beneath the envelope of words. They stand before the Scriptures as the blind before a mirror, holding it in their hand and unable to recognize themselves in it. According to the words of Saint Augustine, 'they are deep in sleep and do not understand the spirit of the Scriptures.' 'They read them,' says Bishop Isidore of Seville, 'and in them find all that Christianity teaches; but they do not see, it being for them the sealed book of which Isaiah has spoken (29:11).' 'They read them literally,' says Martin Leon, 'but without entering into the spirit; the face of Moses is hidden from them, and they cannot see the radiant glory of the Law.' "

PART FOUR

THE AGE OF
THE GHETTO

We are now entering the period when, following the Renaissance, the Western world resolutely takes new paths and important changes appear everywhere. Nevertheless, though science and technology were advancing and the capitalist system was developing, there was no change in the living conditions or the attitude of the great mass of people. Anti-Semitism, as it had crystallized during the preceding centuries, seemed to be an inevitable and integral part of this attitude. Until the approach of the French Revolution, the Jews, too, lived without changing the customs and mores of their ancestors. They were in a state of stagnation or "fossilization." Their special way of existing within a hostile society found its most obvious and complete form in the ghettos of Poland. On the other hand, until the beginning of the eighteenth century, nations like France or England continued to prohibit Jews within their borders. This fact determines the next part of our inquiry.

We shall first consider anti-Semitism and its manifestations in the absence of Jews—in what we may call the pure state, that is, the state unalloyed by the presence of Jews. The situation in Germany will permit us later to study the interdependence of anti-Semitism and the reactions provoked by the presence of the Jews; this we shall call activated anti-Semitism. Lastly, the special circumstances of Polish Judaism will interest us from another point of view: in effect, we shall see European Jews, for the first time since the beginning of the Dispersion, constituting a nation.

eight

Anti-Semitism in
the Pure State: France

First, is it certain that there were no Jews left in France after their expulsion in 1394? Some historians, in particular Robert Anchel, have formulated the hypothesis that some of them continued to live there, either in hiding or as ostensibly converted "marranos" (242). Ingenious arguments have been advanced in support of this idea. We shall see later how public opinion in 1650 still accused the honorable body of Parisian *fripiers* (rag pickers) of "Judaizing" in secret. Yet it is certain that these *fripiers,* whatever they had been in the fifteenth century (there is no information on this subject), were good and loyal Catholics in the seventeenth. We shall thus be dealing with one of those collective fixations *in vacuo,* so persistent and so characteristic of anti-Semitism. The strange case of the Chuetas of the Balearic Islands affords a striking example of this in our own day.[1] But let us not anticipate.

It is certain that after the Renaissance there no longer remained in France any trace of indigenous Jews, save for the survival of a few words and place names. However, colonies of marranos, called "Portuguese," were established at the beginning of the sixteenth century in several ports—Bayonne, Rouen, Nantes, and especially Bordeaux. These Jews ostensibly professed Christianity, which was assuredly less shocking for the sensibilities of the period. They were often per-

---

[1] The "Chuetas" of Majorca, fervent Catholics, are presumably descendants of the marranos, and for this reason are rigorously ostracized by the islanders. This will be discussed further in the next volume.

sons of considerable standing: international merchants for the most part, and as such were protected by the authorities —primarily solicitous for fiscal reasons. It is very probable that some of them went to live inland, in Paris or elsewhere, and that most educated Frenchmen were aware of their existence. The expression "Spanish marrano" (that is, a Spanish Jew who conceals his religion) often occurs in the writings of Du Bellay (243), and Clément Marot writes of "the son of the marrano" (244). But this same Marot is amazed at seeing in Venice

> Des Juifz, des Turcs, des Arabes et Mores
> Qu'on veoit icy par trouppes chacun jour (245).

> (Jews, Turks, Arabs, and Moors
> That one sees here in numbers each day.)

In other words, the sight of acknowledged Jews was apparently quite unusual for a Frenchman of the sixteenth century. Montaigne, too—himself the son of a marrano mother— when he met Jews in Rome and even visited a synagogue, speaks as though this were a curious and exotic spectacle (246). And the poet Sagon (who must have known what he was talking about, since he was the "son of the marrano" Marot referred to) tells us that

> France est entière en sa religion,
> France n'a Juifz dedans sa région
> Ce qu'ont plusieurs nations prochaines (247).

> (France is all of one religion,
> France has no Jews within her region
> As several neighboring nations have.)

In fact, before the reign of Louis XIV and the annexation of Metz and Alsace, there were only two or three instances of Jews in France openly professing their religion. One was Simon Molcho, to whom Francis I offered the chair of Hebrew at the Collège de France (248). In the following century, there was Elijah Montalto, who became the physician of Marie de Médicis. Montalto collected around him a small circle of Jews, converted or not—cabalists, physicians, or merely charlatans "professing to be diviners . . . by the cabala"—at a period when the cabala was fashionable and when many famous persons pursued the philosopher's stone or the elixir of life. Masaïdes, the disquieting cabalist from Lisbon, the product of Anatole France's artistic imagination in *La Rôtisserie de la Reine Pédauque*, might have been inspired by one of the members of this circle, since they were much talked about. Their fate was an unhappy one and deserves to be studied in some detail (249).

At this time (1611-1617), the Italian adventurer Concino Concini and his wife, la Galigai, favorites of the regent Marie de Médicis, virtually ruled France. La Galigai, the demonic member of the couple, was what we call today a psychoneurotic. She suffered from a thousand strange and secret pains and had been treated by the most famous physicians and exorcisers of France and Navarre, without benefit.

Montalto, a physician famous in Italy, was living in Venice. Marie sent for him, but this *Grand Hébrieu et vray Juif*, who "had no intention of dissimulating and counterfeiting his profession," stipulated, as a condition of his coming, the right to practice Judaism freely. He added that "through a single act—his refusal to accept money on the day of the Sabbath—one could recognize his piety." [2] This was granted him. He then arrived, and it appears that his services were more than satisfactory, since he also cared for the regent and remained in France until the end of his days. After his death, his body was embalmed and sent to the Jewish cemetery in Amsterdam. Doubtless Montalto had Jews in his retinue. It is also likely that he summoned others from Holland, as he was accused posthumously of doing.

Meanwhile, in 1615, some scandalous incidents occurred in Paris. Another protégé of the unpopular Concini, the Ital-

---

[2] B. Legrain, *Décade commençant l'histoire du roi Louis XIII* . . . (Paris, 1619), from which the quotations that follow are also taken.

ian Cosme Ruger, abbé of Saint-Mahé in Brittany, refused the sacraments on his deathbed, preferring to die an atheist. His body was therefore "thrown into the fields in unconsecrated ground." "This year seemed to be completely given over to impiety and corrupt ways," concludes the chronicler from whom we quote. "We see at the beginning of the year a great number of sorcerers, Jews and magicians professing their Sabbath and maintaining synagogues with impunity, and insinuating themselves even into the court." (According to Sauval, some had even been caught "preparing a lamb for the Passover of 1615" (250). Energetic measures were immediately taken to put an end to the scandal, especially by the Parliament of Paris.[3] The 1394 edict of expulsion was formally reinstated by letters patent recorded on May 12, 1615. "Considering that the most Christian kings have held in horror all the enemy nations of this name, and especially that of the Jews, whom they have never consented to suffer in their kingdom . . . and particularly since we have been advised that in violation of the edicts and decrees of our said predecessors, said Jews have for some years appeared, disguised, in several places of this our kingdom. . . . We have said, ordered, desired, and declared:

"That all said Jews who are to be found in this our kingdom will be required, on pain of death and the confiscation of all their property, to depart and to withdraw from the same, at once and within the time and term of a month . . ." (251).

The edict of expulsion was not applied to the marranos of Bordeaux and Bayonne, who were too profitable for the royal treasury and who, moreover, superficially satisfied the

---

[3] "That Her Majesty will be very humbly implored to order that the edicts of pacification be maintained, but that the Jews, atheists, anabaptists, and others professing religions not tolerated by the said edicts will be punished by death and confiscation of all property, the half of which will be accorded to the informer. . . ." (22nd session of the Commission of September 1, 1614; cf. the *Registres des délibérations du bureau de la ville de Paris,* Paris, 1927, Vol. 16, p. 67.)

requirements of conforming to Christianity. The edict applied only to the "sorcerers, Jews, and magicians" of Paris.

Two years later, the joint terms of "sorcery" and "Judaism" were very significant in the notorious public trial of la Galigai, after the murder of her husband.

The identification of sorcery and politics in such cases was nothing new, and the Concinis were accused of the crime of *lèse-majesté divine*, as well as of corresponding with foreign powers and espionage. Had there not been "found in their house a book entitled *Cheinuc*, that is, a manual for learning Hebrew . . . and another book entitled *Mahazor*, that is, the Jews' liturgical cycle for the year"? Had not one of her servants "sworn that la Galigai was in the habit of making sacrifices of a cock"? Now, "it appears from two books exhibited by Monsieur le Procureur du Roy . . . that this sacrifice of a cock is Judaic." Finally, had not another witness, Philippe Dacquin, "formerly a Jew and at present a Christian," declared that the accused indulged in even more serious magical practices? [4] And so she was condemned to death and executed on the very same day—to the intense jubilation of the people of Paris. Countless broadsides, pamphlets, and plays commemorated this event, and there was a rumor that she was a Jewess herself, her real name being Sophar (though this was certainly not the case, and this unfortunate practitioner of the black arts died a good Christian). Was the circle of Jewish marranos that surrounded her so powerful and so large? Comparing the available documents, we find several other names, Albarez, Garcia, Veronne, but after 1615 we hear no more about them (except for the erstwhile Jew Dacquin, formerly a

---

[4] ". . . it being noted, according to the testimony of Dacquin, that Conchine [Concini], in the presence of his wife, had taken from the chamber a urinal, and taken from the said chamber the image of the crucifix, for fear of hindering the effect that Conchine and his wife claimed to derive from the reading of several verses of Psalm 51 in Hebrew, which reading they sought to have made to them by Dacquin in the form that it had previously been made to them by Montalto." (Legrain's narrative, *op. cit.*)

rabbi, who sired a line of physicians. His grandson, Antoine, attended the Sun King, Louis XIV) (252). Nonetheless, for a long time to come, some people suspected there were Jews everywhere. In 1627, Malherbe, deeply grieved at being unable to conclude a lawsuit he had begun against his son's murderers, attributed his failure to the Jews and wrote to one of his friends:

"Judaism has spread as far as the Seine. It would be better if it had remained beside the Jordan and if this rabble had not mingled, as it has done, with respectable people. There is no help for it. My cause is a just one. I shall fight everywhere with God's help, even in Jerusalem and with the twelve tribes of Israel" (253).

(It is as if one were reading Drumont!)

Two centuries later, Alfred de Vigny wrote *La Maréchale d'Ancre,* a romantic drama in five acts, in which the Jew Montalto is an important character. According to the conventions then observed, de Vigny strongly accentuated the character's "Jewish" traits, transforming his given name to Samuel and his profession to that of a usurer. Anatole France, as we have remarked, wrote more accurately.

The case of Montalto is typical; thus we have examined it in some detail. The Jewish doctor, who seems to have been a man of rectitude, performed his professional duties for several years at the royal court. He brought his retinue, as well as several friends, to Paris. This was enough to provoke the formal reissuance in 1615 of an edict dating from 1394, to set off a spectacular trial for witchcraft, to make Malherbe burst into vituperation twelve years later, and, two centuries afterward, to nourish the imaginations of a de Vigny and an Anatole France. The reaction to Montalto, moreover, reflects the horror of disbelief or simply of unbelief, which henceforth begins to pose a serious threat to the solidity of the Christian faith.

Thus we see how a "Jewish problem" preyed on men's imaginations, at a period when almost no Frenchman had ever seen a Jew in his life. This was also the period when the words of the national vocabulary acquired their definitive meanings, as Littré, for example, makes clear:

"*Juif,-ive,* s.m. and f . . .

"3) Fig. and familiarly. One who lends at usury or who sells at exorbitantly high prices, and, in general, anyone seeking to gain money by sharp dealings. 'It has been a long time since I have seen young Sancho: he is a young man eager for gain and quite a Jew, in my opinion.' Guy Patin, *Lettres,* Vol. 2, p. 186. 'What the devil! What Jew, what Arab is this? That's more than twenty-five per cent.' Molière, *L'Avare,* 2, 1. 'Farewell, Jew, more Jew than any in all Paris.' Regnard, *Le Joeur,* 2, 14 . . ."

A definition that its theological counterpart, Judas, conveniently completes:

"*Judas,* s.m. . . .

"2) Fig. A traitor. A betrayer. 'He is a Judas. Monsieur Judas is an odd fellow/ Who hotly maintains/ That he has played only one role/ And painted himself only one color.' Béranger, *M. Judas.* Adj. 'Now that is criminal! Now that is Judas!' Molière, *Le Bourgeois Gentilhomme,* 3, 10. Kiss of Judas, a caress given to someone in order to betray him."

How were these stereotypes sustained and strengthened through succeeding centuries? This problem grows increasingly complex and disconcerting as we approach the modern age. As to past centuries, when all education was uniformly religious, the answer is clear. In effect, the family circle, where the child learned to speak and was initiated into moral concepts, played a determining role. As the little Christian grew up and was taught to discriminate between good and evil, he was told of the existence of a strange, impenitent people, guilty of the greatest crime of all time, and hence detestable. Later, when he attended a parish school and learned his catechism, his teachers continued the same lessons, as we can discover by examining the manuals of religious instruction. These assumed their definitive form in the seventeenth century. Their contents assuredly had more influence on public opinion than the reflections of a few scholars or the lofty speculations of a Pascal.

It would be a mistake to assume that these works showed a special emphasis, that they were devoted to long discourses to demonstrate the wickedness of the Jews. This wickedness was taken for granted from the start. It served as a kind of criterion, the absolute zero of evil, in order to set off by contrast the true Christian virtues and to warn the sinner or the libertine that if he did not mend his ways, the fate of the Jews might one day be his own.

Questions and answers: the method was incisive and sure. Rare are the catechisms, among the popular manuals of the time, that do not touch on the subject. This is from Bossuet: "Why did God cause all these miracles upon the death of His Son?—As a testimony against the Jews.—Was this not also a testimony against us?—Yes, if we do not profit by this death" (254).

The celebrated catechism of Abbé Fleury, which in two centuries went through one hundred and seventy-two editions, is more explicit: "Did Jesus have enemies?—Yes, the carnal Jews.—To what point did the hatred of Jesus' enemies go?—To the point of causing his death.—Who was it who promised to hand him over?—Judas Iscariot.—Why was this city [Jerusalem] treated in this way?—For having caused the death of Jesus.—What became of the Jews?—They were reduced to servitude and scattered throughout the world.— What has become of them since?—They are still in the same state.—For how long?—For seventeen hundred years" (255).

Let us imagine, in space and time, the millions of young voices gaily and faithfully repeating their well-learned lesson. Imagine, too, the commentaries that the teacher or curé may have made, according to his own views and fancy. . . .

More laconic, but still more devastating, is the catechism of Adrien Gambart, which, its author expressly tells us, was intended "for the simple-minded," for those who "are not capable of understanding long speeches or reasoning."

"Is it a great sin to take communion unworthily?

"It is the greatest of all sins, because one makes oneself guilty of the body and blood of Jesus Christ, as Judas and the Jews were; and one becomes the object of His judgment and condemnation" (256).

Judas and the Jews, cupidity and betrayal: the identification is always the same. These writers do not strain their imaginations or bother to indulge in an "anti-Jewish propaganda" at this period, when it was implicitly acknowledged by all believers that Judas and the Jews, past and present, are the sworn enemies of the Lord through the unfathomable will of Providence. They have become the permanent tools of the Evil One through supernatural predestination; thus they are distinguished from heretics and sorcerers, who have joined his camp individually and voluntarily.

This same stereotype, enriched by many more suggestive details, may be observed in the lives of Jesus or the saints, as well as in accounts of pilgrimages, which were addressed to a more educated audience.

Here, for example, is a passage from a life of Jesus:

"Some insulted him; others, with the backs of their hands, struck his noble and gentle mouth; others spit into his face (for it was the custom of the Jews to spit into the faces of those whom they cast out from among themselves); others tore out his beard or pulled at his hair, and thus trampled under their accursed feet the Lord of the angels. . . . And still spitting into his noble countenance, they struck his head with a stick, so that the thorns of his crown sank into his head and made the blood flow down his cheeks and over his forehead. . . . Pilate commanded that in this shameful and inhuman state he be led before all the Jewish people, who had remained outside in order not to sully themselves on the day of the Sabbath. But these accursed sons of the Devil all cried out with one voice: Take him away, take him away, crucify him. . . ."

But divine retribution could not be long delayed and was announced by a chapter heading: "Of the vengeance for the death of Our Lord Jesus Christ upon Judas, upon Pilate, and upon the Jews in general."

"Thirty Jews were given for one piece of silver. Ninety-two thousand Jews were sold and scattered into various parts of the world and put into perpetual bondage, in which their race still languishes, and will until the end of the world . . ." (257).

Other works went into greater detail as to the manner in which divine vengeance continued to work upon the Jews. "A race once blessed, today accursed; once holy, today profane; once honored by all men, today detested by men and angels; once heirs to the Holy Land, and now wretched wanderers over the world. . . ." Thus begins the chapter devoted to the Jews by Father Boucher, an Observant friar who had seen a few of them in the Orient. (We shall find later, under Bossuet's name, the same idea, written with remarkable similarity, but there is no need to assume that the Eagle of Meaux plagiarized Father Boucher, since we are dealing with a commonplace of the period.)

Father Boucher then turns to the Talmud and concludes his account—which went into several dozen editions between 1620 and 1735—as follows:

"In conclusion of this discourse, I would say no more about them than that they are odious and loathsome to all the world. The Turks so hate them that they permit all Christians who find them in the square of the Church of Calvary to kill them without being arrested for doing so. The Levantine Christians have such a horror of them that they consider it a mortal sin to eat anything handled by a Jew. We know how they were driven out of England in disgrace in the year 1291, and out of France, first under Philip Auguste [Philip II], then later under Philip the Fair [Philip IV], and finally under Philip the Tall [Philip V].

"They were also banished from Spain under Ferdinand, always in punishment for their impiety and the rage they bear toward all Christians . . ." (258).

More startling statements were made by other pilgrims,

for charlatanism contributed to the perpetuation of age-
old legends. The naïve Franciscan Dominique Auberton reported seeing in 1623, in Jerusalem, in the "house of Pilate,"
Malchus, a Jew who had beaten Jesus Christ with his own
hand: "This man, of an age, so it seems, between thirty-five
and forty years . . . is buried in the earth to his navel, and
speaks only to Christians. . . . He asked us when the Day
of Judgment would come. We told him that the Lord alone
knew. This Malchus beats and strikes at his breast constantly
and never looks at those who speak to him. . . . And I,
Brother Dominque Auberton, certify that this is true, upon
my faith, my word, and my share of paradise" (259).

This eternal Jew was not yet a wandering one! [5]

Stories of miraculous Hosts or of ritual murders—both
famous legends of nationwide currency—were also often
adapted to the taste of the time. Examples are the incident
of the Rue des Billettes in 1290 and minor incidents of local
importance, such as the case of ritual murder in Le Puy in
1320, narrated in various works of 1620, 1630, 1653, and
1693.

Works of this type were accessible only to a literate and
inquisitive minority, but the sermons that priests and friars
delivered from their pulpits affected the entire population.
All trace has been lost of what the humble curés may have
said, but the discourses of the high dignitaries and famous
preachers who served as models are available to us. Turning to these, we can see that two themes—direct vilification
of the Jews, and warnings of the threat they symbolized
for Christians—alternate regularly. This is apparent from a
glance at a few texts not usually found in anthologies (260).

[5] The "wandering Jew" legend, whose spread throughout Europe dates
from the first years of the seventeenth century (see p. 242), was known in
several variants in the Orient from the first centuries of Christianity. We see
how industrious charlatans helped to maintain it.

VILIFICATION

"A monstrous people, having neither hearth nor home, without a country and of all countries; once the most fortunate in the world, now the evil spirit and the detestation of the world: wretched, scorned by all, having become, in their wretchedness, by a curse, the mockery of even the most moderate . . ." (Bossuet).[6]

"The greatest crime of the Jews is not that they caused the death of the Saviour. Does this surprise you? I thought it might. . . . And how could this be? Because God, upon the death of His Son, left them still forty years without punishing them. . . . When He used so sudden a punishment, there was some other crime which He could no longer endure, which to Him was more unendurable than the death of His own Son. What was this crime, so black and so abominable? It is the hardness of heart, it is impenitence . . ." (Bossuet).

"What did the Jews do when they stoned Stephen? Listen to the thoughts of Saint Fulgentius, which will appear to you as solid as they are ingenious: 'Stephen,' says this Father, 'as the first martyr of Christianity, is one of the living stones with which Jesus Christ began to build his Church; and the Jews, who themselves are hearts of stone, striking this mysterious stone, brought forth the sparks of charity and divine love . . ." (Bourdaloue).

"But let us turn from these unbelievers. As they were scandalized by Jesus Christ, they have become, by a just judgment of God, the scandal of all peoples, and they shall be such until God, at the end of time, gathers together the debris of Israel . . ." (Fléchier).

"How far will this foolish people not carry the excesses of its frivolity and its blindness? And how many crimes does it not compound within a single one? First of all, monstrous injustice. . . . Secondly, blind rage. . . . This furious peo-

[6] Compare with the quotation from Father Boucher on p. 182.

ple asks that his blood be upon it and upon all its posterity: it consents, it desires, that this anathema remain eternally upon the heads of its descendants . . . and the outcome corresponds to its desire: even today, having become the opprobrium of the universe, wandering, fugitive, scorned, without altar, without land, without sacrifices, they bear everywhere upon their heads the crime of this blood they have shed . . ." (Massillon).

THREAT

"Yet here, O sinner, I must enter with you into a more detailed discussion: I must examine if you are much less guilty than are the Jews. . . . But, you will say, the Jews have crucified the Saviour. And do you not know, O sinners, that you trample underfoot the blood of his testament? . . ." (Bossuet).

"Death in sin, death with sin, death even, as it often happens, by sin—that, my dear listeners, is what frightens me and what must frighten you even as it does me. That is God's most terrible weapon in the arsenal of His wrath; that is what the Son of God threatens the Jews with today, and what we as well as the Jews must preserve ourselves from . . . (Bourdaloue).

"A crown of thorns is prepared for him, and it is pressed violently down upon his head. His blood flows on all sides, as all the points that pierce him make so many wounds. That is how the Synagogue has treated its King! That is how it treated your King and mine! That is how it treated the Master and the King of all nature. We detest this indignity! But even as we detest it in others, do we not detest it in ourselves? For is it not ourselves, Christians, who have a hundred times behaved in this wise toward Jesus Christ? . . ." (Bourdaloue).

"What kind of terrible beatitude is Jesus Christ announcing to men today, or rather, what judgment is he pronouncing upon them today? . . . They have heard without heeding the words from his sacred lips; they have seen without wonder the brilliant luster of his virtues. . . . Such were once the Jews; such today are the Christians . . ." (Fléchier).

"But such is your work and the consummation of your iniquity and your ingratitude if you are sinners; such is the barbarous act which you repeat every time you consent to the crime; such is the body you dishonor when you corrupt your own; such is the august head you recrown with thorns, when acts of lust, complacently repeated, make dangerous impressions upon your mind; . . . such is Man, *ecce Homo*. Can this spectacle leave you unmoved? Must he ascend Calvary again? Would you mingle your voices with those of the perfidious Jews, and ask again that he be crucified? . . ." (Massillon).

Penitence! Penitence! "Would you mingle your voices with those of the perfidious Jews, and ask again that he be crucified?" But the edifying words of the preachers were applied only to their flocks of perennial scapegoats. Let us recall Pascal's heart-rending cry upon his conversion: "Jesus Christ, Jesus Christ! I have turned from him, fled from him, renounced and crucified him!" That was Pascal. For souls less sublime and less suffering, the only solution psychologically possible was to load again upon the Jews the intolerable guilt of an obsessive and imaginary crime.

Of course, quotations can be deceptive, and it should not be assumed that the preachers of the time had only the Jews in mind. On the contrary, they mentioned them rather rarely; but when they did, it was always in this light. It was, one might say, a "propaganda of reminding" (and not a "propaganda of urging"). The associations are always the same: Crucifixion—indignity; Christian imperfections—Jewish guilt. Here is a final example, quoted from the most powerful popular preacher in France between the Reformation and the Revolution.

The Blessed Grignon de Montfort (1673-1716) exercised his ministry in Brittany, in the Vendée, and in Anjou (and if the Catholic faith is strongest in these regions today, this is attributable to his influence, according to his biographer) (261). Among other gifts, he had that of striking and facile rhyming. He composed a great number of canticles that he set to music, using the popular tunes of the time. This scandalized his contemporaries, but even today we hear children and young people singing these chants in the countryside.

Here is one that may be said to be merely the transposition of a mystery of the Passion of the Middle Ages, with its evocative and bloody images. Though they are no longer performed on a stage, they are still sung.

Here are the chief strophes:

Jesus flagellated

Jésus voit la mort affreuse	Jesus sees a dreadful death
Qui vient d'un air menaçant	Coming upon him threateningly;
Pour être victorieuse	To be victorious
Ainsi qu'il soit le Tout-Puissant.	He must as well be omnipotent.

(Refrain)

C'est moi qui suis le coupable,	I am the guilty one
Mais Jésus est innocent.	But Jesus is innocent.
Ah! que je suis misérable!	Ah! Wretched am I!
Je le dis en gémissant.	I say it, moaning.

Les bourreaux pleins de rage,	The furious executioners
Comme des loups ravissants,	Like ravening wolves
Lui meurtrissent le visage,	Bruise his face
Arrachent ses vêtements.	Tear his garments.

(Refrain)

Il est couvert de blessures,	He is covered with wounds,
Son sang coule par ruisseaux.	His blood flows in rivulets.
Accablé de meurtrissures,	Overwhelmed with bruises,
Sa chair tombe par lambeaux.	His flesh falls in strips.

(Refrain)

Jesus Crowned with Thorns

On met dans ses mains sacrées Into his sacred hands are put
Pour sceptre, un frêle roseau. For scepter, a frail reed.
Chacun en fait des risées Everyone mocks him,
En disant: Ha! Qu'il est beau! Saying: Ha! How fine!

C'est pour nous, ô pécheurs, It is for us, O sinners,
Qu'il endure ces douleurs. That he endures these pains.

On le couronne d'épines. He is crowned with thorns.
Avec des coups de bâton; With blows of a stick;
Un chacun lui fait des mines Everyone makes faces at him
En hurlant comme un démon. Shrieking like a demon.

(Refrain)

Cette couronne cruelle This cruel crown
Lui transperce le cerveau. Pierces his skull.
On voit couler sa cervelle The brain oozes out
Avec du sang et de l'eau. With blood and sweat.

(Refrain)

Jesus Crucified

Cette canaille insolente This insolent rabble
Lui tire tout de nouveau Again tears everything from him;

Sa pauvre robe sanglante His poor bloody robe
Toute collée à sa peau. Sticks everywhere to his skin.

C'est pur nous, ô pécheurs, It is for us, O sinners,
Qu'il endure ces douleurs. That he endures these pains.

Tandis que les plus barbares While the fiercest
Préparent tout pour sa mort Prepare everything for his death
Quelques-uns des plus avares Some of the greediest
Tirent ses habits au sort. Draw lots for his clothes.

(Refrain)

O cruelle barbarie! O cruel savagery!
Ses membres sont disloqués, His limbs are broken,

Sa chair est toute meurtrie,	His flesh is all bruised,
L'on voit ses nerfs tout ban- *dés.*	His nerves laid bare.

(Refrain)

Jesus Dead and Buried

O pécheurs abominables,	O abominable sinners,
C'en est fait, Jésus est mort.	It is done, Jesus is dead.
Nous sommes tous les coupa- *bles.*	We are all guilty.
Que deviendra notre sort?	What is our fate to be?
C'est pour nous, ô pécheurs	It is for us, O sinners,
Qu'il est mort dans les dou- *leurs* (262).	That he died in such pain.

The evocative power of these images is obvious. It is not surprising that Grignon de Montfort was a remarkable rabble-rouser. With other great evangelizers, he felt tempted by the Evil One all his life. On his deathbed, he was still struggling against him; he expired, his biographer reports, exclaiming: "In vain you attack me. I am between Joseph and Mary. I have run my course. It is over, I shall sin no more" (263).

To what extent was this propaganda effective? Could it, in the virtual absence of Jews, provoke great popular movements that are the instinctive and final aspects of anti-Semitism? Our answer must vary with the period. In the sixteenth century, we find no public reaction, no anti-Jewish upheaval. There was an obvious and simple reason for this: in the century of the Reformation, the French Protestants assumed a specifically "Jewish" role, and the traditional "marvelous hatreds" were directed toward them. A persecuted minority, worshiping in secret, devoted to the Old Testament—the analogies are many, and the following passage by a contemporary historian, which carries singularly familiar overtones for a Jewish reader, is characteristic:

"The Protestants lived, individually as well as collectively, in an atmosphere of permanent insecurity. . . . The populace, Catholic or 'atheist,' turned against these men who held secret assemblies. It collected and spread the most damaging stories, which were circulated particularly in the neighborhoods where the secret meetings were held. We can imagine the suspicion aroused by the nocturnal comings and goings of strangers or of persons of high rank through these out-of-the-way districts and on roads through the flat countryside. The people responded with jeers, stones, riots, even fires . . ." (264).

At the end of the nineteenth century, did not Édouard Drumont call the French Protestants "half-Jews"?

Thus, in general, anti-Jewish hatred decreased greatly when other violent passions aroused the social body. Heretics, Turks or other infidels, or simply an "hereditary enemy" in a period of conflict: the substitutes, down through the centuries, were many and varied.

Accordingly, there was a change in the seventeenth century, after the Edict of Nantes put an end to religious wars. We have discussed the eddies stirred up by the Concini case; and though, in the absence of the Jews—the most reliable chroniclers of their own misfortunes—many other cases are unknown to us, in the course of this strange and obstinate shadow war there were some skirmishes of which records survive. The Jean Bourgeois case, which dates from 1652, is an example.

Paris was then in the midst of the *Fronde*—the "court party." Anne of Austria and Mazarin were on one side, while the city people and Parliament were on the other. There were skirmishes and battles; the armed bourgeois temporarily seized *de facto* power, while the guilds assumed police responsibilities in the capital.

On August 15, 1652, the Guild of *Fripiers* (old-clothes dealers) of the Tonnelleris was taking its turn on guard duty. Banners flying, they passed near the church of Saint-Eustache. At this moment, a young bystander named Jean

Bourgeois cried out mockingly, "There go the gentlemen from the synagogue!"

Enraged, the *fripiers* flung themselves on him, beat him with their halberds and the butts of their muskets, and forced him to make honorable amends. Then he was released. This minor incident had a long train of consequences.

Jean Bourgeois, the son of an honorable merchant, did not leave matters there but lodged a complaint with the magistrate against his attackers. One of them was arrested. Furious, the *fripiers* swore vengeance. They lured the young man into an ambush, tortured him cruelly and at great length, and finally blew out his brains with a musket.

A mere incident set against the background of a troubled period? A feud between two guilds? This was not how the public interpreted the matter—and public opinion in this period was remarkably sensitive and active. For four years, as long as the *Fronde* had lasted, public opinion had expressed itself through political pamphlets called *mazarinades,* since they were directly chiefly against Mazarin. Sometimes several appeared in one day, in prose or verse, six or eight pages long; but now Mazarin was forgotten for several weeks, and the world seemed to live under the sign of the "Jewish problem."

First came prose tracts (265). A *Monitory letter published by all the parishes of the City of Paris against the Jews of the Synagogue* . . . (266); a *Simple and true account of the cruel murder and horrible massacre committed on August 26, 1652* . . . (267); and a *Scrutiny of the life of the Jews, of their religion, trade, and associations* . . . (268). "There is no one who does not know that the Jews are the opprobrium of all nations and have been so for sixteen hundred years and more," we read in this last. "Their customs show their malediction no less than their bondage. There is no one who does not know that they have no other profession in life than usury, and that their false witnesses and their infamous practices have sown corruption the world over. . . ." And so on. Then comes: *The true story of what occurred in*

the murder of a young boy, son of a merchant . . . (269);
The reply of the officers of the Synagogue . . . (270), which
defends the *fripiers;* and finally, *The assembly of fripiers
. . . to advise how to remedy the cruelty of their great crime
. . .* (271), a subtle item whose author puts the following
reasoning in the "Jews'" mouths:

"Of what are we guilty? Moses in his day sacrificed animals, and we have sacrificed a man. Is it not said in the same
book that our predecessors had the power to sacrifice Jesus
Christ, their King and ours? Why do we not have the power
to put a man to death? . . ."

Generally, in line with the fashion of the time, these tracts
were in verse, in which the authors gave their imaginations
free rein. They are equally characteristic. Some bordered on
a furious indignation:

Infâmes assassins,	Infamous murderers,
Nation détestable	Detestable nation
Abhorrée des humains,	Abhorred by men,
Chassée de toutes places,	Everywhere rejected,
Fallait-il aujourd'hui	Must you today
Renouveler l'effort	Renew the effort
De vos cruautés inouïes	Of your horrid cruelties
Lesquelles donnèrent la mort	Which put to death
Au Dieu de qui nous tirons vie?	The God by whom we live?

(*True account of the horrible murder committed by the*
fripiers *of the Jewish nation* . . .) (272).

Démons échappés de l'enfer,	Demons escaped from hell,
Race des Juifs, gens détesta-bles,	Race of the Jews, detestable men,
Plus maudits que n'est Lu-cifer	More accursed than Lucifer
Et plus méchants que tous les Diables,	And more wicked than all the devils,
Tigres cruels, retirez-vous,	Cruel tigers, begone,

Indignes de vivre parmi nous.	Unworthy as you are to live among us.
Quand vous serez de sang avides,	When you thirst so for blood,
Craignez donc la punition	You must fear the punishment
Dont la Sainte Inquisition	With which the Holy Inquisition
Doit châtier vos parricides.	Will chastise your parricides.
Déliez les pieds et les mains	Untie the hands and feet
D'un bourgeois mis à la torture.	Of a citizen put to the torture.
Voulez-vous qu'il soit en effet	Would you make of him
D'un Ecce homo *le portrait*	The image of an *Ecce Homo*
Sujet à l'outrage et l'injure?	Subject to insult and outrage?

(*The Synagogue shown in its true colors* . . .) (273).

Here we see the direct identification that our pamphleteers make between the Crucifixion, its temporal extension in the form of ritual murder, and the crime of the *fripiers*.

Having presented the problem in this way, other verses suggest specific remedies. Of course, these are only songs —but it is noteworthy that they advocate the very remedies that were used in Europe during the recent past—for inevitably in such matters, the human imagination is limited. One piece of doggerel suggests expelling the Jews or making them wear special insignia:

Faites sortir de nos murs	Cast out from our walls
Des gens de si mauvaises moeurs.	People of such evil ways.
Ou bien, par l'ordre du monarque,	Or, by the king's command,
Faites-leur porter une marque	Make them wear a sign
Qui les distingue des chrétiens	That distinguishes them from Christians
Et les mette parmi les chiens . . .	And sets them among the dogs . . .

(*The rage of the Jews, dedicated to the Gentlemen of the Synagogue . . .*) (274).

Another simply proposes hanging them:

Faites que l'on voie, pieds et mains	Let there be seen, hands and feet
Liés, ceux de leur troupe	Bound, those of their horde
Suivre les traces à grands pas	Following the footsteps closely
De celui qu'ils ont mis à bas	Of him whom they laid low
Par une mort trop cruelle.	By a death all too cruel.
Faites que l'on voie sur l'échelle,	Let there be seen on the scaffold,
Sans faveur, grâce ni pardon,	With no favor, grace or pardon,
La Synagogue à Montfaucon . . .	The Synagogue at Montfaucon . . .

(*The cruelty of the Synagogue . . .*) (275).

Still another suggests castrating them all "so that their race may be extinguished forever. . . ."

Je crois qu'il est plus juste	I believe it is more fitting
Qu'autrement le fer les ajuste.	That the steel arrange matters differently.
Et qu'on leur ôte tout à fait	And that there be removed from them entirely
Le membre qu'ils ont imparfait.	That member which in them is already imperfect.
Afin que pour punir leur vice	In order that in punishment of their vice
Ils survivent à leur supplice	They may survive their torment
Et qu'au gré de nos justes voeux	And that according to our just desires
Leur nom ici meure avec eux . . .	Their name here on earth perish with them . . .

(*The criminal verdict reached against the Synagogue . . .*) (276).

(The last author, more cautious than his colleagues, nonetheless makes one reservation: "We must see beforehand if they are all whole men, where men may be whole. Or if there has been made some sort of cut whose mark remains within their skin." And then he slips into coarse joking: "Lovely ladies, surmount all obstacles. / I invite you to this spectacle / Where you will have enough choice / To content your every desire. / Consider the perfect model of natural power / Finding long ones, short ones . . ." etc.)

The reader, confronted with so many texts, may well ask whether the *fripiers* of Paris were not, after all, clandestine Jews, marranos professing their religion in the utmost secrecy? What other meaning can we give this campaign? Yet this was not so. All the protagonists, without exception, were good and loyal Catholics. This is proved incontestably by the evidence submitted later at the trial held (for there was a trial), as well as by a number of other texts.[7] The key

---

[7] The father of Jean Bourgeois brought the case before Parliament: the dossier is in the Archives Nationales (*Registres Parlement criminel, arrêts transcrits X2 233-34*). The reporter, M. de Boivin-Vaurony, was severe toward the *fripiers*: "Christendom has been outraged by the outrages committed upon the lamented victim, which . . . only barbarians without the knowledge of God would be capable of inventing and using upon a man of another nation. But that, in the first and foremost city of His Christian Majesty, this barbarism should have been perpetrated by several individuals upon another, *all professing the same religion*, is an occasion in which the offense to God must be a consideration in the deliberation and the judgment of the trial. . . ."

Subsequently, letters of annulment were granted to the accused by the king. "We have received the humble supplication of ——, professing *the Catholic, apostolic, and Roman Religion.* . . ."

Thus neither in Parliament nor on the Royal Council did anyone suspect the *fripiers* of Judaizing. There is no question about their names: Philip Sayde, Jean Forget, Simon Gaultier, Noël Debarque, Gilles Jousseanne, Cahourst the elder, Vivanier, and so on.

Furthermore: How could the *fripiers* be constituted into a guild and bear arms along with the other guilds if they were Jews?

The guild of the *fripiers* of Paris was a very old one. It is listed in the *Livre des Métiers* by Étienne Boileau, and consequently dates back to the fourteenth century. Under Louis XI, the *fripiers* had the fourteenth banner.

to the enigma lies in this definition of the word "Jew," given some fifty years later in Savary's *Dictionnaire du Commerce:*

"*Jew.* 1) This term has various meanings in commerce, but almost invariably is pejorative. . . . In Paris, the term 'Jew' is given to the *fripiers,* either because people believe them to be as deceptive as the Jews were formerly, when they were involved in the second-hand clothing business in France; or because several families among these merchants are suspected of descent from former Jews; yet these suspicions are equally without foundation, there being in their community as many honest men and good Catholics as in any other section of Paris" (277).

Thus we see the issue clearly. The *fripiers* of Paris were "Jews" in the sense that they practiced a traditionally "Jewish" trade; they were called "Jews," and their guild was nicknamed the "Synagogue." Professionally and semantically, they were looked upon as Jews. But they were not Jews, and rejected the imputation with horror.[8] For countless generations they had been Catholics by religion, and nothing in their customs and mode of life distinguished them from other Christians. Yet they continued to be the target of obstinate social suspicion.

Thus they were Jews objectively without being so subjectively. In other words, they were miscast; and though sensitive popular reactions could sometimes provoke short-lived explosions such as that of 1652, the holy rage, meeting with inadequate support, subsided of its own accord. In the absence of fuel, the fire died down.

It was rekindled, however, from time to time. Thus, eighteen years later, in 1670, when a great trial for ritual murder in Metz (where, at the time, there were some Jews) coin-

---

[8] In this connection, the jocular author of the *Criminal verdict* . . . concludes sensibly: "If they have rejected this outrage / With such an extreme rage / It is a sure sign / That the name of whoreson / Would have offended them less / Than this title of Jewry / From which I rightly infer / That they have nothing of the Jew but this false name."

cided with mysterious disappearances of young men in Paris (where there were none), rumors circulated in the capital: they had been kidnaped by the Jews! What Jews? From where? The rumor did not supply details. Then, in the absense of Jews (this time the *fripiers* were not molested), it died out once again.[9]

Horror and contempt. Were the anti-Jewish reactions in this period unanimous? In truth, almost. We can quickly review the rare dissenting voices.

The most famous of the few humanists of independent and critical spirit in France was Jean Bodin. In his dialogue *Heptaplomeres,* seven interlocutors discuss the comparative virtues of the various religions. The conclusion is reached that all are equally good. It is to Solomon the Jew, rather than to Coroni the Catholic or Octave the Mohammedan, that the author's sympathies are given. But Bodin was a cautious man. His *Heptaplomeres* was published only long after his death. We must add that though Bodin was an enlightened spirit, he was a true product of his time and apparently believed in witchcraft.[10] He composed a treatise, *La Démonomanie des sorciers,* which was still regarded as authoritative in the eighteenth century. Unlike most of his colleagues in the field of black arts, he does not mention the Jews in his "demonomania"; his "philo-Semitism" was evident here, too.

[9] *Mémoires tirées des archives de la police de Paris,* by J. Peuchet, police archivist (Paris, 1838): ". . . a terror, motivated by extraordinary disappearances, suddenly spread [in 1670] throughout the chief districts of Paris. . . . Certain gossips claimed that a princess whose life was endangered by a disease sought a cure by bathing every day in human blood. Others attested that the Jews sometimes crucified Christians, in their hatred of the crucified God. This mad notion happily did not prevail" (Vol. 1, pp. 144-45).

[10] In point of fact, this is arguable. Guy Patin, in the next century, was skeptical about the matter: "Bodin's *Démonomanie des sorciers* is worthless. He did not believe in witchcraft himself. He wrote this book only so that it would be thought he did [believe in witchcraft], especially, because, for several rather liberal opinions, and because he favored the Huguenots, he was suspected of atheism." (*Lettres,* Reveillé and Parisse eds., Vol. 1, p. 303.)

(It has been claimed, to explain his views, that Bodin was half Jewish, his mother having been a marrano. Apparently this is pure speculation, without the slightest basis in fact.)

But the chief movement leading to a change of feeling was the Reformation, with all its interest in the Old Testament, Hebrew, and Biblical studies. As a result of being steeped in their subject, many theologians and scholars developed sympathies for the people of the Law, but this interest was directed to them as the people of the patriarchs, rather than as the deicidal race. Active contact with Jewish professors, to whom many Hebrew scholars appealed in order to perfect their knowledge of the sacred language, facilitated this change in attitude. In Germany, during a famous trial, Johann Reuchlin argued as a champion of the Talmud, as we shall see later. We shall consider in some detail the contradictory and characteristic case of Martin Luther. In France, whereas Calvin seemed to remain silent on the question, Théodore de Bèze spoke in a spirit that was already very complex[11] (especially if we consider the actual abasement of the Jews, a situation that could not influence theological judgment).

[11] Especially in his commentaries on the New Testament: ". . . those who today call themselves Christians . . . are very certainly punished and will be in the future, because, solely under the guidance of wickedness and perversity, they have mistreated in every way these people, so holy in their forefathers, actually hardening them further [against Christianity] by setting before their eyes the example of an odious idolatry. As for myself, I gladly pray every day for the Jews in this fashion:

" 'Lord Jesus, it is true that Thou justly punish the scorn that is directed against Thee, and this ungrateful people has deserved Thy severe punishment. But, Lord, remember Thy covenant, and look upon these unhappy creatures favorably, because of Thy Name. As for us, who are the most wretched of men, yet whom Thou nonetheless judge worthy of Thy pity, grant that we may advance in Thy grace, so that we may not be for them instruments of Thy wrath, but that we may rather become capable, through the knowledge of Thy words and the example of a holy life, of bringing them back into the true way by virtue of Thy Holy Spirit, so that all nations and all peoples together may glorify Thee for Eternity. Amen.' "

Nouveau Testament Grec, with Latin translation and commentaries by Théodore de Bèze, 4th ed., 1589 (in the margin of the text of Romans 11:18). Cf. *Foi et Vie*, May-June 1951, No. 3, p. 229.

But in France the Reformation was later overthrown. And apart from several picturesque figures such as the Hebraist Gilbert Gaulmin or the "pre-Adamite" Isaac de La Peyrère, who belong to "subhistory," it was not until a century later that a new voice was heard. This was not yet that of the Encyclopedists; it was the voice of an astonishing forerunner who, because he was too free a spirit for the Catholics and too Catholic for the free spirits, has never been appreciated at his true worth. This was the voice of the Oratorian Richard Simon, the true creator of modern Biblical criticism.

Enormously erudite and a remarkable Hebraist, Richard Simon was intensely interested in the Jews. He even managed to strike up personal acquaintance with two or three: Jonas Salvador, an adventurous Piedmontese tobacco merchant; and a cabalist whose name he conceals but whom he mocked with a *brio* that yields nothing to the best Voltairian sallies.[12] In 1670 he published anonymously a pamphlet in

[12] ". . . I have had in the past several discussions with a Jew who claimed to know the last details of the cabalistic art, having been instructed therein by a rabbi of Damascus. I did all within my power to disabuse him of this vain and superstitious art. But imagining that he might alarm me, he told me that if I would not be afraid, he would summon up his Genie. I replied that I believed nothing of all the astounding things that the cabalists boasted of doing, by means of the secrets of their cabala.

"When he thereupon began to invoke his so-called Genie, I told him that under the pretext of invoking an angel in the service of God, he was going to call to his aid a demon. 'You are still very naïve,' he told me; 'an enlightened cabalist does not believe in that fall of the angels that you assume in your Church, although some of our Directors seem to have acknowledged it.' He claimed that the angels were not called wicked save in relation to those functions in which God employed them. When I asked him what opinions these enlightened cabalists had of the Devil, 'Satan,' he told me, 'is himself neither white nor black: he is somewhat like the first captain of the guards of your king, if this captain were destined by his Prince only to perform bloody executions. Consider,' he added, 'especially what is reported of Satan at the beginning of the Book of Job, and then you will perhaps not be far from my own belief. Satan is in the presence of God with the other angels, and is wicked only in relation to his employment.'

"I confess that this theology seemed quite new to me. But my desire to see how this Jew would manage to call up his Genie caused me to allow him to say whatever he pleased. I urged him then to come to the point in

defense of the Jews, on the occasion of the case of ritual murder in Metz (278). Later, under the name of the "Sieur de Simonville," he published in French the *Cérémonies et coutumes* of the Jews, by the Venetian rabbi Leon of Modena, to which he added a long and erudite preface (279). Here he recalled first of all that "those who composed the New Testament being Jews, it is possible to interpret it only with a knowledge of Judaism": hence the usefulness of studying Jewish traditions and customs. Subsequently he praises the piety of the Jews—"One cannot admire sufficiently the modesty and the inner meditation of the Jews when they go to morning prayers"—and above all, their charity.

"The Jews excel not only in prayers but even more in charity. In their compassion for the poor, we find the image of the charity of the first Christians for their brothers. [Christians then] followed what was practiced in the synagogues. The Jews have retained these practices and customs; whereas at present we [Christians] have scarcely kept the memory of such things. . . ."

This author also reviews the history of the Jews of France. "I may say here a word concerning our French Jews, who once surpassed in wealth all the other Jews, before they were driven from France. . . . Those of France excelled in the knowledge of the Talmud. In those days, Paris was the Athens of the Jews, and they came here from all parts in order to receive instruction. . . ."

But such were the prejudices of the time, or such were the

---

question. He turned to the East; he made several invocations in the Hebrew tongue. But seeing that I laughed and made mockery of his superstitions, he used artifice. 'This land,' he told me, 'is a profane and accursed land. My angel, who is pure and holy, cannot approach it. Let us go to the land which God has given to our fathers, and there you will see the angels descend, summoned by the power of my prayers.' That, Monsieur, is how far the madness of the cabalist Jews may go. I shall send you several observations on these illusions. . . . It is good to disabuse an infinity of men who seriously apply themselves to the study of this cabala. . . . I remain, etc." ("Letter to a Swiss Gentleman"; R. Simon, *Lettres choisies,* Amsterdam, 1720, Vol. 1, pp. 96-98.)

Jews he happened to meet, that Richard Simon subsequently sang a different tune. "I confess to you that I did not know [the Jews] well enough," he wrote in 1684 to a friend, "when I gave to the public in our language the little book by Leon of Modena touching on their ceremonies. I have spoken too much good of that miserable nation in my Preface, as I realized subsequently from the dealings I have had with several of them. They hate us mortally . . ." (280).

Richard Simon also suffered many other disappointments. His concepts of Biblical criticism, too bold for the times, drew down upon him the awful thunders of Bossuet. He was obliged to leave the Oratory and was violently attacked to the end of his days.

Apart from Simon, there was only one other writer in the *Grand Siècle* to offer a somewhat original opinion of the Jews. No less a figure than Blaise Pascal was tormented by the *mystère juif*, as he was tormented by the unfathomable mystery of God. "Men must be sincere in all religions; true heathens, true Jews, true Christians . . ." we read in the *Pensées* (281). And later, apropos of the falseness of other religions: "They have no witnesses. These [the Jews] have. . . . I believe only the stories of those who were slaughtered," he continues (for this celebrated remark occurs in this context). Later, he admires "the sincerity of the Jews . . . , sincere about their honor, dying for it; this has no example in the world, and no root in nature." He marvels: "It is a wonderful thing, and worthy of particular attention, to see this Jewish people existing so many years, always in misery, for it is necessary as a proof of Jesus Christ, both that they should continue to exist, and that they should be miserable because they crucified him; and though to be miserable and to exist are contradictory, they nevertheless still exist in spite of their misery. . . ."

We see how the great thinker was troubled by the extraordinary and decisive role assigned to the Jews by Christian theology, and how from their strange "contradictory" situation, he attempted to draw one more proof.

Then came the century of Enlightenment and the "let us crush out the infamous one."* Nothing is more revealing for our subject than the confusion that then appeared in the minds of the philosophers, some (with Montesquieu at their head) pleading on behalf of the traditional victims of superstition, in the name of justice and reason; others (and Voltaire is the prime example) turning against the mystifying Canaanite race, in the name of that same reason. The debate, a salon diversion in the eighteenth century, was to come into the public domain in the following century; and the argument is far from being decided in our own day. But this will be taken up in our next volume.

* Voltaire in a letter to d'Alembert, dated Nov. 20, 1762. He said: "Whatever you do, crush out the infamous one and only love those who love you." [Ed.]

nine

Anti-Semitism in
the Pure State: England

The Jews were expelled from England in 1290. However, the memory of them remained vivid, and it would be easy to undertake an investigation similar to the one made of France and to show how their ghosts continued to trouble men's imaginations long after their departure. In fact, this has been partially done (282). Had flesh-and-blood Jews managed to penetrate into England before the modern period? There was a royal foundation for converts, the *domus conversorum*, created in 1234, which continued to attract members from Germany, Spain, and even Morocco (283). Also, isolated instances have been found of nonbaptized Jews who entered London fraudulently in the fourteenth and fifteenth centuries (284). This last matter became urgent after the Spanish expulsion (1492), when galleys of exiled Jews filled the seaways. Six years later, on the occasion of his elder son's marriage to Catherine of Aragon, Henry VII took a solemn oath to admit no Jews into his domains (285). This oath was loosely observed by his successors, and there was a marrano colony of thirty-seven homes in London about 1540. It was denounced and dispersed in 1542 (286). It is noteworthy that on the occasion of his historic divorce, which led to his break with Rome, Henry VIII, unable to obtain the pope's approval, tried to gain the support of the Italian rabbis. It was a question of "levirate," and the Old Testament seemed to open the way to a compromise,[1] but the majority of rabbis

---

[1] Henry VIII wanted to divorce Catherine of Aragon, who had previously married the Prince of Wales, his elder brother. On the basis of

Henry consulted were intractable (287). At least the episode contributed to the establishment of Hebrew studies in England, where, as elsewhere, the humanists at this period were infatuated with the holy tongue. A few Jewish converts from the Continent served them as teachers.

Such are the rare contacts that the British had with real Jews in the sixteenth century: contacts unlikely to modify a deep-rooted prejudice. At the same period, English words acquired their definitive meanings and spelling. Murray's Oxford Dictionary defines the word "Jew" as follows: "*Jew* . . . (1) the commonest name for contemporary or modern representatives of the race; almost always connoting their religion and other characteristics which distinguish them from the people among which they live, and thus often opposed to the Christian, and (esp. in early use) expressing a more or less opprobrious sense. . . . (2) As a name of opprobrium or reprobation; spec. applied to a grasping or extortionate money-lender or usurer, or a trader who drives hard bargains or deals craftily . . ." (288).

Let us skip a century. England, which had been to Europe what Ireland was to her—a disinherited island—had transformed herself into the queen of the seas. The reasons for her sudden predominance may continue to tax the wisdom of historians for a long time, but certainly one factor rests in the particular aspect that the Reformation assumed there. Directly or indirectly, Calvinism prevailed in England, leaving its stamp upon the countless sects that proliferated there. It is certain, too, that contrary to the teachings of Martin Luther—who attacked the Jews with unparalleled violence, as we shall see—Calvinistic doctrine was characterized by a marked benevolence toward them. Was this because Calvinism, breaking completely with Roman tradition, embraced a more energetic morality of action than

---

Leviticus 18: 16, which prohibits coveting one's brother's wife, Henry VIII tried to have his marriage declared null and void. But it happens to be Deuteronomy 25: 5 (which prescribes, on the contrary, marrying one's brother's widow) that is recognized as the authority.

Lutheranism, and took the heroes of the Old Testament for its masters in thought and deed? Or because it gave free rein to sects which, faithful to the letter of Biblical teaching, constituted themselves into communities of equal men and eliminated the interceding clergy? However many and subtle reasons there may be (and we might add this one, too: that there were no indigenous Jews in the countries where Calvinism flourished), we are dealing with an almost general situation that prevails even to the present day.

At the beginning of the seventeenth century, certain Puritans, carrying matters to extremes, were converted to Judaism and even had themselves circumcised. Others, by word and pen, demanded the recall of the Jews (289). The numerous active millenarian sects, especially, contributed great interest to the movement, since the conversion of the Jews was requisite for the return of Christ, and to convert them it was necessary to recall them (290). When to the cry of "To your tents, Israel!" the Puritan bourgeoisie overthrew the monarchy and brought Cromwell to power in 1649, the question of an official recall was brought up in a more concrete manner, especially since a small marrano colony had again been established in London, performing many financial and even political services for the government (291). It is characteristic that at the same period alarming rumors circulated in the royalist camp and spread among the population. Was not Cromwell preparing to sell Saint Paul's Cathedral to the Jews for eight hundred thousand pounds? [2] Indeed, was not this Messiah of the Jews of Jewish origin himself? [3]

[2] "They are about demolishing and selling Cathedral Churches. I hear Norwich is designed already: and that the Jews proffer 600,000 pounds for Paul's and Oxford library, and may have them for 200,000 pounds more . . ." Sir Edward Nicholas wrote in April, 1649, to the Marquis of Ormonde, one of the leaders of the royalist camp. (Cf. *A Collection of Original Letters* . . . by Th. Carte, London, 1733, p. 276.)

[3] This rumor is reported in the *Histoire d'Oliver Cromwell* by Abbé Raguenet (Paris, 1691, p. 322), who, moreover, partially accepts it, asserting that a "deputation of Asian synagogues" had come to England "to inquire if Cromwell was not the Liberator they were waiting for. . . . They

Against this background of intertwining Christian and Jewish messianic hopes, of new concepts of religious tolerance heralding the modern age, and of political and economic maneuvers, Manasseh ben Israel, an Amsterdam rabbi with a European education, undertook a mission to Cromwell. Eager to find a haven of refuge for his people, this scholar introduced an eschatological argument. He had identified in the American Indians the ten lost tribes, and thus it only remained, to assure the end of time, to make the Dispersion of the Jews complete "from one end of the earth even unto the other" (Deuteronomy 28:64).[4] He came to London with this plan in September, 1655. Cromwell received him most politely and deliberated with his Council of State. A special commission, consisting of ecclesiastics and representatives of the City of London, was appointed to study the proposition. For his own part, the Protector was quite well disposed, counting on the marranos to help defeat Spain and take her colonies from her. He was at the zenith of his dictatorial power, and a favorable outcome seemed assured.

But Cromwell had not reckoned with the power of the traditional superstitions, which, combined with the opposition of several important London merchants, thwarted his plans. Sinister rumors were circulated with redoubled force. A powerful lord, the Earl of Monmouth, hastened to send the following to one of his mistresses: ". . . The Jews' mouths, though not their eyes, are to be opened; who I do heare are to have two sinagogs allowed them in London, whereof St. Paul's to be one. Well, my heart, God's will must bee done and we must submit to it" (292). As for the good people of London, the following lines give some no-

---

chose for this commission the celebrated Jacob ben Azahel who was ordered to take with him, through Bohemia, David ben Eliezar, rabbi of their synagogue in Prague, who knew all the languages of Europe to perfection . . ." etc.; many other fantastic details follow.

[4] Manasseh ben Israel set forth his argument in his work *Spes Israelis* (*The Hope of Israel*), published in Latin in Amsterdam in 1650. It quickly reached some twenty editions in six different languages. (Cf. *A Life of Manasseh ben Israel* by Cecil Roth, Philadelphia, 1945.)

tion of their alarm: "As I kept on my way . . . in Lincolns-Inne Fields, passing by seven or eight maimed Soldiers on Stilts, who begged me; I heard them say aloud one to another, *We must now all turn Jews, and there will be nothing left for the poor.* And not far from them another company of poor people, just at Lincolns Inne back gate, cried aloud to each other: *They are all turned Devils already, and now we must all turn Jews.* Which unexpected concurrent providences and Speeches, made such an impression on my Spirit, that before I could take my rest that night, I perused most of the passages in our English *Histories* concerning the Jews' *carriage* in England, with some of their misdemeanors in other parts, to refresh my *memory*" (293).

The author of these words, William Prynne, was the man who roused public opinion against the projected recall. This remarkable character, a Puritan Savonarola, used his fertile and erudite pen to bequeath us more than two hundred books and pamphlets. Leading a life of monklike austerity, he hunted down evil in all its forms with indomitable tenacity. He thundered against women who wore their hair too short, against men who wore theirs too long, and against the custom of drinking toasts at table. In 1634 he attacked dancing and the theater, those inventions of the Devil, in terms so violent[5] that he was sued for defamation and *lèse-majesté* and was condemned to have both ears cut off and the letters "SL" (seditious libeler) branded with a red-hot iron on his cheeks. (It appears that on the scaffold itself he composed a caustic epigram against his enemies.) In this way, fitted with the halo of a martyr, this formidable propagandist became enormously popular. When he learned of the new and diabolical threat that, in 1655, hung over his country and

[5] "Dancing is idolatrous, heathenishe, carnal, wordly, sensuall, and misbeseeminge Christians, and the devill himself, who danced in Herodias' daughter, was the first author of the dancing. . . ." As for the theater, the audience (including the royal family) were "incarnate devills, monsters of ympiety, atheisticall Judasses, perjured cutt-throates to their Religion, willful bloody murderers to their own soules. . . ." (*Histrio-Matix, the Player's Scourge or Actor's tragedye.* . . . London, 1634.)

which concerned him vitally "both as a Christian and English Freeman," he did not rest until he had written a vitriolic pamphlet entitled *A short Demurrer to the Jewes long discontinued Remitter into England,* which was prepared, printed and distributed within eight days and enjoyed an enormous success.

Meanwhile, the deliberations of the special commission, which had begun on December 4, 1655, dragged on. From the start, Cromwell had met with unexpected resistance. The representatives of the clergy feared subversion by Jewish ideas; the London merchants were suspicious of competition and hinted that the admission of the Jews would deliver a fatal blow to British commerce. "The most did fear that if they should come, many would be seduced and cheated by them, and little good would be unto them . . ." one impartial witness relates (294). It was in vain that a well-meaning power invoked the beautiful prayer of Théodore de Bèze on behalf of the Jews.[6] Public opinion, roused by Prynne, became increasingly ill-disposed. At the public hearing of December 18, which was to be the last, an openly hostile crowd pressed into the stands. Seeing that tempers were becoming ugly, and moreover not attributing any extraordinary importance to the question, Cromwell closed the debate abruptly, after mocking the adversaries of the project in a brilliant and ironic speech.[7] No new session was scheduled, and matters

6 Cf. p. 198, note 11.

7 "I never heard a man speak so well in his life as Cromwell did on that occasion," reported Sir Paul Rycaut. Cromwell first reminded the ministers that the Scriptures announced the conversion of the Jews, that there was only one means to this end—that is, preaching—and that the Jews must therefore be permitted to reside where the true Gospel was preached. Then, turning toward the merchants, he conceded that the Jews were "the meanest and most despised of all peoples."

"So be it. But in that case, what becomes of your fears? Can you really be afraid that this contemptible and despised people should be able to prevail in trade and credit over the merchants of England, the noblest and most esteemed merchants of the whole world?" (Cf. *Anecdotes*, by the Rev. J. Spence, London, 1858, p. 59; and *A Life of Manasseh ben Israel*, by C. Roth, *op. cit.*, p. 246.)

remained as they were. The Jews were not officially read-mitted.

The war of the pamphlets, however, continued long after-ward. Prynne reprinted his *Demurrer,* adding to it new leg-ends gleaned from the chronicles of past centuries. His friend Clement Walker published *Anarchia Anglicana.* The prolific Alexander Ross published his *View on Jewish Religion,* which was merely a transposition of Prynne's arguments. Meanwhile, in the other camp, Manasseh wrote the cele-brated *Vindiciae Judaeorum,* and his Christian friends ap-pealed to a number of the arguments that from generation to generation are advanced as new concepts. (Thus a certain Thomas Collier argued that by crucifying Jesus, the Jews had merely carried out the divine will and thus had been able to give birth to Christianity.[8]

All this was merely a flash in the pan. The significant fact is that already English political wisdom was finding expres-sion in a suitable style. The Jews, without being officially admitted, were henceforth tolerated semiofficially, and the marrano colony of London was permitted to build a syna-gogue and to increase in numbers, thus creating a situation that contained in embryo the future flowering of Anglo-Saxon Judaism.

[8] ". . . in Crucifying our Lord, the *Jews* did no more than was the Counsel and Determination of God (Acts 4: 27, 28). Tho 'it was *their* Sin, yet it was God's Counsel. Yea it is by Christ Crucify'd that we have life." (Cf. *Anglia Judaïca,* by D'Blossiers Tovey, Oxford, 1738, pp. 278-79, where Collier's arguments are discussed at length.)

ten

Activated Anti-Semitism: Germany

At the end of the fifteenth century, Germany was prosperous and active. Her iron mines and mines of precious metals were the richest in Europe. Her merchants and bankers, solidly established in Antwerp, in England, and on the Baltic, controlled the trade of northern Europe and, after the discovery of America, dominated the spice market in Lisbon and were to equip the Indies fleets. The discovery of printing also contributed to the prestige of Germany: German printers spread the new art to Spain and Scandinavia, to Turkey and Scotland. Gutenberg's contemporaries were keenly aware of the significance of his invention. "There is no invention or creation of which we Germans can be more proud than of the invention of printing, which has made us the propagators of Christian doctrine and of all human and divine knowledge, and thus the benefactors of humanity," wrote the humanist Jacob Wimpheling (295). But in other areas, too, at the crucial period when nationalities were being determined, the Germans were already loudly proclaiming their sense of their own supremacy. Thus Felix Fabri, burgher of the city of Ulm: "If one wishes to have a masterwork made in bronze, stone, or wood, he entrusts it to a German. Among the Saracens, I have seen wondrous work done by German jewelers, goldsmiths, stonemasons, and coachbuilders. . . . They surpass the Greeks and the Italians. . . ." (The author also cites other examples: the Sultan of Egypt employed a German engineer; the Venetians bought their pastry from German bakers, etc.) (296).

The skill of German artisans and the activity of German

merchants, increasing the wealth and spreading the love of luxury among all strata of society, in turn created a demand for money. The discovery of America and of the trade route to the Indies opened further possibilities for trade and speculation. This was the period when the great corporations, the Fuggers, Welsers, Imhofs, and Hochstätters, monopolized raw materials and risked bold coups, sometimes making millions overnight, sometimes going bankrupt just as quickly. These fluctuations caused rises in the prices of goods and artificial shortages; hence the people cordially detested these magnates, often calling them by the unflattering term "Christen-Juden." In Germany the word *Jude* had come to signify both "Jew" and "usurer," the word *Judenpiess* being used as a synonym for *Wucher* (usury). Thus the resentment of the little people against the great, henceforth turned against the possessors of money, encompassed in the same hatred "Christen-Juden" and "Juden," a vast indefinite group, whose irreducible core was represented for Christians, emotionally, by Jews themselves, even though the Jews played only a minor role in the economic life of the period. As soon as Jews were present, the traditional hatred erupted; moreover, this was given a new impetus as the Germans discovered that the deicidal (i.e., homicidal) and usurious race was at the same time a foreign people. Many texts by clerical and lay authors, theologians and humanists, show how during this period the three motifs—religious, economic, and national—had become amalgamated.

Thus in 1477, Peter Schwartz, a burgher, explains the persecutions of the Jews: "The Jews have been punished severely from time to time. But they do not suffer innocently; they suffer because of their wickedness, because they cheat people and ruin whole countries by their usury and secret murders, as everyone knows. That is why they are so persecuted, and not innocently. There is no people more wicked, more cunning, more avaricious, more impudent, more troublesome, more venomous, more wrathful, more deceptive, and more ignominious" (297).

Johann Reuchlin, a scholar to whom we shall return, sees things in a more traditional light. He ascribes the punishment of the Jews to their hard-heartedness rather than to their crimes. "Every day, they outrage, blaspheme, and sully God, in the person of His Son, the true Messiah Jesus Christ. They call Him a sinner, a sorcerer, a criminal. They treat the sainted Virgin Mary as a witch and a fury. They call the apostles and disciples heretics. They regard us Christians as stupid pagans" (298).

Less prolix, other humanists disinterred from Tacitus the "enemies of the human race" argument:

"No people have so hated others as the Jewish people have; in turn, no people have been so loathed or have so justly provoked implacable hatred . . ." (Beatus Rhenanus) (299).

"Relegated to perpetual exile, and scattered throughout the entire universe, the Jews outrage and disturb the society of the human race" (Conradus Celtes) (300).

Theologians, who argued against Jewish usury, sought to put the Jews to work, using social and patriotic arguments:

"We understand that the small and the great, the learned and the naïve, the princes and the peasants, are all filled with animosity against the usurious Jews, and I approve all legal measures taken to protect the people against such exploitation. Should foreign people who have settled among us dominate us; dominating not as a result of a greater courage and virtue, but solely by means of crass wealth amassed from all parts and by all means, and whose possession seems to them the supreme blessing? Are these people to grow fat with impunity, on the labor of the peasant and the artisan?" (Johannes Tritheim) (301).

"Are the Jews then better than the Christians, that they should be unwilling to work with their hands? Are they not under the word of God: 'In the sweat of thy face shalt thou eat bread'? To practice usury is not to work, but to flay others, while wallowing in idleness . . ." (Geiler von Kaiserberg) (302).

A few rare authors observed that the "Christian-Jews" were much more deleterious to the social body than the Jews proper—for instance, Jacob Wimpheling, who exclaimed: "Dreadful is usury, as it is practiced by the Jews and by many Christians even worse than the Jews!"—or the mocking Sebastian Brant, in his famous *Narrenschiff*:

Gar lidlich war der Juden Gsuch	Forsooth the wound of the Jews was great
aber sie mögen mit nie bleiben	but they can no longer remain among us
die Kristen-Juden sie vertreiben	for the Christian-Jews have driven them out
mit Judenpiess dieselben rennen	and they abandon themselves to Jewry.
ich kenn vil die ich nit wil nennen	I know many such I shall not name;
die triben doch wild Kaufmanschatz	they practice unfair and barbarous trades
und schwig dazu all recht und gsetz.	and both law and right are silent.

A foreign observer, the Frenchman Pierre de Froissart, best summarized the general opinion, noting: "Hatred of the Jews is so common in Germany that the most peaceful men become agitated when it is a question of the Jews and their usury. I should not be surprised to see a sudden outbreak of bloody persecutions against them and in all countries at the same time. They have already been expelled forcibly from many cities . . ." (303). If Froissart was a bad prophet, since the simultaneous persecutions he expected did not break out, the "Jewish question" appeared in the foreground of German and even European current events during the famous dispute over Jewish books. This incident, at the beginning of the sixteenth century, contains in embryo the entire Reformation. It contrasted the innovators, the humanists, with the pious monks, guardians of the traditional faith. Although both camps made it a point of honor to declare their anti-Jewish sentiments, it was, contrary to common belief, the innovators who were more venomous.

The altercation broke out when, in 1516, a converted Jew, Johannes Pfefferkorn, who seems to have been a moderate and sincere man, in a pamphlet called *Der Judenspiegel* (The Mirror of the Jews) demanded the suppression of the Talmud, it being the chief advocate of Jewish resistance to Christianity. Pfefferkorn had the support of the Cologne Dominicans, whose important role in witch-hunting and demonomania has been discussed. As to the sacred people, the Jews, the program of this missionary and his protectors was limited to three points: prohibition of usury, obligation to attend Christian sermons, and suppression of Jewish books. The *Judenspiegel* denied the accusation of ritual murder in categorical terms and protested against the bloody persecutions of which the Jews had been victims. Pfefferkorn was received by the Emperor Maximilian and obtained from him a commission to seize and destroy the Talmud wherever found. He began immediately in the city of Frankfurt, whose Jews appealed to their direct suzerain, the archbishop of Mainz, winning from him the authorization to have the allegedly blasphemous character of the Talmud re-examined by a commission of scholars. One of them, the famous Johann Reuchlin, the first and for some time the only German Hebraist, vigorously defended the venerable and mysterious writings. He even asserted that in a close examination of the Talmud and of the cabala one could find a striking confirmation of Christianity. An exchange of violent polemics between the two camps ensued (Pfefferkorn's *Hand Mirror, Mirror of Fire,* and *Tocsin;* Reuchlin's *Mirror of the Eyes* and *Letters of Obscure Men*). The matter was finally taken to the pope, who hesitated a long time before rendering his verdict, which was an equivocal one. Meanwhile, all European men of letters had sided with or against Reuchlin. He was approved by Erasmus and all the humanists, but condemned by many universities, above all by the University of Paris.

Thus began a great general debate on the right of free discussion and free research that continued for ten years, heralding, in its religious aspect, the various reform movements; and in its secular aspect, the modern scientific spirit. In fact, this debate may be said to have established the principle of free inquiry, especially since Reuchlin won his case, practically speaking. But there was at least one question on which the two opposing camps were in agreement. Both were openly hostile to the Jews, though with this nuance: the humanists, though they had become champions of the Jewish books, attacked the Jew Pfefferkorn and all his coreligionists, baptized or not, even more violently; whereas the Dominican inquisitors and their allies, though consigning the books to the flames, showed greater Christian charity toward their zealots. Reuchlin himself attacked the "baptized Jew Pfefferkorn, who gaily abandoned himself to a perfidious revenge, according to the traditional manner of his ancestors the Jews" (304). One of his greatest partisans, Ulrich von Hutten, the principal author of *Letters of Obscure Men*, took a still more violent stand, and in particular rejoiced that Pfefferkorn was not a German. "Germany could not have produced such a monster. His parents are Jews, and he remains such, even if he has plunged his unworthy body into the baptism of Christ" (305). As for the venerable Erasmus, he was scarcely less "racist" (to use our current terminology): "Pfefferkorn is revealed to be a true Jew," he wrote to his friends. "He appears quite typical of his race. His ancestors attacked Christ only, whereas he has attacked many worthy and eminent men. He could render no better service to his coreligionists than by betraying Christendom, hypocritically claiming to have become a Christian. . . . This half-Jew has done more harm to Christendom than all the Jews together" (306).

The Dominicans and their partisans, included under the heading "obscurantists," seem in comparison more clement, with their faith in total redemption by baptism.

At this period there were few authors who openly championed the Jews. Luther, in his youth, was one of these, but in his later years he felt a correspondingly greater hatred for them. It is important to consider the figure of the great reformer in some detail in order to gain a clearer picture of the first and most important panel of the infernal triptych: religion, money, and race.

Luther

In 1542 Martin Luther published his celebrated pamphlet: *Against the Jews and Their Lies* (307). In it he advised never entering into an argument with a Jew. If it was impossible to avoid, one was to say: "Listen, Jew, don't you know that Jerusalem and your kingdom, the Temple and your ministry, were destroyed over 1460 years ago? . . . Give this nut to the Jews and let them break their teeth on it and dispute as much as they like. For the cruelty of divine wrath shows all too clearly that they are surely in error and are on the wrong path: a child would understand this. . . ."

Then for nearly two hundred pages[1] the reformer rails against the Jews in his powerful, lusty style, with a torrential outpouring of passion that makes the diatribes of his predecessors seem languid, and that no one else, perhaps, has matched to this day. Reproach and sarcasm addressed to the Jews alternate with transports of love and of faith in Christ; and between the lines we may glimpse a kind of anguished admiration. Sometimes Luther attacks the usurers and the parasites from foreign countries, and we see how, in forging the German language, he implanted at the same time a certain style of argument and thought. "In truth, the Jews, being foreigners, should possess nothing, and what they do

---

[1] Pages 100 to 274 in the complete Erlangen edition (Vol. 32), from which these quotations are taken. Luther's relations with the Jews have been studied in detail by Reinhold Lewin in his monograph *Luthers Stellung zu den Juden*, Berlin, 1911.

possess should be ours. For they do not work, and we do not give them presents. Nonetheless, they keep our money and our goods and have become our masters in our own country and in their Dispersion. When a thief steals ten guldens, he is hanged; but when a Jew steals ten barrels of gold through his usury, he is prouder than the Lord himself! He boasts of it and strengthens his faith and his hatred of us, and thinks: 'See how the Lord does not abandon His people in the Dispersion. We do not work, we are idle, and we pass the time pleasantly; the cursed *goyim* must work for us, and we have their money: thus we are their lords and they our servants!'

"To this day we still do not know what devil brought them into our country; surely we did not go to seek them out in Jerusalem!

"No one wants them. The countryside and the roads are open to them; they may return to their country when they wish; we shall gladly give them presents to get rid of them, for they are a heavy burden on us, a scourge, a pestilence and misfortune for our country. This is proved by the fact that they have often been expelled by force: from France (which they call Tsarpath), where they had a downy nest; recently from Spain (which they call Sepharad), their chosen roost; and even this year from Bohemia, where, in Prague, they had another cherished nest; finally, in my own lifetime, from Ratisbon [Regensburg], Magdeburg, and from many other places. . . ."

Sometimes Luther makes use of one of his unique and imaginative comparisons: "They did not live so well in their countries under David and Solomon as they live in our countries, where they steal and pillage every day. Yes, we hold them captive, just as I hold captive my stone [calculus], my ulcers, or any other disease I have caught and must endure: I would rather see [these miseries] in Jerusalem, with the Jews and their following!

"Since assuredly we do not hold them captive, how have we provoked such enmity by such noble and saintly characters? We do not call their wives whores, as they do Mary, the mother of Jesus; we do not call their children sons of whores, as they do our Lord Jesus Christ.

"We do not curse them; we wish them all the good in the world, in flesh and in spirit. We give them shelter, let them eat and drink with us, we do not carry off and kill their children, nor poison their wells, we do not slake our thirst on their blood. Have we then deserved the fierce anger, the envy and hatred of these great and holy children of God?"

He then shifts to the religious level: to the defense and glorification of Christ, the only matter that really counts for Luther:

"Know, O adored Christ, and make no mistake, that aside from the Devil, you have no enemy more venomous, more desperate, more bitter, than a true Jew who truly seeks to be a Jew [*als einen rechten Juden, der mit Ernst ein Jude sein will*].

"Now, whoever wishes to accept venomous serpents, desperate enemies of the Lord, and to honor them, to let himself be robbed, pillaged, corrupted, and cursed by them, need only turn to the Jews. If this is not enough for him, he can do more: crawl up into their —— and worship the sanctuary, so as to glorify himself afterward for having been merciful, for having fortified the Devil and his children, in order to blaspheme our beloved Lord and the precious blood that has redeemed us. He will then be a perfect Christian, filled with works of mercy, for which Christ will reward him on the Day of Judgment with the eternal fire of hell [where he will roast together] with the Jews. . . ."

On a practical level, Luther proposes a series of measures against the Jews: that their synagogues be burned, their books confiscated, that they be forbidden to pray to God in their own way, and that they be made to work with their hands; or, better still, that the princes expel them from their lands and that the authorities—magistrates as well as clergy —unite toward these ends. As for himself, having thus done his duty, Luther is "excused." (*Ich habe das meine gethan: ich bin entschuldigt!*)

A few months later another pamphlet appeared: *Schem Hamephoras,* in which Luther's curses became even more frenzied. Here he is not concerned with the Jews' usury and graft, but only with their captious reasoning and their witchcraft. This is, then, a theological polemic, but in what a tone! In the preface, Luther specifies that he is not writing to convert the Jews but merely to edify the Germans: ". . . so that we Germans may know what a Jew is. . . . For it is as easy to convert a Jew as to convert the Devil. A Jew, a Jewish heart, are hard as wood, as stone, as iron, as the Devil himself. In short, they are children of the Devil, condemned to the flames of hell. . . ." Later he contrasts the apocryphal gospels of the Jews, which are specious and false, with the four canonical Gospels whose truth is evident. His exegesis is interspersed with remarks of this kind:

"Perhaps some merciful and holy soul among us Christians will be of the opinion that I am too rough with these poor and pitiable Jews, mocking and deriding them. O Lord, I am much too feeble to mock such devils. I would do so, but they are much stronger than I in raillery, and they have a God who is a past master in this art; he is called the Devil and the wicked spirit. . . ."

In other passages Luther indulges in obscene buffoonery: ". . . Cursed *goy* that I am, I cannot understand how they manage to be so skillful, unless I think that when Judas Iscariot hanged himself, his guts burst and emptied. Perhaps the Jews sent their servants with plates of silver and pots of gold to gather up Judas' piss with the other treasures, and then they ate and drank his offal, and thereby acquired eyes so piercing that they discover in the Scriptures commentaries that neither Matthew nor Isaiah himself found there, not to mention the rest of us cursed *goyim.* . . ."

Elsewhere we seem to hear a cry from some deeper level of his tormented soul:

"I cannot understand it except by admitting that they have transformed God into the Devil, or rather into a servant of the Devil, accomplishing all the evil the Devil desires, corrupting unhappy souls, and raging against himself! In short, the Jews are worse than the devils. O God, my beloved father and creator, have pity on me who, in self-defense, must speak so scandalously of Thy divine and eternal Majesty, against Thy wicked enemies, the devils and the Jews. You know that I do so in the ardor of my faith, and in Thy Majesty's honor; for in my case, the question is one that involves all my heart and all my life. . . ."

Such are the depths into which Luther allowed himself to fall, wherein scatology that outraged his most faithful colleagues[2] followed closely upon authentic religious anguish. He concluded this work by proclaiming:

"Here I break off, and I would have nothing further to do with the Jews, neither write upon them, nor against them. They have had enough of me. If there are some among them who would repent, may God take them into His mercy. . . ." A drunkard's promise: many letters attest to Luther's efforts to have the Jews expelled or their privileges withdrawn. (He was successful in this respect in Saxony, Brandenburg, and Silesia. "Truly, he has made our position very perilous!" noted Yosel [Joseph] of Rosheim at this time in his *Memoirs*) (308). Luther's last sermon at Eisleben, the city of his birth, four days before his death (February 18, 1546), was entirely devoted to the obdurate Jews, whom it was a matter of great urgency to expel from all German territory.

It would be easy to explain these excesses in the light of

---

[2] This stands out especially in a correspondence between Bullinger and Martin Butzer: "If the famous hero Capnio [Reuchlin] came back to life, he would say that the spirit of [the inquisitors] Tungern, Hochstraten, and Pfefferkorn was incarnated in Luther," wrote the first-named. Even the loyal Melanchthon, in a letter to the preacher Osiander, showed his disapproval. As for the Swiss congregations, they openly declared that ". . . even written by a shepherd of pigs and not by a celebrated shepherd of souls, the *Schem Hamephoras* would be difficult to excuse." (*True Confession of the Servants of the Churches in Zurich.*) Cf. R. Lewin, *op. cit.*

what is known of the aging Luther, of his bitterness and inner conflicts, his hallucinations that made him see the Devil everywhere, and his incessant obsession with the end of the world. Such comparisons, which we have already made several times with respect to other prophets, would nowhere be better justified than in Luther's case. We might also, apropos of his verbal lack of restraint, cite some relevant psychopathological considerations. For instance, the reformer was a man who slipped into blasphemy, as in his stating that at certain moments and during certain temptations, he no longer knew who was God and who was the Devil, and he actually wondered if the Devil was not God! At times he called God infinitely foolish (*stultissimus*) and described the Christian religion as the most absurd of any. On one occasion he proved that Christ must necessarily have been an adulterer, and on still another proclaimed the suppression of the Ten Commandments. One might describe him as an unbalanced genius and find in him astonishing anticipations of Freudian theory. We know, too, that he expressed himself about the pope, his archenemy, even more vehemently and obscenely than about the Jews. Such invectives, temptations, and outbursts of aggression certainly seem to combine quite naturally with the hatred of the chosen people. But Luther's character is too rich and complex, and the imprint he left on the history of his country and of our whole civilization is too profound, for us to be content with an over-simplified, unidimensional interpretation, limited to the level of individual psychology.

As we have said, Luther was not always the enemy of the Jews. At the zenith of his activity, during the heroic period when this rebellious monk, sustained and justified by his faith, defied pope and emperor and for some time attained the dizzy peaks of total freedom, he had a very different attitude toward the Jews. Apparently he hoped for some time to convert and rally to his cause the people of the Bible. This hope moved him to publish in 1523 a pamphlet with a significant title: *Jesus Christ Was Born a Jew* (*Das Jesus Christus ein geborener Jude sei*). This was a missionary text intended to show the Jews, with the help of the exegesis of various verses from Genesis and Daniel, that Christ was indeed the true Messiah. Commentaries on the meaning of the Dispersion and the servitude of the Jews were cited in support of this view. The author sympathizes with the Jews and mocks their enemies: "Our imbeciles, the papists and the bishops, the sophists and the monks, have treated the Jews in such a way that a good Christian would seek to become a Jew. If I had been a Jew, I should have preferred to turn pig before I became a Christian, seeing how these imbeciles and ignorant louts govern and teach the Christian faith. They have treated the Jews as if they were dogs and not men. They have done nothing but persecute them. The Jews are the blood relatives, the cousins and brothers of Our Lord; if His blood and flesh could be boasted of, the Jews belong to Jesus Christ much more than we do. Hence I beg my dear papists to call me a Jew, when they are tired of calling me a heretic. . . .

"That is why I advise being considerate of them. So long as we use violence and lies and accuse them of using Christian blood to eradicate their own stink, and I do not know what other absurdities; so long as we keep them from living and working among us, in our communities, and force them to practice usury—how can they come to us? If we seek to aid them, it is the law of Christian love that we must apply to them, and not the papist law. We must welcome them in friendship, let them live and work with us, and they will be of one heart with us. . . ."

To understand Luther's complete reversal between 1523 and 1543, we may note primarily that his propaganda met with no success among the Jews. Although he had some discussions with them,[3] there were very few who "came to him"

---

[3] Especially during the crucial days of the Diet of Worms, when two Jews had come to visit him in his lodgings. It would seem that the hopes inspired by this visit caused Luther to write the pamphlet *Jesus Christ Was Born a Jew* (cf. R. Lewin, *op. cit.*).

and accepted conversion, and most of these seem to have re-canted subsequently. "If I find a Jew to baptize, I shall lead him to the Elbe bridge, hang a stone around his neck, and push him into the water, baptizing him with the name of Abraham!" he sneered one day in 1532. "These dogs mock us and our religion!" And when, five years later, the indefatigable Yosel of Rosheim tried to intercede with him apropos of the expulsion of the Jews from Saxony, Luther refused to receive him and informed him in writing of his disappointment. His heart, he told the Jew in substance, remained kindly disposed toward the Jews, but such kindness must serve to convert them, not to confirm them in their errors. Shortly thereafter, troubling news reached him from Bohemia. On the instigation of the Jews, some reformed Christians were Judaizing, celebrating the Sabbath, and even having themselves circumcised. This news seemed to upset Luther greatly; thereafter, in conversation, he referred more often to the Jews: "I hope I shall never be so stupid as to be circumcised!" he exclaimed one day. "I would rather cut off the left breast of my Catherine and of all women!" And he wrote a missive, "The Letter of Dr. Martin Luther against the Sabbatarians," in which he polemicized against the Jewish law. On December 31, 1539, he announced to his friends: "I cannot convert the Jews. Our Lord Christ did not succeed in doing so; but I can close their mouths so that there will be nothing for them to do but lie upon the ground." Three years later he put his plans into operation.

Such were the successive stages of Luther's reversal. To be sure, the Jews had profoundly disappointed him. But there was something else: during these years he himself had changed a great deal.

Between 1521 and 1543 lay the gap that separates dream from reality. There had been the war of the knights, the bloody peasant revolts, the countless sects and heresies, put down by fire and sword, with Luther's express approval. His very success had made him aware of the measure of human imperfection and of his own political responsibilities.

Forced to choose, he had sided with the mighty of this world, the princes, since it was upon them that the future of the Reformation depended. Thus the splendid purity of his doctrine was tarnished. Blood was shed in his name, crimes were perpetrated to which he must accommodate himself, for better or worse. ("You do not acknowledge the peasants, but they acknowledge you!" Erasmus wrote him.) Certain aspects of his thought developed as a consequence: to inner freedom he opposed the immutable order of things established in the world by God. The necessity of obedience was emphasized: the Christian must remain loyal and submissive. Hence, by an inescapable dialectical reversal, the doctrine of total freedom becomes one of total servitude. The archangel of rebellion is transformed into an embittered and despotic bourgeois, excommunicated and banished from the empire, confined in the small territory where his prince protects him.

We can readily see that his failure among the Jews tormented Luther all the more since his rejection by the people of God was symbolic of the countless failures and disappointments that darkened his last years and which he attributed to the intervention of the Devil—and of the Jews. Did he not make them responsible (even if it was said jokingly) for the chill that, in 1546, was to carry him off in three weeks? The Devil tormented him only in dreams; the Jews were living scapegoats, within easy reach.[4]

The consequences of Luther's position with regard to the "Jewish question" were incalculable, less from the direct ef-

---

[4] This symbolic role of the Jews, the exceptional importance accorded to their testimony, is also found in other religious leaders: Paul of Tarsus and Mohammed speak this same language and go through the same reversal, rancor succeeding the urgent—but fruitless—entreaties of the early period. A curious parallel! And one that we might extend to the collective reactions of nations, which received the Jews favorably at the beginning of their colonization, a favor inevitably followed by the fatal rise of anti-Semitism. Both mirror and catalyst, the souls of the great leaders recapitulate the evolution of the social body, just as ontogeny recapitulates phylogeny. What fascinating speculations for those bold enough to trace these problems further!

fect of his savage texts—which during his lifetime enjoyed only a limited circulation and which subsequently, until Hitler's advent, were practically hidden under the bushel [5]— than as a result of a certain internal logic of German Lutheranism. In that species of polyphonic passion which is anti-Semitism, the religious motif of justification by faith implies the rejection of justification by works, an essentially Jewish doctrine (*jüdischer Glauben*, wrote Luther; and we have seen that for him the "Jew who truly seeks to be a Jew" is the "enemy of Christ"). The social motif of unconditional obedience to the authorities, combined with identification with a national prophet—the reformer had specified many times that he was addressing himself to the Germans alone —paved the way for the Hitlerian heresy four centuries later. In all this, Luther's ardent spirit had roused some secret yearning of his people, provoking a gradual crystallization of national awareness. In essence, "the Jewish problem was for Luther the reverse of the problem of Christ," as one of his German commentators has recently pointed out (309). This is an appalling contrast; for minds not trained to the subtleties of dialectics, but that look upon moral questions as black or white, it inevitably comes down to contrasting "good" and "evil," "God" and "Devil," with consequences we have discussed at length.[6] "If to be a good Christian is

---

[5] *Against the Jews and Their Lies*, in Luther's lifetime, went through two editions; the *Schem Hamephoras* (part of which was later destroyed), three. On the other hand, *Jesus Christ Was Born a Jew* was reprinted nine times during the first year after its appearance (cf. R. Lewin, *op. cit.*). During the following centuries there were few reprintings of these pamphlets (cf. *Bibliotheca Hebraica* of J. C. Wolf). In the nineteeth and twentieth centuries they were to be found only in editions of Luther's complete works, until the appearance, under Hitler, of many popular editions, widely circulated among the people.

[6] This contrast is obviously not limited to Lutheran theologians; even to the Catholic theologians of our generation, it seems essential to the understanding of what they regard as the "mystery of Israel." Thus the brilliant dialectician Father G. Fessard refers to the "negative mission" or the "negative power" or the "negative unity" of Israel. He even writes: "Judaism, to the very extent that it rejects Christ, cannot help but be the enemy of all that is specifically Christian, of all that is human." (*Pax Nostra*, Paris,

to detest the Jews, then we are all good Christians," Erasmus had said. Perhaps a true Christian who worshiped his God in the manner of a Martin Luther inevitably ended by detesting the Jews with all his soul and opposing them with all his strength.

Moreover, we must take the customs and usages of the period into consideration. We must consider the actual role of the Jews and the stereotyped notions about them. We have seen what these were before Luther; now we shall see how the question was to develop after him.

Germany after Luther

There is not much to say about the German Jews of the sixteenth century. Hunted and impoverished, they led an obscure life at the very period when their Spanish and Portuguese coreligionists, temporarily safe behind a Christian mask, were entrenching themselves in the financial markets of the Low Countries and Italy and becoming the pioneers of Levantine and transatlantic trade. (The breaking-up of a ghetto always seems to coincide with a vigorous phase of Jewish finance.) Thus, an insurmountable barrier separated the German Jews from these glamorous marranos, whom they refused to regard as Jews at all. "It is a country where there are no Jews," the celebrated Yosel of Rosheim laconically notes at the time of his visit to Antwerp in 1531 (310), though a

---

1936, p. 219.) This comes very close to the Lutheran dialectic. M. Jacques Maritain sees in "Israel's suprahuman relation to the world . . . a kind of reversed analogy to the Church," but from it derives quite different conclusions: "Israel, we believe, is assigned, in the order of temporal history and its own finalities, a work of *terrestrial activation* of the world's body . . . it does not leave the world in repose; it keeps it from sleeping; it teaches the world to be discontent and uneasy so long as it does not have God; it stimulates the movement of history." (*Les Juifs parmi les nations,* Paris, 1938, p. 21.) Obviously, the implicit moral judgment here is of a very different order.

From Dostoevski to Berdyaev, including Soloviev and Rozanov, we shall find the same differences among scholars of orthodox Christianity.

flourishing marrano colony had been established there since the beginning of the century.

It is noteworthy that Yosel of Rosheim is the only sixteenth-century German Jew whose name has come down to us. Yet he was neither a learned rabbi nor a cunning financier, but a tireless agent, a *shtadlan* (in Hebrew: intercessor, mediator) struggling to safeguard the meager rights of his coreligionists and initiating new tactics of relationships with the government. He began his career early; at scarcely twenty-five he was the spokesman for the Jewish communities of Alsace. After 1520 we see him intervening with the authorities on behalf of all the German communities. Soon afterward, Charles V authorized him to assume the title of "commander and regent of all the Jewries of the Reich." [7] He was remarkably skillful in manipulating the two chief arguments that men of his kind have invariably resorted to: the plea of the moral and theological order, and the knowingly apportioned jug of wine. This latter method permitted Yosel to avoid the worst during the peasant revolts, when there were many occasions when rebels or regular troops were about to massacre the Jews. Throughout the Diet of Augsburg he polemicized against Pfefferkorn's competitor, the renegade Anton Margaritha. He blocked the expulsion of the Jews from Hungary and Bohemia and convened an assembly of rabbis who adopted a ten-point program of commercial ethics for the Jews. [8] His reasoning showed both

[7] "Befehlshaber and Regierer der gemeinen Jüdischkeit im Reich." Following a curious trial that took place in 1535, Charles V forbade Yosel of Rosheim to call himself "Regierer" since this title was reserved to himself as emperor; thus Yosel was merely "Befehlshaber," or "commander." (Cf. Dubnow, *History of the Jews in Europe* [in Russian], Vol. 3, p. 32.)

[8] The Jews were to be obliged: not to demand too high an interest; not to camouflage interest by artifically increasing the price of merchandise; not to collect compound interest; not to accept stolen objects as pledges; not to buy household articles from children or servants without the parents' or masters' knowledge; not to take action against the heirs of a deceased Christian debtor except after verification of the debt by representatives of the Jewish community; to excommunicate Jews who owed money to Christians and who tried to avoid payment by changing residence; to

common sense and forcefulness. "I shall cause this program to be observed," he said in substance, "if the authorities do what is necessary to let us live in peace, to put an end to the expulsions, to permit us to move about, and to curtail their bloody accusations. For we, too, are human beings, created by almighty God to live beside you on the earth." Yosel of Rosheim pursued his activities for almost half a century, intervening with Protestants and Catholics alike. Charles V showed him great favor, but he suffered a complete defeat against Luther. This remarkable man was a precursor, and his technique of intervening with the authorities was to be adopted in the centuries to come—nor is it likely to be relinquished in our own time.

But otherwise, until the end of the eighteenth century, the Jewish communities remained virtually frozen in their traditional way of life, while the surrounding world was experiencing increasingly rapid changes. This way of life and the Jews' strange customs have been described in an earlier chapter. Yet we must emphasize the curiously anachronistic aspect of these communities, these conventicles that, more successfully than the ecclesiastical establishments, than the guilds striving to save their superannuated privileges, kept intact amid the general molting that was taking place in the manners and customs of medieval civilization.[9] The old ways were maintained all the more easily because the new order of things introduced a modicum of stability. Expulsions and sudden changes became rarer, although they persisted just enough to remind the Jews from time to time of their very special status as hostages of Christendom.

Nonetheless, time slowly did its work. Gradually, the

---

examine with scrupulous honesty the suits brought against Jews by Christians; not to attempt to conceal the dishonest actions of Jews against their debtors. (Cf. Dubnow, *op. cit.*)

[9] This has led certain historians, for example Arnold Toynbee, to speak of Jewish civilization as a "fossilized Oriental civilization." As a matter of fact, it was a civilization in which the Oriental elements were mingled with medieval ones, with the latter predominating.

enormous capital of skill and tenacity amassed by the Jews down through the centuries began to bear fruit for some. The new opportunities can be explained by many factors: among them, the disappearance of the patrician trade dynasties, especially after the devastations that followed the Thirty Years' War; a new social differentiation, carrying in its wake a social differentiation within the Jewish communities; and above all a new mentality, that of the age of political absolutism, in which the prince, the chief of state, released from traditional structures and contexts, entered into open conflict with those structures. Greedy for power and money, the countless German potentates rapidly discovered that the Jews were ideal auxiliaries: they were willing and humble, they had vast international connections, they were free of all connection with Christian society, and they shared none of its prejudices. Thereupon, a new character appeared on the scene, leaving a strong imprint on all German history of this period: the court Jew (*Hofjude*).

Each royal or princely court had its own Jew: the new Midas with the reputation of turning everything he touched to gold, at a period when gold was sovereign, since it procured free and uninhibited power. Certain contrasts are extremely suggestive. In 1670, Emperor Leopold had pitilessly expelled the Jews from Vienna. The guilds had long since demanded this expulsion, and the empress' miscarriage, for which the Jews were blamed, supplied the pretext. This decree, symbolic of the old days, was countered three years later by a sign of the new. In 1673 the same emperor summoned a Heidelberg Jew, Samuel Oppenheimer, to the court and assigned him the responsibility of provisioning his armies. For thirty years Oppenheimer acquitted himself of this task with singular felicity, especially during the Turks' siege of Vienna in 1683 and in the endless wars against France. Max von Baden wrote that without him, the Austrian army would have been annihilated. Prince Eugene refused to do without his services. To estimate the extent of his activity, it suffices to quote this passage of a letter that Oppenheimer wrote in his old age to a dignitary of the court:

"As long as I lived in Vienna, I provisioned, almost every year, the two armies engaged against the French and the Turks, supplying flour, oats, horses, and money for recruits, as well as munitions, powder, lead, cannon, artillery, wagons, horses, and oxen, and there were never any losses . . ." (311).

Behind the clatter of arms and the subtle interplay of diplomatic intrigues, we find the court Jew everywhere at this period. It was the court Jew Leffmann Behrens who transported in hogsheads the subsidies that Louis XIV paid to the Duke of Hanover. It was the court Jew Bernd Lehmann who brought about the election of his prince, August, as king of Poland, thanks to judicious distributions of wine. The court Jew Süss Oppenheimer, called "Jud Süss," the most famous of all, the favorite of Duke Karl Alexander, reorganized the administration and finances of the duchy of Würtemberg and became the most powerful man in the country, before ending on the gallows. It mattered little whether the court was Protestant or Catholic, whether the prince was a bigot or a libertine. We find Jewish "agents" or "commissioners" or "factors" at courts controlled by the Jesuits and at the side of bishops and cardinals. Their functions were enormous and enormously diversified. They administered finances, provisioned armies, raised money, furnished textiles and precious stones to the court, introduced new industries, manufactured textile or leather articles, leased out tobacco or salt taxes, and so on. Sometimes they entered into genuinely friendly relationships with their employers and masters, especially since the Jew lived on the fringes of society and the prince, inaccessibly high above it, was alien to it, too. They understood each other all the more readily since they both led a marginal existence. Great lords, famous captains, and even royalty ate at the Jews' table, slept at their homes while traveling, received them in their palaces, attended their marriages. Here is the vivid description of a marriage of court Jews, quoted from the memoirs of Glückel von Hameln, that priceless document about the lives of German Jews at the end of the seventeenth century.

"We were more than twenty who went to Cleves, and we were received there with honor. We arrived in a house that in truth resembled a royal palace, and that was admirably furnished. Great preparations had been made for this marriage. At this time the prince [the future King Frederick I of Prussia] happened to be in Cleves. . . . Prince Maurice [of Nassau] and other lords and important personages were also there. They all let it be known that they wished to be present at the wedding. . . . Thus Elias Cleve, the father of the groom, did all that was needful for such noble visitors. The wedding day, immediately after the nuptial blessing, an excellent collation of delicacies and choice foreign wines was served. One can imagine the difficulties involved, and how Elias Cleve and his people did their best to lodge and care for these noble guests. This is why they had not even time to put aside and count the dowry, as is customary.

"When the couple was standing under the canopy, it appeared that in the confusion, someone had forgotten to write down the *ketubah* [marriage contract]. What was to be done? All the nobles and the young prince were already there and ready to watch the ceremony. The rabbi then said that the groom must furnish a surety and promise to write the *ketubah* immediately after the marriage. And he read aloud the *ketubah* from a book. After the nuptial blessing, the nobles were led into the festive hall of Elias Cleve, hung with gilded leather. There was a great table in the center, covered with the choicest delicacies. Thus the nobles were treated according to their rank. My son Mordecai was five years old at the time; there was no lovelier child in the world, and we had dressed him with care and skill. The nobles nearly devoured him with their eyes, and the prince especially held him by the hand the whole time. After the nobles had eaten the sweetmeats and fruits and had drunk the wines, the table was taken away. Masked actors then appeared, were gracefully presented, and provided every kind of amusement, in order to divert the guests. Then the actors executed a *danse macabre*, which was a very rare thing. . . ."

Of course, such friendships lasted only so long as the Jew remained useful and rich. He was continually at the mercy of a coup or a caprice of fate, and his good fortune was always precarious. No court Jew founded a dynasty; many, on the other hand, ended their days in poverty. The sons of Bernd Lehmann were expelled from Saxony; the grandsons of Leffmann Behrens spent many years in debtors' prison; and the trial of Jud Süss, the joy his fall provoked throughout all Germany, his last-minute return to Judaism and his tragic end, are virtually the symbol of the fate of a court Jew. Perhaps the following sally, attributed to Friedrich Wilhelm, the soldier-king, appropriately depicts their situation and the interest shown them. Passing through a Prussian town, he was requested to grant an audience to a delegation of Jews. "I shall never receive those dogs who crucified our Lord!" he exclaimed. A chamberlain then whispered to him that the Jews had brought him a valuable present. "In that case, let them come in," he added. "After all, they weren't there when he was crucified. . . ." True or false, the little story reflects quite accurately the mixed feelings the Jews provoked in the baroque age.

Court Jews dressed in the fashion of the time, wearing short tunics of bright colors and powdered wigs. They built magnificent homes, sometimes even small chateaux. Wolf Wertheimer, court banker of Munich, gave hunting parties on his estate, which great lords, the British ambassador, and Prince Eugene himself did not disdain to attend. Süss Oppenheimer even had a titled mistress. Despite this, these Jews were not "emancipated," and they usually remained closely attached to their Jewish orthodoxy. Champions of their less fortunate coreligionists, they did everything possible to have residence prohibitions repealed and expulsion orders revoked. Like Yosel of Rosheim, they were all *shtadlanim*. As such, they played leading roles within the

J. Community no longer democratic

Jewish communities, ruled them tyrannically, and even sent their overbold adversaries to prison.

Thus the Jewish communities lost their egalitarian and democratic character. A marked social differentiation was established at their core.

At the top of the scale, the court Jews formed a caste apart; at the very bottom, the Jewish rabble was organized in its own way and left its stamp on the entire German lower social strata.

The appearance of many Jewish bandits at this period should also be noted. Court Jew and Jewish bandit had, in fact, this in common: that each in his own way sought to overcome his pariah condition and braved the society that oppressed him. The former by exercise of cunning, the latter by cruder and more direct means. This Jewish banditry, whose first 'traces appear at the beginning of the sixteenth century, was an odd and very characteristic phenomenon, unduplicated elsewhere in the age-old history of the Dispersion. Its beginnings are obscure: we only know that in Luther's time the German criminal-class argot was already larded with Hebraisms.[10] In the following centuries we find records of organized gangs, some exclusively Jewish, others mixed Judeo-Christian, about which the police officers made some remarkable statements. Jewish bandits, we learn from these, were good fathers and husbands, often led a settled family life, showed exemplary piety, and never robbed on Saturdays and holidays.[11] Though they constituted only

[10] The oldest known German work that deals with banditry and thieving, the *Liber vagatorum* . . . , published in 1499, already contains a little lexicon of *Rothwelsch*. Many words are of Hebrew origin. In a preface to a new edition of the book published in Frankfurt in 1520, Martin Luther wrote: "I consider it useful that this little book be widely read, so that it may be seen and understood how the Devil rules in this world, so that men may become wise and guard against him. It is true that this *Rothwelsche Sprache* comes from the Jews, for it contains many Hebrew words, as those who know Hebrew will observe."

[11] The terms in which a German police commissioner expressed his virtuous indignation have an undeniable flavor.

a tiny minority within the German criminal classes, they set the tone. They implanted their special language, the *Gaunersprache*, or *Rothwelsch*, a strange adaptation of Hebrew. (Furthermore, as is often the case with slang, many words made their way into common speech and at present form part of the German linguistic heritage.) The customs and religion of the Jews seem to have exerted a lively attraction on many German delinquents. The Christian prisoners in a Berlin jail demanded the right to attend Jewish ceremonies. On the scaffold, Domian Hessel, the most famous highwayman of the eighteenth century and a former seminarist, requested the attendance of a rabbi. Upon reflection, this is scarcely surprising. In taking a position outside the law, the Christian bandit flouted society, its moral values, and its religion. Judaism flouted that society by the mere fact of its existence.

Like the court Jews, Jewish bandits were an exceptional phenomenon. Until the era of emancipation, the great majority of German Jews continued to live according to the old order, perpetuating, in the eighteenth century, customs established in the Middle Ages. From generation to generation,

---

"If it is somewhat comforting and beneficial to find in the most perverse characters the slightest trace, even the smallest spark, of what we might call virtue, that is, in the case of the Jewish bandit, the affection he bears his wife and his children, the respect he shows his parents. . . . Skillful investigators, moreover, will be able to use this character trait to advantage in interrogations. . . .

"For six days [the Jewish bandits] do not fear to sin against the laws, both human and divine, laying hands on the property of others, and they would know no scruples on the seventh day if their rabbinical dogmas did not forbid them all dealings on the Sabbath. Yet their dealings are theft, on which they live, and it is only because theft is a form of commerce, not because it is a crime, that they abstain from stealing on Saturday. . . . Even before the stars appear on the horizon, the Jewish thief interrupts his journey and eagerly makes his way to an inn where he may celebrate the Sabbath, since he is forbidden to travel on that day. . . ."

These lines are taken from *Die jüdischen Gauner in Deutschland*, by A. F. Thiele (Berlin, 1842), the last of a long series of studies about Jewish bandits in the eighteenth and early nineteenth centuries by German police officials of various ranks.

age-old hopes enabled them to endure every abasement, every catastrophe. From year to year they awaited the coming of the Messiah. Thus when, in the second half of the seventeenth century, a false Messiah, Sabbatai Zevi, appeared in Turkey, he was acclaimed not only by the rabbis but by a goodly number of the faithful—artisans, laborers, or usurers—who ceased to attend to their business and hurriedly sold their property in order to embark for Constantinople. The memoirs of Glückel von Hameln, mentioned above, have left us a vivid picture of this episode. This naïve and colorful narrative, written by a warmhearted woman, carries us intimately into the Jewish home and enables us to understand (better than any concept of "sublimation" or other abstraction could do) how the Jews, throughout their tribulations, could preserve an extraordinarily strong faith and ethics, endure the blows of fate and endless humiliations, without ever losing confidence in the Lord—or in men, even Christian men.[12]

[12] Glückel von Hameln's memoirs, discovered in the family archives at the end of the nineteenth century, have subsequently appeared in several German and English editions. Here is the beginning of the work:

"In the year 5451 of the Creation [1690-1691 of the Christian era] I began to write this book in my great distress and grief. May God give us joy and send us our liberator! . . . My dear children, I have begun writing this after the death of your pious father, in order to soothe my soul somewhat when dark thoughts came to me, when grave anxieties oppressed me, because we had lost our faithful shepherd. I then spent many wakeful nights, and often got up from my bed in order to shorten my hours of sleeplessness. My dear children, I am not attempting to write an instructive book for you, for I am not capable of such a thing; our wise men have written many works for instruction, and we have our holy Torah in which we may see and understand all that is useful for us, and all that leads us from this world to the one to come.

"It is my intention to leave you the story of my life in seven little books, if God permits me to live. Certainly it is best to begin with my birth. It was, I believe, in the year 5407 [1646-1647] that my pious mother gave birth to me in the community of Hamburg.

"I was not yet three years of age when the Jews were driven from Hamburg and obliged to leave for Altona, which belongs to the king of Denmark, from whom the Jews possessed safe-conducts. This Altona is merely a quarter of an hour from Hamburg. Twenty-five Jewish families were already living there; we had our synagogue there and our cemetery.

This fascinating book fails to mention the series of new vexations and cunning abasements devised for the Jews in her day, perhaps because the author found such things entirely natural. Though massacres and pogroms became rarer

---

We lived thus for a certain time in Altona, then with difficulty succeeded in obtaining from Hamburg passports for the Jews of Altona, so that they might go to the city to tend to their affairs. Each passport was valid for four weeks, it was received from the burgomaster, it cost one ducat, and when it had expired it was necessary to purchase a new one. But the four weeks often became eight when one knew the burgomaster or other officials. Oh, the people often had a hard life! For they had to seek in the city all that pertained to their trade, yet frequently many poor and miserable men tried to enter the city surreptitiously and without passport. But when they were caught by the officials, they were cast into prison. All this cost a great deal of money, and it was difficult to obtain their release. At dawn, as soon as they left the temple, the men set off for the city, and at evening, when the gates were about to be closed, they returned to Altona. Often, when they set off on the road, the poor wretches feared for their lives on account of the hatred of the Jews among the soldiers, boatmen, and other common people, so that each wife thanked God when her husband had happily returned to her side. In those times, forty households at the most had come from Hamburg to Altona. There were no particularly rich people among them, each earned his bread in all honesty. The richest of the time were: Haim Fürst, with 10,000 thalers as his fortune; my late father with 8,000 thalers; others with 6,000 thalers; and some with 2,000 thalers as well. But they lived together in friendship and great attachment, and all in all led a life better than the richest of our time. Even he who had only 500 thalers could enjoy himself, and each had more joy with his lot than the wealthy of today, when there is no means of satisfying oneself, and when it is said: 'No one dies who has fulfilled even the half of his desires.' Of my father, I remember that he was a man full of trust in God, a man without equal, and if the gout had not troubled him, he would have made his way still better. Still, even thus, he provided well for his children in all honor.

"I was about ten when the Swede waged war against the king of Denmark. May God grant him great renown! I cannot say much that is new of this, because it happened in my childhood, when I was still going to the *heder*. In those days we suffered great hardships in Altona, for the winter was very cold, such as had not been known for some fifty years. It was called the Swedish winter. It froze so hard that the enemy could move about everywhere. Suddenly, on the Sabbath, cries of grief and pain rang out: 'The Swede is upon us!' This happened at dawn, we leaped from our beds and, all undressed, ran to the city [Hamburg], and were obliged to find succor with either the Portuguese or the Hamburgers. We thus made a brief sojourn [without authorization] until the moment when at last my

at this period, when administrative and police institutions
had evolved, these new institutions showed great ingenuity
in harassing the Jews without bloodshed. The municipality
of Frankfurt, renewing the old ordinances—such as requir-

[handwritten marginalia: end of 17th C]

---

father managed [that is, obtained the right of domicile] to settle once again
in Hamburg. Afterwards, an increasing number of Jews gradually managed to come to the city. And almost all the fathers of Jewish families were
established in Hamburg, except for those who had lived in Altona before
the expulsion.

"At this time, few taxes were paid to the government, each man reach-
ing an agreement for his own account with the officials. But we had no
synagogue in Hamburg, nor the right of sojourn, and remained there only
by the grace of the council. Still, the Jews assembled and held their prayer
meetings in their rooms, as best they could. If the council had some wind
of this, they were willing to close an eye. But when the priests discovered
the matter, they did not tolerate it, and drove us from those lodgings.
Then, like timid lambs, we were obliged to go to the temple in Altona.
This lasted some time, after which we returned to our 'Schülchen.' Thus,
sometimes we were left in peace, sometimes we were pursued, and the
same was true until this very day, and I fear that this will last always, so
long as Hamburg is governed by its burghers. May the merciful God take
pity on us soon and send us His Messiah so that we may serve Him with
a pious heart and so that we may once again make our prayers in our
sanctuary in Jerusalem, amen!

"They remained, then, in Hamburg, and my father trafficked in precious stones and in other things—a Jew who deals in almost everything.
The war between Sweden and Denmark grew ever more savage, and the
king of Sweden had great fortune, so that he took all from the king of
Denmark, marched upon the capital, and laid siege to it. A little more,
and he would have taken it, if the king of Denmark had not had such
good advisers and subjects who aided him with their goods and their
blood, so that he managed to save everything. In truth, this happened only
by the special aid of God, for he was a just and pious king, in whose land
we had been happy, we Jews. Although remaining in Hamburg, each of us
had only six thalers of taxes to pay to Denmark, no more. Thereafter the
king was aided by the Dutch; they crossed the Sund in their ships and
put a stop to the war. Yet never since have Sweden and Denmark been at
ease together; even as friends or relatives by marriage, they never stop
pecking the one at the other.

"My father was not so rich, as I have said, he had great trust in
God, never owed anything to anyone, and led a hard life in order to feed
himself and his family honestly. Having already endured many ordeals, he
was in haste to marry off his children. When he took my mother, he was
a widower, having spent sixteen years of conjugal life with a woman of
the name of Reitze, of great spirit and distinction, and who ran, it was

ing distinctive insignia and forbidding Jews to employ Christian servants—added new ones that were astonishingly petty. Jews were forbidden to linger in the streets without a specific purpose, to walk in pairs, to use certain streets, to appear during Christian festivals or when a prince visited the city. They were allowed to market only after the Christians. Detailed orders, the *Kleiderordnung*, prescribed the demeanor of the Jews and their manner of dress. It was expressly stated that Jews were not "burghers" but merely "protégés" or "subjects" of the city of Frankfurt—a distinction that the Nazis were subsequently to adopt upon Hitler's accession to power (312). The city of Hamburg, in consultation with the leaders of the Jewish community, passed a still more exacting *Kleiderordnung*. This even limited the number of guests at a wedding banquet, as well as the kind of presents that could be given, and prohibited certain dishes such as capons and preserved or jellied foods, ritually irreproachable but regarded as too extravagant (313). Of

said, a great and good household. My father had no children by her. But from her first marriage she had a single daughter of matchless beauty and virtue. This girl knew French fluently, from which my father one day gained great advantage. He had received, in fact, against a loan of fifty thalers, a pledge from a man of quality. Some time after, this gentleman came to my father with two associates and sought to release his pledge. My late father, without suspecting anything, went in to find the object. His stepdaughter was standing by the clavichord and began to play so that the fine gentlemen would not find the time too long. They, standing beside her, whispered together: 'When the Jew returns with the pledge, we shall take it back without money [without paying] and be off.' They spoke French, not suspecting that the young girl understood them. When my late father returned with the pledge, she began to sing at the top of her lungs, in Hebrew: 'For the love of Heaven, no pledge. Here today, gone tomorrow!' In her haste, the poor creature could think of nothing else. Then my late father said to his distinguished visitor: 'Sir, where is the money?' Thereupon the other replied: 'Give me back my pledge!' To which my late father replied: 'No money, no pledge!' Then one of the fine gentlemen said to the others: 'Brothers, we are betrayed! The girl must know French.' The next day the borrower returned alone, paid my father in exchange for his pledge, the capital and the interest upon it, and declared: 'It was a great advantage and a wise measure to have your daughter taught French.' So saying, he went on his way."

course, the Jews did not have many occasions for diversion, and those they did have were severely restricted. At the
beginning of the eighteenth century the Austrian government invented a brand-new regulation: one on marriages in
general. In order to prevent too rapid a growth of the Jewish
population, the court of Vienna decreed in 1726 that only
the eldest son of a Jewish family had the right to marry
within the law; the other sons were obliged to remain bachelors. As a method of birth control, this tribute to the fecun-
dity and morality of the Jews was both simple and radical.
Called "reduction," it was applied first in Bohemia and Mo-
ravia and later adopted in Prussia, the Palatinate, and Alsace, and resulted in the emigration of many young Jews to
Poland or Hungary.

Of course, the majority of German Jews led a humble and
laborious life. But the exceptional careers we have mentioned, fermenting in the social body and accelerating the
economic changes already under way, inevitably produced
a profound impression upon contemporaries. In this sense,
the "Jewish problem" appeared in Germany as a real problem—in contrast to the abstract anti-Semitism of the other
Western nations—one nourishing and multiplying anti-Jewish hatreds.

We have quoted earlier the French and English definitions
of the term "Jew." Here, a faithful and impartial mirror, is
the German etymological definition, with an even stronger
emotional charge, one more concrete and more suggestive.
We take it from the famous *Deutsches Wörterbuch* of the
Brothers Grimm (whose tales have enchanted so many
generations of children):

"*Jude* . . . 3) Among their offensive characteristics, emphasis has been primarily on their slovenliness as well as
their greed for money and their usury. *Dirty as an old Jew;
he stinks like a Jew;* whence: *to taste like a Jew* and, *a for-
tiori, to taste like a dead Jew: one must first grease one's
throat, otherwise this food tastes like a dead Jew,* Lehmann, 149; to lend money, cheat, borrow like a Jew: *that is*

worthless, neither a Jew nor a priest would lend anything on it, Fischart, 92b; . . . Jew, a prickly beard; thus, in Thuringia: *I have a real Jew in my face, I must get shaved;* in eastern Frisia, Jew is the name given to a meal without a meat course, Fromm., 4, 132, 82. In the Rhineland, Jew is the name of a part of a pig's spinal column; in the Tyrol, to the spinal column in general, Kehr, 212 . . ." (314).

The Brothers Grimm also tell us that a verb was derived from the root *Jude: jüdeln,* whose various meanings were: to talk like a Jew; to bargain like a Jew; finally, to smell like a Jew, to have the odor of a Jew. . . .

The invention of printing made it possible to popularize countless variations and commentaries on this main theme. Every year many pamphlets and weighty treatises appeared. J. C. Wolf, a diligent German bibilographer of the early eighteenth century, lists in his *Bibliothecae Hebraeae* over a thousand works of *Scriptores Anti-Judaici,* and this enumeration is far from complete. We can thus appreciate the vigor with which the "Jewish question" preoccupied men's minds. This was no longer abstract rhetoric, as in France or England; German expressions of anti-Semitism are combined with urgent social problems. All genres and styles are represented: missionary texts intended to convert the Jews; huge erudite works about Jewish customs, in the "believe it or not" category; and learned treatises on the disturbing juridico-theological question: Is it permissible to tolerate Jews in a Christian society? Does not the Christian conscience demand their immediate expulsion? [13]

But most important are the incendiary pamphlets whose prototype Martin Luther had provided, both as to form and content. They usually had impressive titles, such as *The*

---

[13] For example: *Geistliches Bedencken ob die Juden und ihr Wucher in dem Römischen Reich zu dulden? ob nicht ihrer Gotteslästerungen wegen sie sich aller Privilegien entsetzt?* Darmstadt, 1612; *Etlicher Theologen Bedencken, wit christliche Obrigkeit Juden unter den Christen zu wohnen gestatten könne,* Giessen, 1614; *Discurs über die Frage: ob wahre Christen mit gutem Gewissen die Juden als Juden im äusserlichen weltlichen und bürgerlichen Stande erdulden?* n.p., 1695.

*Enemy of the Jews; The Scourge of the Jews; Jewish Prac-
tices, a Study of Their Impious Life; Jewish Delights; A
Brief Catalogue of the Horrible Jewish Blasphemies; The
Sack of Jewish Serpents,*[14] or even *Inflamed Poison of the
Dragons and Furious Bile of the Serpents;*[15] or *The Jewish
Baths, in which is publicly shown the secret practices and
Jewish knavishness, how they drink the blood of Christians,
as well as their bitter sweat.*[16] (This last title emphasizes the
close connection between the imputation of ritual murder
and that of usury.) Sometimes current events gave rise to
especially large numbers of such works; thus the fall and
execution of Jew Süss were celebrated in dozens of pamphlets, with titles too detailed or too florid to be translated
here.[17]

The great success of these publications and the special
kind of imagination they show seem to correspond to the
quasi-erotic titillation, the compelling psychological need,
that characterize the modern anti-Semite. The general
themes, of course, remain those of the great demonological
myths of the Middle Ages, in which religious dread spontaneously gives rise to a libidinous imaginative outpouring.
It is always a question of the Jews' secret vices and crimes,

[14] *Judenfeind,* Giessen, 1570; *Judengeissel,* n.p. 1604; *Kurzer Auszug
von den erschrecklichen jüdischen Lästerungen,* Giessen, 1604; *Juden-Prac-
tick oder Bericht von ihrem gottlosen Leben,* Augsburg, 1610; *Deliciæ
Judaicæ . . . ,* Darmstadt, 1613; *Jüdischer Schlangenbalg,* n.p., 1702.

[15] J. Schmid, *Feuriger Drachen-Gift und wütiger Ottern-Gall,* Rotzen-
burg, 1634.

[16] Adrian Warner, *Der Juden Bad-Stub, darinnen eigentlich der Juden
heimliche Practick und Schelmestück öffentlich bewiesen werden, wie sie
den Christen das Blut und den sauren Schweiss, etx. aussaugen . . . ,* n.p.,
1611.

[17] Here are three examples: *Das lamentierende Jud süssiche Frauen-
zimmer unter dem grossen eisernen Galgen vor Stuttgardt draussen,* n.p.,
1738; *Des justifizierten Juden Joseph Suess Oppenheimer Geist in den
elysæischen Feldern . . . ,* Frankfurt, 1738; *Guthe Arbeit giebt herrlichen
Lohn, in einer Predigt über das Evengelium Math., XX, 1-16, in einer einge-
flossenen Anweisung, wie die an dem verurtheilten Juden Joseph Suess Oppenheimer geschehene Execution anzusehen und zu gebrauchen sei, samt
einiger Nachricht von dessen kläglichen und schmachlichen Ende, gezeigt
von M. Rieger, Pfarrherrn in Stuttgart,* Esslingen, 1738.

their shameful diseases, bizarre sexual attributes, and above all, their special relationship with the Devil. But in this period these themes are usually treated in a bookish and pedantic manner, sometimes even with pretentious references to natural history that subsequently led to so-called "racial" anti-Semitism. In this period of restriction, when prohibitions and repressions of all kinds were emphasized, such themes acquired a vicious tinge, a corrupt flavor utterly alien to the naïve and spontaneous soul of medieval man.

More subtle and poetic, an obscure and ancient legend suddenly enjoyed tremendous popularity at the beginning of the seventeenth century. The *Brief Account and Description of a Jew Named Ahasuerus* first appeared in 1602 and within the year went through eight editions in German.[18] It was quickly translated into every European language. Thus originated the myth of the wandering Jew, witness of the Crucifixion and condemned by Jesus to wander endlessly until the Second Coming (i.e., the Last Judgment). This myth conformed to the traditional conceptions of the Church,[19] as well as to the unstable and vagabond lot to which Christendom had condemned the Jews. We know the literary fortunes of this impressive theme, transposed to all keys and illuminated from all angles by such illustrious authors as Goethe, Schlegel, Shelley, Andersen, Edgar Quinet, and Eugène Sue. It contributed powerfully, in all nations and all *milieux,* to the concept of the mysterious destiny and providential mission of the Jews.

Against this checkered background several more special-

18 The first known edition was published by Christoff Crutzer in Leyden in 1602.

19 We may recall the bull of Innocent III of January 17, 1208: "God made Cain into a vagabond and a fugitive upon the earth, but marked him, making his head tremble, lest he be killed. Thus the Jews, against whom the blood of Jesus Christ calls out, although they are not to be killed, so that the Christian people may not forget the divine law, must remain vagabonds upon the earth, until their faces be covered with shame and they seek the name of Jesus Christ the Lord . . ." (Migne, *Patrologiae* [Latin], Vol. 215, p. 1,291, No. 190).

ized works of marked influence stand out. German theologians plunged into the depths of the Talmud, seeking instruction from rabbis or consulting apostates, and eagerly communicated their discoveries to the public. Their attitude toward the Jews was usually much less favorable than that of the French Hebraists. Some, such as J. Wulfer (*Theriaca Judaïca*) or J. Wagenseil (*Tela ignea Satanae*) (315), sought primarily to uncover anti-Christian blasphemies, to that end laboriously analyzing Jewish prayers. At the same time, they were eager to refute the great demonological accusations of ritual murder or poisoning. Others adapted these accusations for their own purposes, such as the Orientalist I. A. Eisenmenger, author of *Judaism Unmasked, a True and Accurate Report*.[20] The history of this work is interesting, since for the first time we see a court Jew intervening in one of these polemics. The powerful supplier of the Austrian armies, Samuel Oppenheimer, actually succeeded, for a consideration, in having the work banned. Its two thousand copies were confiscated as soon as they were printed, and the author died, apparently of grief. Shortly after his death, however, his heirs had the work reprinted in Königsberg, with the help of King Frederick I of Prussia, and it has subsequently served as a source of inspiration and a treasury of arguments for generations of German anti-Semites.

The influence of the court Jews was also expressed in another way. Though expulsions of Jews had decreased, they still occasionally occurred; quite naturally, the court Jews tried to have them annulled through the influence of their international connections. A typical example is the expulsion of the Bohemian Jews, decreed in 1744 by the Most

---

[20] The complete title of the work, printed in Frankfurt in 1700, is: *Entdecktes Judentum oder gründlicher und wahrhafter Bericht, welchergestalt die verstockten Juden die heilige Dreieinigkeit erschrecklicherweise verlästern und verunehren, die heilige Mutter Christi verschmähen, das neue Testament, die Evangelisten und Apostel spöttisch durchziehen und das ganze Christentum auf das äusserste verachten und verfluchen. Dabei noch vieles andere. Alles aus ihren einigen Büchern erwiesen. Allen Christen zur treuherzigen Nachricht verfertigt.*

Catholic Empress Maria Theresa, on the pretext that they had been engaged in espionage for the Prussians during the War of the Austrian Succession. A concerted action was initiated immediately, its leading spirit being Wolf Wertheimer, who had excellent Christian connections. The Jewish communities of Frankfurt, Amsterdam, London, and Venice were alerted. That of Rome was urged to intervene with the pope. Those of Bordeaux and Bayonne were requested to take up collections for the benefit of the expelled Jews. Even the king of England and the states general of the Low Countries made representations to Maria Theresa, and a number of courtiers also intervened. Hence, in spite of her previous insistence, the empress finally yielded and authorized the Jews to return to their homes— to be sure, in return for the payment of the enormous sum of 240,000 florins.

Thus ended the last great expulsion of the German Jews, and this denouement is at the same time a fine example of their growing international influence. As for the expulsions spontaneously carried out by the people themselves, the last occurred in Frankfurt in August, 1616; it too must be viewed in the context of the last major rebellion against the constituted authorities. Under the leadership of a hog butcher, Vicenz Fettmilch, the artisans of the city laid siege to the ghetto. After an improvised defense that lasted several hours, the gates yielded at nightfall and the townspeople rushed in, pillaging and burning, furiously destroying the acknowledgments of debts as well as the scrolls of the Torah. The Jews, unharmed except for several beatings, were authorized to leave the city, ruined but safe and sound, and scattered into the countryside. A few months later the city of Worms followed Frankfurt's example and expelled its Jewish community. To counter such disorders, the provincial and subsequently the imperial authorities tried to intervene but for a long time were unsuccessful. The troublemakers enjoyed considerable support, to such a degree that the German faculties of law, when asked for their views, decreed that the assault, made both in daylight and by the light of torches, fell into no known legal category and consequently was not punishable. It was only twenty months later that the Jews were able to return to the city, under the protection of the imperial army, and their return —to the sound of fifes and trumpets, in ranks six deep, preceded by two carriages, one of which was occupied by a venerable, white-bearded rabbi, and the other blazoned with the imperial bearings—constituted a spectacular and symbolic ceremony for which the years following the Nazi massacres in Europe provided no counterpart.

After the Frankfurt incident, whatever the popular animosity, there were no longer any open anti-Jewish excesses of this kind in Germany. The authorities were opposed to them, and the German people were already giving evidence of their traditional qualities of discipline and obedience. These qualities were to assure generations of German Jews of peaceful existence, so long as it was the will of the *Obrigkeit,* the authority, and were to facilitate greatly the Jews' methodical extermination when, in the twentieth century, a new authority decided upon such a course.

eleven

Poland:
the Autonomous Center

Although it was particularly in the East, in the hospitable regions of Poland and Lithuania, that the German Jews sought refuge as their condition grew worse, we cannot conclude that the Polish Jews were solely of Western origin. On the contrary, it is quite probable that during the first millennium of our era the first Jews to penetrate into the territories between the Oder and the Dnieper came from the southeast, from the Jewish kingdom of the Khazars, or even from the south, from Byzantium. We are not sure about the relative proportions of the two groups; what is important is that the superior culture of the German Jews permitted them rapidly to impose their language and customs as well as their extraordinarily sensitive historical consciousness.

In a country of agrarian economy, whose population consisted only of nobles and serfs, the Jews rapidly assumed the chief role in all activities relating to the circulation of merchandise and to money. It is certain that they lived initially on excellent terms with the Christians. This is an observation we have already made many times over. One can discern a constant link between the intellectual status of a crude people, scarcely touched yet by the teachings of Christianity and not having learned to harbor special prejudices against the deicidal race, and its poor state of economic development; this permitted the Jews to assert themselves in a domain where they did not have any competition. We shall not therefore elaborate upon this subject, except to note that the first part of our thesis is reflected by a popular tradition, according to which a Jew was temporarily elevated to the throne of Poland,[1] and that the second part is illustrated by the fact that many ancient Polish coins were minted with Hebrew letters on them.[2] The early history of the Polish Jews, taken from obscure chronicles and accounts of travelers, is vague and scanty. It is only after the thirteenth century that we have any definite information about them. In 1264 King Boleslav of Kalish (Boleslav V) granted the Jews a charter whose broad outlines were similar to those granted by the German princes in the preceding centuries. It served as a model for subsequent charters, some of which were even more favorable; thus, that of Casimir the Great (1364) equated the Jews with the nobility, in case of injury or murder, and imposed identical punishment upon the guilty. Just as in the Carolingian Empire four or five centuries earlier, such preferential treatment provoked the resentment and vehement protests of the clergy, probably with reason. The severe decrees of the Council of Breslau in 1267 specifically concerned Poland, as appears from its twelfth article: "Poland being a new settlement of the Christian body, it is to be feared that the Christian population will be all the more easily influenced by the superstitions and wicked customs of the Jews, since the Christian religion has only recently been established in the hearts of the faithful in this country" (316). From the second half of the thirteenth century, the Polish ecclesiastical authorities were to legislate against the Jews just as actively as the authorities of Western Europe. In 1279 they attempted—unsuccessfully, to be sure

[1] According to this legend, the Polish nobles, unable to agree on the choice of a king, decided to put on the throne the first foreigner to visit Poland. This was a Jew named Saul Wahl, according to one version, or Abraham Porochovnik, according to another. He apparently reigned one day and then abdicated.

[2] Some of these coins bear, in Hebrew, the name of the king ("Meshko the Great"; "Meshko the Just"), others the names of Jewish founders ("Abraham Duchs," "Rabbi Abraham, son of Rabbi Zevi," or even "Rejoice, Abraham, Isaac, and Jacob"). They date from the eleventh and twelfth centuries.

—to impose the wearing of distinctive insignia. At the end of the next century there appeared in Poland the first accusations of profanation of the Host and of ritual murder. In 1454, apparently yielding to the urging of the ubiquitous John of Capistrano, King Casimir Jagello (Casimir IV) abrogated some of the Jewish privileges. Thirty years later the expulsion of the Jews from Warsaw took place, followed by the expulsion from Cracow (Kraków) and by an attempt to expel them completely from Lithuania.

While history thus seemed to repeat itself, with a gap of several centuries corresponding to the gap in intellectual development between Eastern and Western Europe, it was nonetheless to take quite a different turn for the Polish Jews. Not that the hostile reactions of the Polish or Slavic populations were slow to appear and to gain momentum; on the contrary, they became, if possible, even more violent than in other countries. But the economic and even administrative positions in which the Jews rapidly entrenched themselves were so deeply rooted in the social foundations of the country that it was impossible to oust them until modern times. Contrary to what was to happen in the West, where the small numbers of Jews ultimately facilitated their economic and cultural assimilation, in the East, the existence of a Jewish social class culminated in the emergence of a nation in a class by itself.

To grasp the reasons for this strange difference, we must first consider the constant influx of refugees from Western Europe, which permitted many Jews to establish themselves solidly in commercial and financial activities at a period when they had not yet encountered any competition (except from German colonists, immigrants like themselves). This influx became even greater after the Black Plague. It is significant that except in territories adjacent to Germany, the Polish Jews did not suffer greatly from this scourge. Insofar as we have any statistical records about this period, it would seem that in the fifteenth century the number of Jews in Poland already approached a hundred thousand—a somewhat questionable figure[3]—but the first systematic census, taken about 1765, shows that they constituted 10 percent of the country's population.

Strengthened by so solid a demographic base, they practiced all trades and monopolized several, and organized themselves like a state within the state. This organization acquired its definitive forms in the sixteenth century, and from this period onward, Poland was the chief world center of Judaism for many centuries. Without lingering over the Polish Jews' previous tribulations, which were not very significant, we shall now consider their way of life in the period of their prosperity.

"In these regions, masses of Jews are to be found, who are not subject to the scorn they meet with elsewhere. They do not live in abasement and are not reduced to menial trades thereby. They own land, engage in commerce, study medicine and astronomy. They possess great wealth and are not only counted among respectable people but sometimes even dominate them. They wear no distinctive insignia, and are even permitted to bear arms. In short, they have all the rights of citizens." In these terms the papal legate, Commendoni, described the status of the Polish Jews about 1565 (317). Indeed, there was no possible comparison between the condition of the Polish Jews and that of their less fortunate coreligionists in the other European nations.

They did not live in ghettos but in a neighborhood or a street of their choice. The scope of their occupations was as broad as possible, including not only all types of commerce and trade, but also administrative offices (collecting taxes and customs), industrial management (development of salt mines and forests), and even agriculture, either as

---

[3] This is the figure arrived at by I. Schipper, the chief specialist in the economic history of the Polish Jews. Until the middle of the eighteenth century we have no valid data for our estimates; the usual source—that of tax records—is of no help in this case, since the Polish Jews were taxed as a group.

overseers or as managers on their own account. In other words, a certain proportion—a proportion that was to increase—lived in the country. Many rich Jews, bankers to the nobility, had become important landowners; they even owned entire villages. Others were the stewards, tradesmen, and commercial agents of the Polish lords, of the *shlakhta:* "To each lord, his Jew," says one Polish adage. In effect, these were "court Jews"—to be sure, of very small courts, given the confused division of power in Poland at the time. Others were important merchants, importers, and above all exporters of wood, wheat, skins, and furs; but the majority were small tradesmen and artisans, having to compete with the rising Polish bourgeoisie; or, in the country, they were innkeepers, retail dealers, and even simple farmers. On the whole, then, it is accurate to say that in Poland the Jews formed an entire social class—that urban middle class which, in this nation, took so long to become established. In contrast to the great flexibility shown by their ancestors, who had rapidly adopted the language of the various European nations in which they settled, the Polish Jews continued to speak German, which became Yiddish. It isn't possible to say whether this difference was attributable to their great numbers, to the cultural superiority of their country of origin, or even to their heightened self-awareness, their tremendous attachment to their past, which the German Jews had acquired as a consequence of their shocking tribulations. Doubtless it was a combination of all three of these factors. In any case, this special feature raised an additional barrier between them and their Christian neighbors.[4]

It is not surprising, therefore, that the Polish Jews enjoyed a high degree of self-government on both local and

---

[4] As we know, the same situation is found among the Sephardic Jews, who have continued to use "ladino" more than four centuries after their expulsion from Spain. In both cases, it may be that the collective trauma arising from their persecutions contributed to a collective self-awareness that found expression in a loyalty to the language of adoption. This language was thus—paradoxically—that of the nations where the Jews had suffered the worst persecutions.

national levels. They practically administered themselves, in accordance with a constitution that might be described as customary and federative. Its basis was the community or "kahal" that corresponded to a geographical unit including both the Jews of any important city and those who lived in its environs. The government of the kahal was oligarchic. Sworn electors, whose names were drawn by lot from among the richest and most influential members of the community, were named to select the administrators each year. The latter were given very broad powers. Among their responsibilities were the collection of taxes and customs, internal policing and maintenance of public order, synagogue affairs (that is, the organization of worship and public education, which were indissolubly linked), as well as careful control of the labor market. An interesting feature of the labor market was that only those artisans who were fathers of families could open a new workshop; also, except in unusual circumstances, this was forbidden to the members of a foreign kahal. (The local cohesive spirit of the kahals was also manifested by the endless "border" disputes over some village or hamlet whose administrative jurisdiction was contested: for example, the case of Zabloudovo, which from 1621 to 1668 kept the kahals of Grodno and Tykoszin at odds) (318). The kahal also appointed the rabbi, a personage of great importance, since his moral authority was reinforced by his powers in judiciary matters. He was by rights president of the judiciary council, the tribunal of the kahal. Elected commissions, various half-philanthropic, half-religious guilds, counterbalanced the "protectionist" leanings of the kahal and devoted themselves to numerous works of charity and Jewish solidarity: ransom of prisoners, care of the sick and aged, aid to the needy and the homeless, to impecunious students, and above all honor to the dead and the worship of their memory. The pious brotherhoods (*khevrot kedishah*) were concerned with assuring a dignified burial and care of the deceased's family.

An organization so detailed and so concentrated was favored by the Polish authorities, who found it convenient to collect taxes *en bloc* and therefore to deal with a strong community organization. Subsequently, these authorities realized that it was even more convenient to impose a single total annual payment upon all Jews and to charge them with allocating this tax among the various communities themselves. Hence the consultations and meetings of the kahal representatives, at first sporadic and irregular, soon became extremely important. From the second half of the sixteenth century, these representatives gathered at semi-annual conferences—at the Lublin fair in the spring and the Yaroslav fair in Galicia in the fall—and determined tax quotas, settled conflicts among kahals, published new laws and decrees (*takkanoth*), and discussed other important questions pertaining to Polish Judaism. The federal chamber thus improvised, a veritable Jewish parliament with about thirty members, received the name "Council of the Four Nations," [5] and there was some justification for its being compared by contemporaries to the Sanhedrin of Jerusalem. As a matter of fact, never had the Jews enjoyed such autonomy in Europe. In all these matters, involving unprecedented situations and conflict of interests, the role of the rabbi—as moral authority, professional mediator, and interpreter of the subtle and often obsolete Talmudic laws—was of utmost importance. Rabbinical learning was thus vindicated.

Under these circumstances Talmudic learning—knowledge of the countless rules, judgments, and arguments dating from Parthian Babylonia or from Europe of the Crusade era, together with skill in applying these to new conditions —reached incomparable heights in sixteenth-century Poland. "Pilpul" (literally, pepper) was the name given to the spicy dialectic whose object was to find two Talmudic texts that

[5] In Hebrew: "Vaad Arba Aratzot." The "four nations" were Greater Poland (Posnan), Lesser Poland (Cracow), Red Russia or Ruthenia (Lvov), and Lithuania. Subsequently Volhynia was added, while in 1623 the Jews of Lithuania seceded and formed their own council.

logically contradicted each other, and after having clearly established their incompatibility, to reconcile them with the aid of some subtle sophistry, however finely the hairs had to be split. Pilpul tournaments, held at fairs, markets, and political meetings, became the national pastime of the Polish Jews. (How this apparently sterile mental gymnastics trained the mind, how it increased the capacity for intellectual work, is understandable only to those who have attempted it themselves, for to the uninitiated, Talmudic reasoning usually presents insurmountable difficulties.[6])

Under these circumstances, erudition, even if it remained uniformly Talmudic, was even more highly prized, if possible, by the Polish Jews than by their German ancestors. Furthermore, the priority accorded to intellectual values served as a corrective to the great social inequalities within the Jewish community, in which the rich were the chief possessors of municipal power. It is true that traditional Jewish philanthropy broadly made up for grave inequalities. Understandably, throughout the Dispersion the lot of the Polish Jews

---

[6] Hence it is very difficult to give examples. Few authors have tried to make Talmudic reasoning accessible to educated Europeans. We refer those interested in this question to an old but hitherto unequaled study by the philologist Arsène Darmesteter ("Le Talmud," in *Reliques scientifiques,* Paris, 1890, republished in "Aspects du génie d'Israël," *Cahiers du Sud,* Paris, 1950). *Ad usum populi,* the following example may serve to illustrate the thesis that Talmudic reasoning is, in the last analysis, an exercise in common sense:

A *goy* insisted that a Talmudist explain to him what the Talmud was. The sage finally consented and asked the *goy* the following question:

"Two men climb down a chimney. When they come out the bottom, one has his face covered with soot, the other is spotless. Which of the two will wash himself?"

"The one who's dirty," answers the *goy.*

"No, for the one who's dirty sees the other's clean face and believes his is clean, too. The one who's clean sees a dirty face and believes that his is dirty, too."

"I understand!" the *goy* exclaims. "I'm beginning to understand what the Talmud is . . ."

"No, you have understood nothing at all," the rabbi interrupts. "For how could two men have come down the same chimney, one dirty and the other clean?"

was regarded at this period as so privileged that—according to one of those puns so common among them—Polonia was to be read *po lan ia* ("God resides here").

It is apparent that in such a situation Polish anti-Semitism arose quite early, and in a very different fashion from elsewhere in Europe. Hitherto we have been dealing with mythological anti-Semitism, that composite of hatred and religious fervor whose effects were so strangely disproportionate to its apparent cause, and which remained active even in the absence of Jews. In the case of Poland, even though the first hostility may have had the same origin as elsewhere, the Jewish group ultimately became so numerous, and its functions so indispensable, that the nature of the conflict was altered. In Poland the Jew was a permanent element of his neighbor's daily existence, an integral part of the social body. The Christian Pole, whether nobleman or laborer, peasant or city dweller, turned to the Jew to buy or to sell, to borrow or to pay taxes, to travel or to patronize a tavern. This Jew, whether proud or humble, rich or poor, hard or compliant, was an omnipresent human reality, behind whom the accursed Satanic likeness gradually began to disappear. Thus the original and fundamental aspect of anti-Semitism was somehow conjured away. On the other hand, this Jew, though part of the Christian's familiar background, was associated with certain functions and operations of everyday life that were all part of the struggle for existence. Thus with regard to Judeo-Christian hostility, we are now concerned with tensions that are in no way exceptional, are not disturbing or unprecedented, that do not shock the sensibilities, since they do not differ essentially from other tensions and conflicts of social, national, or religious groups throughout the history of our civilization. At most, some specific Jewish characteristics we have frequently mentioned, especially their absolute disdain for physical exercise and prowess ("It's as useful to you as a sword to a Jew," says one Polish proverb), mark them with a special stamp. This, combined with the Jews' scornful rejection of Christ, made it even easier to assign to them the traditional role of scapegoat. It is difficult to know whether anti-Semitism gains or loses in violence under such conditions, especially since we are dealing with incommensurable quantities, the same word being used for two rather different phenomena. We may try to see the matter more clearly by considering in turn the attitudes of various social classes toward the Jew.

As chief beneficiaries of Jewish enterprise, the Polish nobles were their natural protectors. There could be no conflict of interest here, except in the case of some small, needy landowners, competing with the "court Jews" for the favor of a magnate. The nobility treated the Jews with greater disdain than that reserved for other classes of society, but it did not show much malice in doing so. It is characteristic that in the early days of printing, when the custom of defaming the Jews, of describing their vices in books and pamphlets, spread throughout Poland as everywhere else, no text of this kind came from the pen of a noble.

Usually these works were written by members of the Christian bourgeoisie. Big-city dwellers, especially, were in permanent conflict with the Jews, in an attempt to oust them from trade or prevent them from becoming artisans. A special commission from the elected magistrates of Cracow caused Sebastian Miczynski to write his *Mirror of the Polish Crown*[7] in 1618, in which the wealth of the Jews, as well as their commercial techniques, were described at length for the first time. Religious accusations are of minor importance in this work. This is also true of the numerous writings of the physician Shleszkowski, who had undertaken to expose the fraudulent practices that he ascribed to his Jewish colleagues and rivals.[8]

The clergy confined itself to religious charges. At the end of the sixteenth century, its leader was the famous Jesuit Peter Skarga, the most illustrious Polish preacher of all time,

---

[7] *Zwierciadlo Korony Polskiej.*

[8] *Odkrycie zdrad zydowskich,* 1621; *Jasny dowod o doktorach zydowskich,* 1623.

author of the *Lives of the Saints* (*Zywoty Swietych*, 1579), which for centuries was the bedside reading of the Polish people. In it the miraculous biography of Simon of Trent figured prominently, and Skarga later officiated in person as prosecutor in a trial for profanation of the Host. He had many imitators who, from generation to generation, launched attacks of this kind. Scholars and students, pupils of the Jesuits, were the chief artisans of slanders and riots that degenerated into pogroms, so that the custom was established among the Jews of paying an annual fee (*kozubales*) as protection against systematic molestation.

The common people, the oppressed and illiterate peasants, had no voice in the matter, nor any means to hand their opinions down to us, unless we regard as such the countless sayings and proverbs that serve as a traditional repertory of popular wisdom. Some of them seem to sound an ambiguous note. For instance: "We peasants are always in misery: we must feed the noble, the priest, and the Jew" (319). Or: "What the peasant earns, the noble spends and the Jew profits by" (320). Or again: "The Jew, the German, and the Devil, a fine trio and all sons of the same mother" (321). Judging by such adages, the people made few distinctions among their exploiters.

The Deluge

In 1648 the disturbances known in Polish history as the Deluge broke out. These heralded the decline of Poland and were to put an end to the golden age of the Polish Jews and to have enormous consequences for all of Judaism.

The Deluge began with the uprising of the Ukrainian peasants, serfs settled on the vast trans-Dnieper plantations of the Polish nobility. These peasants, of Greek Orthodox religion, hated equally their Catholic masters and the Jewish stewards and agents. As one contemporary Jewish chronicler noted: "The Greek people (the Cossacks) . . . were scorned and humiliated by the Polish people and by the Jews. . . . Even the humble sons of Israel, usually in servitude themselves, flaunted their power over them" (322). It is noteworthy that the chronicler should call the rebels "Greeks" (and not "Russians" or "Ukrainians"); the conflict was religious as well as social and national. The flag of the rebellion was raised by the famous Bogdan Chmielnicki, who for a time was able to unite the anarchic Cossack groups and form an alliance with the Crimean Tartars. "Remember the insults of the Poles and the Jews, their favorite stewards and agents!" Chmielnicki exclaimed in his "appeals" to the Ukrainian population. "Remember their oppressions, their wickedness, their exactions!" The resentment of the serfs must have been violent. One Ukrainian chronicle states that certain *pans* (title of nobility) assigned even the churches located on their lands to Jewish agents, so that their authorization was required for baptisms, weddings, and funerals (323).

Chmielnicki's troops poured over all of southeast Poland and reached the very gates of Lvov, massacring Poles and Jews indiscriminately as they passed, sometimes granting mercy to those willing to be converted. This irresistible popular uprising was marked by mass exterminations described by eyewitnesses in that traditional and hieratic style we have already noted so often (one of them compares the catastrophe to the "third destruction of the Temple"); but their content is realistic and detailed.[9] During the following

---

[9] Together with descriptions of scenes of horror ("Nurslings were murdered in their mothers' arms, gutted like fish. The wombs of pregnant women were laid open and the unborn infants replaced by a living cat that was sewn into the womb, while the victim's arms were cut off so she could not remove the creature . . ." etc.), certain passages of these chronicles have an aura of things seen and noted very accurately. For example:

". . . The leaders of the communities of Ostrog declared that no Jew should remain in this city or in Mezherich, for the enemy was only two leagues away, and we were not certain of avoiding attack by the local Orthodox inhabitants. And the flight began again. He who had horse and cart set out by horse; he who had none set out on foot with his wife and children, abandoning house and property. That Saturday the horse-drawn carts advanced in three rows along the road from Ostrog to Dubno, extend-

years, riots and massacres were broken off and begun again
several times until Chmielnicki decided to seek Muscovite
protection. A Polish-Russian war followed, aggravated by
Swedish intervention, and the conflict degenerated into a
free-for-all, with unfortunate Poland as its permanent theater.
The tsar's troops invaded White Russia and Lithuania and
abused the Jews in the same fashion as their Cossack allies
farther south. The Swedish army invaded Poland proper and
occupied Warsaw and Cracow. This was a better disciplined
army, and its leaders did not kill the Jews; instead, they
forced them to provision their forces—as a result of which
the Poles, when they returned, accused the Jews of treason
and exercised a summary justice upon them in many localities.
Thus, between 1648 and 1658 there was virtually no Jewish
community that was completely unharmed. There was no
longer a single Jew on the left bank of the Dnieper (those
who had been spared were sold as slaves to the Turks), and
only a handful of survivors on the right bank. In the interior
the losses were less serious; nonetheless, the total number of
victims amounted to several tens of thousands, perhaps to
one hundred thousand.[10] Of course, the country as a whole
suffered the full force of the Deluge, and Poland henceforth
ceased to be a great power. But the blow to the Jews was even
worse, both because they were the first victims of the mas-

---

ing over seven leagues. . . . On the way we were joined by three horsemen, the Jew Moses Tzoref of Ostrog and two Polish *pans* who said to
us: 'Why do you drag along so slowly? The enemy is catching up, they are
now in Mezherich, we shall never be able to escape.' An incredible panic
then spread among our brothers: each sought to lighten his cart, and threw
to the ground silver and gold objects, garments, books, mattresses, and
cushions, so as to travel more rapidly and to save his own life. Many men
and women, seeking refuge in woods and caves, lost their children in the
confusion." (From the chronicle *Yeven Metzulah* by Nathan Hannover,
Venice, 1653.)

[10] From 100,000 to 500,000, according to the testimony of the Jewish
chroniclers of the period; these figures are certainly exaggerated. The statement that nearly seven hundred communities were totally or partially destroyed is more reasonable. In any case, as S. Dubnow rightly points out,
"the number of victims exceeded that of all the catastrophes of the Crusades and of the Black Plague in Western Europe."

sacres and lootings and because the economic foundations of their life were more precarious than those of the other social classes. They were never to recover.

By the second half of the seventeenth century, the Jews were no longer the country's chief bankers. This role had passed to Christian capitalists, especially to religious communities—churches and monasteries—whose wealth, consisting chiefly of lands, had remained intact. The Jews, both communities and individuals, contracted debts to these. The chronic indebtedness of the kahals, in the course of their desperate efforts to re-establish the Jewish economy, became a major social problem in Poland and grew worse until the end of the eighteenth century.[11] In 1765 the Polish diet, with a stroke of the pen, suppressed the Council of the Four Nations, considering it more advantageous to impose upon the Jews an individual poll tax of two zlotys, instead of the former group tax. Thus ended the Jewish semistate autonomy.

Impoverishment spread little by little. The Jewish "social class" deteriorated and was ultimately liquidated (very broadly, a Marxist interpretation is applicable here). Seeking a means of livelihood, many Jews left the country, while others took refuge in the countryside as innkeepers, artisans, and laborers. The majority stagnated in extreme poverty.

New spiritual and religious currents coincided with these social transformations, and left a characteristic stamp on the mentality of the Polish Jews, and were to have vast repercussions among all the Jews of the Dispersion. This was a remarkable process of interaction, having the whole of Europe as its base, and in which the infiltration of Christian concepts was to play its part. (This time these currents were to affect not only details of life and customs, but to leave their imprint on the new messianic movements.) Thus the Jewish

[11] In 1719 the debts of the kahal of Cracow were more than 500,000 zlotys. Those of the kahal of Posnan reached 400,000 zlotys in 1760. The "floating" debt of the Council of the Four Nations was some 3 million, or about the same as the annual budget of the Polish state. (Cf. Dubnow, *History of the Jews of Europe* [in Russian], Vol. 4, p. 131.)

nation assumed its definitive form, solidly established on the banks of the Vistula and in the forests of the Carpathians.

In 1650 the Council of the Four Nations had proclaimed national mourning in memory of the first victims. Polish Jews were forbidden to wear silk or velvet garments for three years. An annual fast was instituted on the twentieth of Sivan, the anniversary of one of the first massacres, perpetrated by the Cossacks at Nemirov. This has continued to be observed faithfully to the present time. New elegies, *selihot* and *kinot*, were composed by the rabbis and recited in the synagogues following those that traditionally commemorate the massacres of the Crusades. Traditionally, too, the Jews did penance, seeing in their misfortunes the just retribution for their sins, seeking to expiate them by a greater piety and austerity. "Gravely have we sinned before our Lord . . ." proclaimed an appeal of the Council of the Four Nations in 1676. "Troubles increase daily, life becomes ever more difficult, our people has no importance among other peoples. It is even surprising that, despite all the disasters, we continue to survive. The only thing left for us to do is to unite in a single alliance and obey the commandments of God and the precepts of our pious teachers and leaders" (324). Fugitives, however, scattered to the four corners of Europe and spread the sad news; everywhere the Jewish communities vied with one another to help. Renowned rabbis went into exile and were welcomed with open arms because of their learning. Some were itinerant sages, such as the Talmudist Zevi Hirsch Ashkenazi—himself son of a celebrated rabbi of Vilna—who lived and taught successively in Budapest, Sarajevo, Vienna, Venice, Prague, Altona, Amsterdam, and London, returning in his old age to Lvov. Others chose a more stable life and for some time virtually monopolized the rabbinical posts, especially in Germany. In the words of the historian Graetz, all of European Judaism "was Polonizing." [12] Common people emigrated by thousands into Hun-

[12] "Das Judentum . . . wurde sozusagen polonisiert." (Graetz, *Geschichte der Juden*, Vol. 10, p. 76.)

gary and Rumania, rapidly submerging the small local Jewish colonies. Collections were taken everywhere to feed the immigrants, but especially to ransom the Jews sold into slavery, who were concentrated in great numbers in Constantinople. Alms collectors combed Europe, and even the traditional sum for the Jews of Jerusalem was neglected for a time (325). Not since the beginning of the Dispersion had Jewish solidarity had occasion to function on such a vast scale. All minds were impressed by the disaster suffered in 1648 by the chief European citadel of Judaism.

By a curious coincidence, 1648 was a date that already had a special meaning for many Jews. The cabalists, in fact, had long since declared that this year would see the coming of the Messiah, according to the *Zohar*.[13] And in the tragedy of Poland they saw a striking confirmation of the prophecy. Deliverance being at hand, they claimed, these must be the unendurable labor pains of its birth. . . . (One notes that Karl Marx's famous image about the "labor pains of history" had its precursors.) Furthermore, a simple acrostic, consisting of the name of Chmielnicki written in Hebrew, read: "The sufferings of the Messiah's birth will come upon the world," and thus confirmed that the supreme hour, so passionately awaited, was indeed approaching.

Now, there have been frequent claimants to the title of

[13] Probably written in the thirteenth century, but "predated" from the first, the *Zohar*, in many passages, predicted the coming of the Messiah at the beginning of the fourteenth century. Since the Messiah had not appeared at this date, the cabalists fell back on another passage (139b) that predicted the resurrection of the dead (but not the coming of the Messiah) in the year 5408 of the Jewish calendar, which corresponds to the year 1648 of the Christian era. For those who are interested in the cabalistic reasonings and calculations, we may add that the passage 139b of the *Zohar* reads: "In the sixth millennium, after the expiration of 408 years, the dead will return to life, for it has been said: 'This year, each of you shall return to his property.'" "It has been said," refers to Leviticus 25:13, regarding the year of jubilee: "In the year of this jubile ye shall return every man unto his possession." *This* year: in true cabalistic style, each word and each comma has its meaning, and especially a numerical meaning: according to the Hebrew numerical alphabet, the word "this" (*hazoth*) can represent 5408.

Messiah in Jewish history, but in general they have met with more jeers than rejoicing. For nearly a thousand years none had achieved any broad recognition or set off a lasting movement within Judaism itself. For one of them to succeed, it was necessary to have this remarkable chain of circumstances, and above all, a great despair. The fact that another famous prediction—this one of purely Christian origin—fixed the apocalyptic year as 1666 [14] merely facilitated Sabbatai Zevi's career.

In another volume we shall discuss this remarkable person: bigamist, though wedded to the Torah; Moslem, though king of the Jews. His entire public life was pursued among the Sephardic Jews. The essential facts are that this most illustrious of the false Messiahs revealed himself to the Jewish crowds of Smyrna, his native city, in 1648. He married with great ceremony a young Polish Jewess who had escaped from a Christian convent (predestined bride of the Messiah, according to some; a woman of ill repute, according to others) and in 1666, after many adventures, demanded the sultan's throne and ended his days as Mehmet Effendi, gatekeeper of the Sublime Gate. His promises and his new theology stirred up hope and agitation among the Jews of Hamburg and Amsterdam. The response was just as great in Avignon, Venice, Cairo, or Salonica, and it was even stronger, if possible, in Poland, where the Jews had suffered so cruelly. The

---

[14] 1666: According to the Revelation of Saint John (13:18), 666 was the number of the apocalyptic beast. (The figure was obtained by adding the numerical value of the letters in the name of the Emperor Nero, transcribed in Hebrew.) Then to 666 was added 1000 (the year Mil), and 1666 became the messianic year. Or again, recourse was had to figurative interpretation: ". . . the triumph of the Church, which must follow the persecution of Antichrist, will begin in the fortieth hour after the Ascension of Jesus Christ, taking twenty-four hours for 1000 years . . ." and therefore forty hours were figuratively equivalent to 1,666 years. (Cf. *Les Remarques sur les principales erreurs* . . . by M. Arnaud, 2nd ed., Paris, 1735, p. 68.)

These calculations continued to excite men's imaginations for a long time. Witness the passage in Tolstoy's *War and Peace* where 666 could be applied equally well to the Emperor Napoleon as to l'Russe Besuhof (proper French, "le Russe", produced 671); as a result, Pierre Bezukhov plans to kill Napoleon.

greater the misery, the more essential the need for imminent salvation. One Christian witness assures us that in Poland in 1666 ". . . the Jews rejoiced and began to hope that the Messiah would place them upon a cloud in order to transport them to Jerusalem. During this time they fasted several days a week, deprived even their young children of food, washed in cold water after breaking the ice upon it, and recited some recently composed prayer. When the skies above some town were covered with clouds, the Jews would boast in front of the Christians and tell them that the Messiah would bear them off straightway to settle them in the country of Israel and in Jerusalem . . ." (326). This caused disturbances and riots, so that King John II Casimir had to publish a special decree, forbidding the Jews to make demonstrations or to circulate sensational propaganda, and forbidding the Christians to indulge in reprisals on this pretext . . . (327).

This year 1666 is equally memorable in Christian religious history. It was the year in which a schism split the Russian Orthodox Church, leading to the proliferation of sects of "old believers," certain of which (especially the *shlysty*) have so many features in common with Sabbathaianism that it is impossible to avoid assuming reciprocal influences and personal contacts (328). Thus this heresy found new material to feed on. In contrast to events in the West, where the downfall of the false Messiah quickly put an end to the euphoria of the Jewish masses, the Sabbathaian movement in Poland sent down deep roots; the resurrection of Sabbatai was expected from year to year. As late as 1700, a group of zealots, numbering over a thousand men, set out for the Promised Land and managed to reach Jerusalem. Braving the threat of anathema, the *herem*, other agitators tried to spread the good word in Poland or even in Western Europe. A statement by the rabbis of Amsterdam, dated 1725, complained: "Once the Torah came from Poland, and now this nation is a source of infection for the other nations" (329). At this period the cabalistic charlatans and religious reformers, the pseudo-Messiahs and pseudo-Zevis abounded in Poland, especially in the strife-torn Ukraine. The most famous of them was Jacob Frank, high priest of a new cult in which Jewish traditions and the belief in the Holy Trinity were curiously fused— an easy transition toward complete conversion. But it was the powerful Hasidic movement that afforded the best answer to popular hopes and which imposed itself irresistibly. Under the pressure of social necessity, the severe rabbinical teaching, product of a thousand years of urban life and an intensive intellecutal culture, yielded throughout most of Poland to a gentler, simpler religion, filled with mysticism and tinged with imperceptible Christian borrowings, better adapted to the needs of the poverty-stricken and often ignorant masses scattered in towns and countryside.

Little is known about the creator of Hasidism, the legendary Baal Shem-Tob (BEShT). What is known about this authentic founder of a religion is so vague and obscure that his figure is comparable to that of Jesus Christ. As in the case of the Nazarene, the first biography of BEShT appeared two generations after his death (330), having long circulated by mouth, embellished with ever-new details and miracles. Like Christ in the Gospels, BEShT's teachings were preceded by a long retreat "in the desert," where he lived as a hermit deep in the wild forests of the Carpathians. Like Christ, he taught a simple doctrine understandable by all and illustrated with parables. Like Christ, he supported it by direct and irrefutable proofs: miraculous cures and exorcisms. He preached faith, hope, and the search for God, omnipresent in nature in the form of a "sacred spark" that is the one true reality. To recognize this reality is to be convinced that the so-called tangible world of earth, with its miseries and pains, is only a tissue of illusory phantoms.

Crowds eager to hear such a consoling message soon gathered around BEShT. From Miedzyboz, in Podolia, where he lived, disciples went out to spread the new gospel. His doctrine was received even more eagerly since it corresponded to the popular resentment against the despotism of the rich and the rabbis. (Yet their ousting ultimately led to the institution of a still more despotic government.) Communities of Hasidim sprang up in all Polish cities and townships, with a "tzaddik," a "just man," at their head. The great uniqueness of Hasidism rests on the existence of the just man, a man with direct access to the Supreme Power and even exercising some influence over it. Obviously, ordinary mortals could not do this, rooted as they were in their earthly cares. A deep and solemn fundamental concept of Judaism—that each man must confront his Creator, alone and face to face—was thus destroyed. The new views undoubtedly were derived from Sabbathaianism, that is, from the faith in a Messiah descended to earth. (Podolia, where Hasidism was born, had been a fruitful field of Sabbathaianism and from 1679 to 1699 had belonged to Turkey.) As one authority observes: "Not only the doctrine of the new pietists, but also many aspects of their behavior—the loving attachment to God, the enthusiasm, the victory over sorrow, the songs and hand clappings—all these had derived from the customs of the Sabbathaian sect. . . . The just man is merely the reincarnation of the Sabbathaian prophet as the vital center of the community . . ." (331). In short, the just man is only a Messiah struck off in many copies. But I shall not attempt to explain so briefly an original and fruitful doctrine with some Sabbathaian roots, others generally cabalistic, some perhaps even Christian. (Like the Catholic priest, the just man is an intercessor with the Divinity, a function that Judaism had hitherto refused to admit.) What matters to our inquiry are the social consequences of the new movement.

One of the first was to provoke within the heart of Judaism a veritable schism, such as it had not known for a thousand years, since the Karaite schism. Orthodox rabbis attempted to nip in the bud a sect whose heresy was obvious to them. For over thirty years, from 1772 to 1804, a desperate struggle was waged by means of decrees, solemn anathemas, and even denunciations to the authorities. The Hasidim were completely identified, with some justification, with the Sabbathaians; and also, quite unjustifiably, with the Frankists. They were censured for their disdain of the sacred rites and customs, their ignorance and their strange ways; they were even suspected of secret crimes. Here is an excerpt from one of these pastoral letters by the famous sage of Vilna, the Gaon Elijah.

"You have already learned, our brothers in Israel, of this news that our fathers never dreamed of, which is that a suspect sect has appeared, known as the Hasidim. . . . In praying, they utter dreadful alien cries [in Yiddish], behave like madmen, and explain their behavior by saying that their spirits are wandering in distant worlds. They use painted prayer books and shriek so that the walls shake; heads down, feet in the air, they pray moving in a circle. . . . They completely ignore the study of the holy Torah, and are not ashamed to say that it is useless to devote oneself to study and that one need not excessively deplore sins already committed. . . . That is why we write as follows to our brothers in Israel . . . that they may prove their ardor by exterminating them, destroying them, banishing and anathematizing them . . . so that there will be not even two such heretics left, for their suppression will be a benefit to the world" (332).

Sometimes the charges were even more serious, and certain puns on the root *hesed*, which can mean grace and disgrace, love and crime, made it possible to accuse the Hasidim of incest and other debaucheries. "Horror be upon me!" exclaimed one of the opponents, "upon me, who am obliged to hear what mysteries they have invented! Do they not thereby introduce impure thoughts into the Holy of Holies! Their prayer becomes a kind of dream, for it is only in dreams that man learns of his hidden desires (*Berakhot*, 54). And to repress such thoughts, the Hasidim uttter deafening cries and in the course of prayer scream words that have no part in them . . ." (333).

We shall not discuss in detail the obscure and desperate struggles during which recourse to the government, Polish or Russian—in other words, denunciation—played the role of supreme argument, leading the Russian government in 1804 to regulate the Jews' use of anathema rigidly. It is enough to say that all the efforts of orthodox rabbis were futile. Hasidism progressed invincibly and finally won over the majority of Polish and Ukrainian Jews. The just men, usually persons of extraordinary vitality, were organized into veritable dynasties and exercised complete control over their flocks. Their counsel and intercession were sought on every occasion: questions of conscience, health, business; and usually their good offices were liberally rewarded. Payments to the interceding clergy assumed a kind of hieratic and institutional form. We have mentioned the religious significance that money had acquired for the Jews down through the centuries. In good doctrine, ". . . the just man who serves God in all sincerity is comparable to the honest agent who stands between buyer and seller" (334); from this came the just man's absolute right to collect his agent's fee. According to a Hasidic parable, its author BEShT's own grandson, ". . . guardians of the gates of the gods, the just men are comparable to the gatekeepers of a royal palace. If one would be received by the king, he is first stopped by a guardian of inferior rank, and can pass the first gate only after having given him a coin. The closer one approaches the royal apartment, the higher the gatekeeper is in rank and the greater the sum he receives. When one presents oneself before the supreme gatekeeper, who stands on the threshold of the royal apartment, one is obliged to be lavish with one's money in order to gain access to the king" (335).

The meaning of this parable is clear. And another celebrated just man, the miracle-working rabbi of Lublin, seriously explained that he could intercede with God only in return for a remuneration: "When a just man undertakes to invoke the Sacred Name for another man, this may be considered [by Heaven] as an overweening presumption, and he may be asked why the interested party does not make his own invocation. If the just man is remunerated beforehand, he can ward off the celestial prosecutor's accusation by answering: 'I am praying for him because I have been paid by him and am merely carrying out my contractual duties'" (336). In a certain sense, today's psychoanalyst proceeds in similar fashion.

In fact, like good psychiatrists, the just men greatly lessened men's miseries. They took upon their own broad shoulders the pains, cares, sufferings, and the fears of their flocks. They taught the faithful to turn from harsh realities, which were only appearances, and to seek out the hidden melodies of the universe, to instruct themselves in the secret mechanisms controlling the visible and invisible worlds. This left an impression of comfort (for man is so made that when he believes he understands his destiny, he also believes he can control it). Above all, they instilled a sublime and optimistic faith in God that they considered the basic factor in the success of their interventions. If you believe in God (and in me), I shall be able to make God grant your prayer, but if you doubt divine clemency and omnipotence (and my abilities), you will have only yourself to blame for your failure. The essential faith was stimulated by the mechanical behavior—cries and contortions—that so outraged the opponents of Hasidism. The Hasid's prayer became ecstatic: a mystic ecstasy, a loving union with God, assumed a new status, weakening orthodox Judaism.

Similarly, the roles of study and intellectual speculation were relegated to the background, while simplicity, humility, and gentleness were extolled as cardinal virtues by most of the just men. Some even served as examples. For instance, it is told that Wolf of Zbarasz, presiding over a circumcision feast, suddenly remembered that it was a very cold night and that he had left his coachman outdoors. He hurried into the courtyard and persuaded the coachman to come indoors to get warm while he himself took care of the horses. When, after an hour, his absence was noticed, he was found half-frozen on the coachman's seat. It is also told that Moses Loeb of Brody insisted on washing the heads of mangy children with his own hands, saying: "He who does not have the courage to care for the abscesses of Jewish children and to wash away their pus with his own hands has not half the love for Israel that is needed" (337).

This suggests Saint Francis of Assisi. Naïve and touching, countless stories of this kind have thus been incorporated into Jewish folklore.

The tales, the imaginative fables that dramatized a moral teaching much better than a long sermon could have done, are very characteristic of Hasidism. Some of the stories, deeply significant, can be read in several different ways. For example, this one, which can be applied to every religion:

"When the Baal Shem had a difficult task before him, he would go to a certain place in the woods, light a fire and meditate in prayer—and what he had set out to perform was done. When a generation later the "Maggid" of Meseritz was faced with the same task he would go to the same place in the woods and say: We can no longer light the fire, but we can still speak the prayers—and what he wanted done became reality. Again a generation later Rabbi Moshe Leib of Sassov had to perform this task. And he too went into the woods and said: We can no longer light a fire, nor do we know the secret meditations belonging to the prayer, but we do know the place in the woods to which it all belongs—and that must be sufficient; and sufficient it was. But when another generation had passed and Rabbi Israel of Rishin was called upon to perform the task, he sat down on his golden chair in his castle and said: We cannot light the fire, we cannot speak the prayers, we do not know the place, but we can tell the story of how it was done. And, the story-teller adds, the story which he told had the same effect as the actions of the other three" (338).

Lingering as I have done over the customs of the Hasidim and the tales of their just men, perhaps I have strayed too far from my subject. Insofar as the customs and conduct of the Jews traditionally serve as a stimulus to the anti-Semitic obsessions of their adversaries, the digression does not seem irrelevant. For we are concerned with the forms that Judaism assumed at the final stage of its evolution, in the mountains and plains of Poland, tempering certain Jewish characteristics, accentuating others, and raising to the maximum their dynamism and their optimism, within a traditionally hostile environment.

At this same period, Polish anti-Semitism found its most characteristic expression in frequent sporadic massacres in the troubled confines of the East, the permanent site of ethnic and religious discord, as well as in countless trials for ritual murder in the very heart of Catholic Poland.

In the East, in the continuously disputed regions of the Ukraine and White Russia, imitators of Bogdan Chmielnicki continued to appear. One of these bold mobsters and implacable murderers, Basil Voshtchilo, presented a coherent political program in a manifesto in which he stated that the constituted authorities must be obeyed and could be opposed only when they had been corrupted by the Jews. He proclaimed himself "Ataman Voshtchilo, grandson of Chmielnicki, grand hetman of the troops, charged with the extermination of Jewry and the defense of Christendom." His manifesto continued:

"In their petitions, the Jews claimed that I am fomenting disturbances and that I oppose the government with violence. This is a base lie. I have never had such an intention. I am a Christian. In this region, infidel Jews have not only deprived Christians of their means of existence, but they carry out aggressions, murders, robberies, and oppress the holy sacraments [the churches]. Without their sanction and their written authorization for the priest, no newborn child can be baptized. They bewitch the *pans*, the lords of the nobility, and thereby gain their acquiescence. They rape Christian women and do many other things that are difficult even to list. Impelled by my fervor for the holy Christian faith, I have decided, in company with other men of honor, to exterminate the cursed Jewish people, and with the aid of God I have al-

ready done away with the Jews in the districts of Krisht-
chev and Popoisk. Although the Jews have armed the government's troops against me, God's goodness has protected me
in every case . . ." (339).

On the eve of the first partition of Poland, in a context of
civil war, the massacres became more frequent. Under cover
of a so-called imperial decree, the "Gold Charter," falsely
attributed to Catherine the Great, insurgents proceeded to
the systematic extermination of the Jews and the Polish lords,
in the name of the Pravoslavic faith. Russian and Polish
troops intervened, re-established order, and the authors of
the forgery were exiled to Siberia.[15] But a bloody tradition
was perpetuated, as evidenced by the pogroms of the late
nineteenth century, the massacres of 1918-1920, and the co-
operation given to the Nazis a generation later.

Reports of ritual murder and profanation of the Host increased from the beginning of the eighteenth century. The
more widely they were believed, the more belief found to
feed on. Proofs and new demonstrations appeared in its support. There was even at this period a witness, Michael the
Neophyte, who swore that as a Jew he himself had been a
murderer! This half-lunatic, a converted Jew who claimed
to have been the former grand rabbi of Lithuania, swore on
the crucifix not only that ritual murder was an absolute commandment of Judaism, but that he himself had murdered
Christian children. His writings, *Revelations of the Jewish
Rites before God and the World* (340), filled with sadistic
details, were the favorite catechism of the maniacs of anti-
Semitism for two centuries, and before the Nazis introduced
a new thesis and terminology, high prelates and university

[15] The chief author of the forgery appears to have been Father Mel-
chizedek, prior of an Orthodox monastery. The so-called decree reads:
"Observing the scorn and impudence with which the Poles and the Jews
treat our Pravoslavic faith, we hereby order Maxim Jelesniak, colonel and
commander of our territories of the Lower Zaporozhe, to enter Poland, in
order to put to the sword and exterminate, with God's help, all the Poles
and Jews, blasphemers of our holy faith." (From *History of the Jews in
Europe* by S. Dubnow [in Russian], Vol. 4, p. 319.)

professors drew from it the essentials of their information and convictions (341). From the very beginning, the Neophyte's confessions and the agitation of his protectors were given even royal approval: "The blood of Christian children, shed by the infidel and perfidious Jews, cries out to Heaven!" exclaimed August II, ordinarily so skeptical (342). As for the dignitaries of the Polish Church, they remained faithful to their traditional role of instigators and propagandists.

Under these auspices, it is not surprising that the great majority of cases of ritual murder that appeared annually during Easter week ended in executions. These were veritable ritual inquisitions which, this time, were concerned only with the Jews. The accidental or contrived disappearance of a Christian child was of vital concern to the nearest Jewish community. It had to be redeemed by Jewish blood or at the very least by Jewish money, which sometimes permitted the matter to be dropped. A secret fund, the *aliloth seker* (fund for bloody calumnies), set up by the Council of the Four Nations, served chiefly for this purpose. The Council finally decided to appeal to the Holy See about the ritual inquisition by the Polish clergy. An emissary went to Rome in 1758, and after a great many preliminaries obtained from Cardinal Ganganelli (the future Pope Clement XIV) a learned judgment that is a model of detailed criticism of sources and texts. In his memorandum, Ganganelli reviews the historically known cases of ritual murder, and with the exception of two cases, he establishes the lack of basis for the accusation. It is true that he had to proceed with some care, for the Church had already beatified the two boys in question.[16]

But this remarkable document had no great effect. Rumors,

---

[16] These were the Blessed Andrew of Rinn (†1462) and the Blessed Simon of Trent (†1475) (cf. pp. 62 f.). In a remarkable study (*La Question du meurtre rituel chez les Juifs, Études de critique et d'histoire religieuse,* Paris, 1913), Abbé Vacandard showed the correspondence between the Vatican's decisions and Ganganelli's historical work. A certain margin of appreciation was accorded it, since the two children had been merely beatified (and not canonized).

arrests, tortures, and executions continued worse than before, which is certainly not surprising.

There are a large number of separate considerations, any one of which proves simply and obviously that there is not, and cannot be, any Jewish rite prescribing the consumption of human blood. On the contrary, no religion inculcates in its believers such horror of blood in general.[17] Some of these considerations are based on easily observable facts; but unfortunately, if these are viewed in bad faith, they only contribute to a deeper entrenchment of the bloody superstition.

Thus, the practice of ritual slaughter of animals, expressly intended to prevent the consumption of blood, the use of special knives and professional "sacrificers" to administer a mysteriously "ritual" death to beasts and fowls, helped aggravate suspicion. Other rites or customs may have had the same effect.[18] On a more psychological level, the Jews' fearful and respectful attitude toward blood (and toward human life in general) may have contributed its share. If they made so much of blood, if they attributed so much value to it, then they desired it, just as they desired money.[19]

[17] The essential point is found in Leviticus 17: 11-13: "For the life of the flesh is in the blood: and I have given it to you upon the altar to make an atonement for your souls: for it is the blood that maketh an atonement for the soul. Therefore I said unto the children of Israel, No soul of you shall eat blood, neither shall any stranger that sojourneth among you eat blood. And whatsoever man there be of the children of Israel, or of the strangers that sojourn among you, which hunteth and catcheth any beast or fowl that may be eaten; he shall even pour out the blood thereof, and cover it with dust."

We know how the restrictive interpretations of the Talmudists have aggravated and infinitely complicated these prohibitions.

[18] Thus the custom of drinking *red* wine at the beginning of the Jewish Passover. This is why, in the second half of the seventeenth century, the Talmudist David ben Samuel Halevy, author of the critical commentary *Turey Zahav*, insisted that this custom be abandoned in Poland; also the custom of using red liquid palm resin to stop bleeding after circumcision. The connection is evident.

[19] It is curious that the plural of the Hebrew word *dam*, which means blood, is the homonym of the word that means money (*damim*). Some

Furthermore, since magical virtues had always been attributed in the popular imagination to human blood, who, then, would be better able to take advantage of these than the Jews, those cunning sorcerers? Finally, in the hidden depths of men's souls there functioned that terrible mechanism that consists in attributing to the loathed people of God one's own blasphemous desires and unconscious corruption.

Corroborated in many ways, obvious because salutary and salutary because obvious, it is thus understandable that belief in ritual crimes committed by the Jews became so powerfully anchored in Christian hearts.[20]

---

authors (such as the Protestant theologian Strack) have tried to see in this fact an additional source of the legend of ritual murder. Christians with some slight knowledge of Hebrew had "confounded" the Jews' pursuit of wealth with a thirst for blood. This seems to me a very fragile line of reasoning. But the homonym is a striking one.

[20] Need we add that the belief has not entirely disappeared, sometimes spread by authors professing to be historians? Here are two examples:

In his *History of Witchcraft and Demonology* (London, 1926), Montague Summers writes that the Jews were persecuted ". . . not so much for the observance of Hebraic ceremonies, as is often suggested and supposed, but for the practice of the dark and hideous traditions of Hebrew magic: . . . In many cases, the evidence is quite conclusive that the body and especially the blood of the victim was used for magical ends" (p. 195).

Similarly, in his *Histoire de la Magie* (Paris, 1949), M. Louis Chochod writes that from "1071 to 1670 in France, England, and Germany, there were thirty-six ritual murders reported and attributed to the Jews. A Catholic prelate, Monseignor Konrad, bishop of Padeborn, has stated that to repudiate these stories would be to erase from history thirty to forty clearly established facts described in detail" (p. 247, note). He adds: "It is not proved that the Jewish community as a whole was associated with such practices. And we have quoted passages from Leviticus clear enough to show that they are just as contrary to the spirit as to the letter of the Mosaic law. It is nonetheless appropriate to note that according to the Talmud, it is lawful to put heretics to death, and that Maimonides considers the commandment forbidding murder as concerning only Jews. It would therefore not apply to those who are not Jews" (p. 250).

twelve

The Case of Russia

We have emphasized throughout the preceding chapter the way in which the history of the Polish Jews was constantly determined by the scope of their economic functions. It is not surprising that many writers, indulging in one of those simplifications so satisfying to the human spirit, have tried to reduce everything to economics and, by extrapolating, have sought to enclose the entire history of the Jews within an economico-social outline, generally Marxist-inspired. But whatever may be valid with respect to the history of Western society in general, Jewish history cannot be considered in this way.

The case of Russia affords a remarkable example. In fact, from a simplistic point of view, Russia's backward state of development and her geographical location to the east of Poland would be adequate and essential conditions for the formation of a "social class" of Jews, after a suitable time lag. Yet the fearful superstitions of the people and the influence of the ruler combined to prevent the Jews from even attempting to enter the territory. Thus in order to study the problem from the point of view that interests us, if it was helpful to study the persistence of anti-Semitism long after the departure of the Jews, as we did in France and England, it is even more helpful, in the case of the Muscovite Empire, to study its action and effects before the arrival of the Jews. More precisely, at a decisive moment in Russian history some random Jews risked going to the Kremlin to preach new ideas, and this sufficed to instill in the souls of the Orthodox a great fear of the Jews, resulting in their civil quarantine.

The reign of Ivan III (1462-1505) was in fact the crucial period when the Muscovite grand duchy definitely threw off the Mongol yoke of the Golden Horde. This cautious and cunning potentate then seized Novgorod, quadrupled his territory, and concentrated autocratic power in his hands, while his councilors dazzled before his eyes the succession to fallen Byzantium and the vision of Moscow as a third Rome. It was during his reign, too, that the first Jews ventured into Muscovy.

One of them, Messer Leon, was a physician;[1] another, Khoza Kokos, a diplomat;[2] a third, Skharia (Zechariah?) became an active missionary of Judaism, under vague circumstances but with results that we shall discuss.

In fact, it is not known whether there was a single Skharia or if there were two different ones, and the circumstances in which "the heresy of the Judaizers" appeared are little known. Some Russian chronicles mention Skarguina, some Skharia, some Zechariah, and give his country of origin as Lithuania around 1470 or as the Crimea around 1485, so that we begin to wonder if this is the real name of a historical person or a group of legends centered around some obscure travelers. This case is all the more open to question since there had been another legendary apostle of Judaism in the same part of the world, the sage Isaac, who, six centuries earlier, apparently taught the Law of Moses to the king of the Khazars. He is sometimes nicknamed Sangari, sometimes

[1] Messer Leon was a Jew from Venice. His medical career in Moscow ended most unfortunately. The son of Ivan III having fallen ill, the Jew offered to cure him and wagered his head upon his success. The young prince died soon afterward, and the Jew had to accept the consequences of his presumption and was publicly decapitated in 1490. Such was the fate of the first physician to be mentioned in Russian chronicles.

[2] Khoza Kokos was a Crimean Jew who served as an intermediary between Ivan III and Mengli-Guiray, Khan of the Crimea. In a curious message, a copy of which has been preserved in Moscow, Ivan III asked him to write no longer in Hebrew characters, but to use Russian or "Basurman" (Turkish?) characters.

Zambria, sometimes Samvria; thus we may wonder if these two mythological persons do not reflect the same tradition, and if it is not a question of some kind of archetypal name. Whatever the case, here is all that is known for certain about the man called Skharia.

He arrived in the free city of Novgorod about 1470. The city, which was soon to be annexed by Moscow, was torn between the Lithuanian camp and the Muscovite camp and was in the grip of the heresy of the *Strigolniki*, enemies of the ecclesiastical hierarchy. Skharia, a man of erudition, sided with the members of the clergy and managed to convince certain of their number of the superiority of the Jewish faith. Pope Denis, Pope Alexius, as well as several others, were secretly converted to Judaism. Other Jews, Joseph Chmoilo Skariavy (*sic!*) and Moses Khapuche, joined Skharia. The propaganda was successful, and soon a kind of Judaism was practiced openly; but once this was the case, we hear no more of Skharia and his various coreligionists, of whom all trace is lost, as if they had never existed (343).

The "Judaizers" did not recognize the divinity of Christ, denied the Trinity, and broke the sacred icons. Some even had themselves circumcised. This was not Judaism strictly speaking, since the Judaizers glorified Jesus: but "How can God descend to earth and be born of a virgin in human form? This cannot be the case. . . . He is like Moses, he is not like God the Father . . ." (344). This, transmitted in mysterious ways, was the teaching of the Marcellians and the Photinians of fourth-century Byzantium; these were also the ideas which, as we have seen, appeared to take root quite naturally among newly baptized peoples; and finally, this was a Jewish heresy.

From Novgorod, the heresy spread to Moscow and there rapidly became extraordinarily strongly entrenched. It seeped into the immediate entourage of Ivan III: his favorite, Feodor Kuritzin, and his daughter-in-law Helena joined the sect, and even the Muscovite Metropolitan Zossima, according to the chronicler, "seduced the simple, plying them with Jewish poison" (345). "Since the time when the Pravoslavic sun first shone in our country, there has never been such a heresy. In the home, in the streets, in the markets, clergy and laymen debated the Faith and no longer trusted the teachings of the Prophets, the Apostles, and the Fathers of the Church; but on the arguments of the heretics, renegades of Christianity, sided in friendship with them and accepted instruction in Judaism . . ." notes the same chronicler (346). The religious dispute was also a dynastic one, for the Princess Helena sought the throne for her son Dmitri, while Prince Basil, son of Ivan III's second marriage, claimed the throne for himself. For a long time, Ivan's favor seemed to incline toward Helena and Dmitri. What direction would the destiny of Holy Russia then take?

Ultimately, the Pravoslavs triumphed. In effect, Ivan III intervened relentlessly when he realized that the heresy, which was also the expression of the centrifugal forces within the nascent empire, was firmly implanted in rebellious Novgorod and was becoming a state matter. A long and confused struggle ensued, ending with the complete victory of the autocracy. In 1504, after a council held in Moscow, the principle leaders of the sect were burned. Princess Helena died in prison that same year. The heresy was still not uprooted: it went underground, to reappear in the course of the following centuries, influencing the various religious movements and sects that have always proliferated on the soil of Holy Russia; or combining with them in order to accept Sabbathaian heresies, as we have already seen; and, finally, manifesting itself as *molokanes* or *dukhobors* in the nineteenth century.

It was under these circumstances, and in order to protect themselves thereafter from the Jewish contagion, that the Muscovite authorities decided to quarantine the Jews—a decision they were to enforce with an astonishing constancy. As we know, the tsarist regime from the first was traditionally suspicious of all foreigners, the *inoviertzy* (those who believe differently), considering them all as unbelievers. Until the reforms of Peter the Great, all foreigners in Moscow or in Archangel lived in a special isolated region, a *sloboda*, quite comparable to a ghetto; as for the Jews, they were feared and regarded as the quintessence of evil and depravity; suspicion of them survived all reforms.

"The Jews revolt us most of all, and the very mention of their name horrifies us. We do not permit them to enter our lands, for they are vile and evil-doing men. Have they not recently taught the Turks to cast cannons in bronze?" declared Dmitri Guerassimov, Russian envoy to the Holy See in 1526 (347). In 1550, Ivan the Terrible (Ivan IV), urged by his Polish ally, King Sigismund Augustus, to admit several Jewish merchants into Moscow, took an even stronger position.

"Apropos of what you write to persuade us to allow your Jews to enter our lands, we have already written you several times, telling you of the vile actions of the Jews, who have turned our people away from Christ, introduced poisonous drugs into our state, and caused much harm to our people. You should be ashamed, our brother, to write us about them, knowing their misdeeds all the while. In other states, too, they have done much evil, and for this have been expelled or put to death. We cannot permit the Jews to come into our state, for we do not wish to see any evil here. We pray that God may permit the people of our country to live in peace, without any disturbance. And you, our brother, should not write us in the future concerning the Jews" (348).

The successors of Ivan the Terrible scrupulously held to this same policy. Only the period known as the "troubled years," between 1605 and 1613, is an exception. Many Polish Jews seem to have come to Moscow at this time in the retinue of the false Dmitri. The manifesto published at the time of the accession of the first of the Romanovs, Michael Feodorovich, expressed indignation at the appearance in Moscow of "wicked heretics, Calvinists, Lutherans, Armenians,

Roman Papists, and deicidal Jews, profaners of our churches."
As for the false Dmitri, he was openly called a "bandit of
Jewish origin" (*vor, rodom zhidovin*) (349).

Nevertheless, a handful of converted Jews (some of whom
Judaized in secret) were able to settle in Moscow during the
seventeenth century. But when the king of Poland asked
Tsar Michael to let Aaron Markovich, the "agent" of his
court, come to the Russian capital, the Tsar replied: "The
Jews have never come to Moscow, and the Christians must
not communicate with them" (350). Similarly, the treaty between Tsar Feodor III and John III Sobieski signed in 1678
expressly stipulated that Catholic Polish merchants could
settle in Moscow, but that Jewish merchants could not. In
1698, Peter the Great, during his sojourn in Amsterdam,
was solicited by the burgomaster of the city, Witsen, to admit
certain Jewish merchants or specialists. According to one
chronicler, he replied as follows:

"You know, my friend, the character and customs of the
Jews; you also know the Russians. I, too, know them both,
and believe me: the time has not yet come to unite these two
peoples. Tell the Jews that I thank them for their offers and I
understand the advantages I might have derived from them,
but I would have pitied them for having to live among the
Russians" (351).

Though Peter the Great, who was without doubt an enlightened spirit—"Whether a man is baptized or circumcised,
it is all the same to me, provided he is a man of honor and
knows his business," he wrote on another occasion (352)—
preferred not to admit Western Jews into his empire, at least
he was not concerned with those who had lived for generations in newly annexed or conquered territories: the Ukraine
and the Baltic countries. This was not the case under his
successors. Two years after his death, his widow, Empress
Catherine I, published the following edict:

"The Jews of masculine sex and those of feminine sex who
are found in the Ukraine and in other Russian cities are to be
expelled at once beyond the frontiers of Russia. Hence-

forth they will not be admitted into Russia upon any pretext, and a very close watch will be kept upon them in all places" (353).

These were the Jewish businessmen and artisans whose roots in the local economic life I have already described. As soon as they began to be expelled, serious complications arose, and civil and military authorities were obliged to grant numerous stays in order to avoid a more serious disorganization. During the following years, many conflicts pitted the officials and offices concerned with national prosperity against those concerned with the salvation of souls. In 1743 the state senate submitted to Elizabeth Petrovna, daughter of Peter the Great, a documented report emphasizing the profits the imperial treasury could derive from admitting Polish Jewish merchants to the markets of Kiev and Riga. The empress' reply was brief and peremptory. "From the enemies of Christ I wish to derive neither interest nor profit," she wrote in her own hand on the margin of the report (354).

Such were, in brief, the origins of the famous "pale of settlement" and of the legislation which until the revolution of February, 1917, confined to the western periphery of the tsarist empire all Jewish subjects who had been deprived of their hereditary residences. Their number greatly increased after the partition of Poland.

In the history of anti-Semitism, a certain specifically feminine bigotry has played a decisive part. Like the wife and the daughter of Peter the Great, Isabella of Castile, Margaret Theresa of Austria, and Maria Theresa of Austria[3] made themselves famous by upsetting a delicate balance at a given moment. It is noteworthy that absurd decisions, weighty with consequences, were characteristic of the female ruler. In this instance, the consequences were especially far-reaching. Another policy, permitting the immense Russian Empire to absorb the overflow of Polish Jews, would have offered a remedy for their indescribable concentration in a tiny region

[3] Expulsions from Spain (1492), Vienna (1670), and Bohemia (1745).

—the quadrilateral bounded by Warsaw, Odessa, Vienna, and Berlin—where, from the end of the nineteenth century, passions began to boil as in a crucible, with the consequences now known to the world.

appendix a

The Origin of the Jews in
the Light of Group Serology

It is widely known, especially since blood transfusion has become a part of common medical practice, that there are four different blood types, designated by the letters O, A, B, and AB, transmitted from parents to children according to the laws of Mendelian heredity. We find these four groups among all the peoples of the earth, but in different proportions. Thus for example:

	Type O	Type A	Type B	Type AB
Among 1000 Frenchmen	440	453	74	33
Among 1000 Japanese	305	382	219	94
Among 1000 Senegalese Negroes	432	224	292	50

A great number of studies undertaken during the last decades have shown that these distributions correspond approximately to traditional racial classifications; that is, the differences are much greater between whites and Mongols, for example, or between whites and Negroes, than between Frenchmen and Englishmen or between Chinese and Japanese. This is shown quite clearly in R. Kherumian's graph (see pp. 292-293), where the percentages of type O are shown by ordinates and the difference A— (B + AB) by abscissas.

We see from this graph that the Jews of Tel-Aviv, who are known to be of extremely varied origins, but mostly European, correspond to the European group. As for the Jews of the Dispersion, the figures, country by country, are remarkably close to those of the peoples among whom they live, and the variation between Jews of different countries is approximately the same as among the non-Jewish population of the same countries, as shown by the following table:[1]

	O	A	B	AB
German Jews	42.1	41.1	11.5	4.9
German non-Jews	39.1	43.5	12.5	4.9
Polish Jews	33.1	41.5	17.4	8
Polish non-Jews	33.7	38.4	19.4	8.5
Russian Jews	28	42.3	23.5	6.2
Russian non-Jews	32.9	35.6	23.2	8.1
Yemenite Jews	56.0	26.1	16.1	1.8
Yemenite Arabs	55.7	32.3	10.7	1.3
Tunisian Jews	41	31	15.5	12.5
Tunisian Berbers	46.4	32.4	15.8	5.4

Such data are all the more remarkable since this analysis avoids the vagueness or ambiguity inherent in other criteria of the classification of human beings. In effect, as R. Kherumian writes,[2] "(1) These are objective criteria: tests of blood groups admitting of no ambiguous interpretation; (2) the blood groups are absolutely fixed for each individual and completely independent of the milieu; (3) there is no reason to believe them adaptative: they confer neither advantage nor disadvantage, and their frequencies cannot undergo, through selective adaptation, sudden and important modifications in the course of evolution; (4) they are determined by a simple genetic mechanism, which permits one to predict the results of crossing in families and ethnic groups; (5) their rate of mutation is practically negligible."

Let us also note that in the case of populations inhabiting the same territory for centuries but not intermingling, the frequencies in question offer striking divergences. Thus (still following R. Kherumian), in the case of Hungarian

[1] From R. Kherumian, *Génétique et Anthropologie des groupes sanguins*, Paris, 1951, p. 71.
[2] Kherumian, pp. 62-63.

gypsies and of German settlers in Hungary, ". . . the distribution of frequencies is much nearer the proportions characteristic of their countries of origin than of the Hungarian population, despite the duration of their settlement in Hungary (860 years for the gypsies, 200 for the Germans)."

	O	A	B	AB
Gypsies	34.2	21.1	38.4	8.5
Hindus	31.3	19	41.2	8.5
Germans in Hungary	40.8	43.5	12.6	3.1
Germans	39.1	43.5	12.5	4.9
Hungarians	31	38	18.8	12.2

To return to the Jews, there is a remarkable correlation between the serology data and those that can be derived from their history. With regard to the Jews of Western Europe, we have noted that their blood groups correspond to those of the European average. This bears out our assumption of an almost total "panmixia" effected in the course of the first thousand years of our era. As for the Jews of Eastern Europe (Poles, Russians, etc.), it has always been assumed that they descended from an amalgamation of Jews of Khazar stock from southern Russia and German Jews (the latter having imposed their superior culture). Group serology confirms this assumption, since here the percentages of blood groups approach those of the native population, which is itself the result of a mixture of Slavic and Mongol tribes. In the present case, it is natural that the divergences between Jews and non-Jews should be more accentuated. Except for several small Jewish "islets," such as occur in certain oases of southern Morocco, we obtain analogous results with respect to the Jews of North Africa, those of the Near East, etc. (For further details, see R. Kherumian's work, as well as J. Brutzkus' study, "Blood Groups among Jewish Populations" in *Races et Racisme*, No. 5, 1937, and the work by William Boyd, *Genetics and the Races of Man*, Boston, 1950.)

Let us now consider the reservations that might apply to the above.

(1) The studies undertaken up to the present on the different Jewish groups are not sufficiently numerous. Thus, we still lack data on the Hungarian and Italian Jews, on the Sephardic groups of France and the Low Countries, etc. Additional studies may well afford enlightenment on certain details.

(2) In recent years, other factors of differentiation in human blood have been discovered ("M," "N," and "P" antigens, Rhesus antigens, etc.) that are inherited according to the same laws as the O, A, and B antigens, but entirely independent of them. The data collected about them are still much too few for us to be able to draw any general conclusions. Nevertheless, the results of research among the different groups of the Canadian population[3] are somewhat disconcerting, in that they seem to contradict those of the ABO system. As a matter of fact, with respect to the Rh factor, Canadian Jews are noticeably different from the rest of the population, whereas according to the ABO system, Canadian Jews are similar to Polish and Ukrainian groups having the same geographical origin.

Doubtless we must wait for further studies to resolve this apparent contradiction and to reach more general and more precise results in this interesting field.

[3] Kherumian, p. 91.

Note for the American Edition (1965)

Since the writing of this appendix some ten years ago for the original French edition, there has been an appreciable increase in knowledge about blood serology. Although the new findings do not clearly invalidate the earlier information, given above, they do suggest to scholars that considerable caution must be used in determining facts of Jewish history from biological data.

Professor L. C. Dunn of Columbia University, who has devoted himself since 1955-56 to a study of the Jewish community of Rome, believes that this population can be identified by its *blood-group gene frequencies* and distinguished not only from non-Jewish Italians but also from other Jewish Italians.[1] But in this instance the evidence suggests that the population's individualization is of recent date—the Roman ghetto had not been severely isolated by the pontifical government until after the Counter Reformation in the sixteenth century—and does not disprove the hypothesis we have mentioned of "panmixia" at the beginning of the Christian era. The same observation can be made in the other instances where "genetic individualization" of Jewish communities has been demonstrated.

More recently the crucial point of the matter was raised by

[1] L. C. and S. P. Dunn, "The Roman Jewish Community," *Scientific American*, March, 1957; "The Roman Jewish Community, A Study in Historical Causation," *Jewish Journal of Sociology*, 1959, Vol. 2; "Are Jews a Race?" *Issues*, 1961, Vol. 15.

Professor A. E. Mourant, director of the Lister Institute of London, at a conference on human population genetics held in Israel in 1961. Among other things he said, "The study of the blood groups and other genetic characteristics of the Jews has thus far solved comparatively few problems." It seems best to quote his conclusions;[2] in particular it will be seen that Professor Mourant finds a contradiction, in the case of the Eastern European Jews, between Rhesus factor and fundamental ABO system evidence.

(Ashkenazic Jews) ". . . We can say that the great majority of the Jewish population of eastern Europe show a close approach to uniformity. The average blood group gene frequency of all the Jews of the region as a whole are similar to the average frequency of all the non-Jews of corresponding nationalities. This finding might lead to a superficial interpretation that the Jews are simply a cosmopolitan mixture of all the nationalities concerned. In fact, however, the resemblances between the ABO frequencies of Jews as a whole and non-Jews as a whole are deceptive and probably accidental, as will be seen when the Rh blood groups are considered. There is, nevertheless, a slight and by no means accidental tendency for the blood group frequencies of the Jews in any country to diverge from the average Jewish frequency in the direction of the frequency shown by non-Jews in that country, which probably is a genuine effect of intermarriage of Jews with non-Jews, though it might be accidental and could, indeed, in theory, be the result of the parallel operation of natural selection on Jews and non-Jews in a common environment. . . ."

(Sephardic Jews) "The only Jewish community in western Europe for which we have adequate data is that of the Netherlands, with the lowest known B frequency of any Jewish community, and with both A and B frequencies almost identical with those of the local non-Jews; there can be

[2] "Blood Groups of Jewish Communities," *Proceedings of a Conference on Human Population Genetics Held at the Hebrew University, Jerusalem* (Ed. by E. Goldschmidt), New York, 1963, pp. 256-62.

hardly any doubt that the Jews here have acquired a large number of non-Jewish genes by intermarriage.

"Data for the Sephardic Jews, apart from those tested in Israel, are very scanty. We can be certain that the Jews of the Netherlands just mentioned, though probably in part of Sephardic descent, differ very widely from their Spanish or Sephardic ancestors. The only known data for Sephardim tested in Europe are those of Yugoslavia, showing 21 per cent of A genes and 15 per cent of B genes. These figures agree well with the 23 per cent of A and 15 per cent of B genes of Sephardim tested in Israel. Rather similar figures are found, as we have seen, for the Jewish communities of North Africa. It is to be noted that, although the frequency of B in the Ashkenazim is comparable to that found in most central and eastern European peoples, the frequency in the Sephardim is higher than in any of the autochthonous peoples of western Europe, and that B frequencies are particularly low among Spaniards. Thus, it appears likely that the B genes in the Sephardim are derived mainly from their east Mediterranean ancestors. . . ."

(Jews of Asia) "The diagram for the Jews of Asia is even more confusing than that for Europe. A and B frequencies are high, as are the corresponding frequencies of the peoples among whom they live or from whose regions they take their name. But in Asia the Jews appear to have more diversity of frequencies than the non-Jews. One is tempted to see in this an effect of inbreeding, each Jewish community tending to develop somewhat extreme gene frequencies as a result of genetic drift. The explanation, however, probably is that non-Jewish communities of southwestern and central Asia differ more widely from one another in blood group frequencies than the currently available data indicate, and that the Jews reflect these differences.

"Entirely distinct from other Jewish communities in Asia so far examined are the Yemenite Jews and the Samaritans, both communities having very low frequencies of both A and B, similar to those of the Arabs of Arabia. . . .

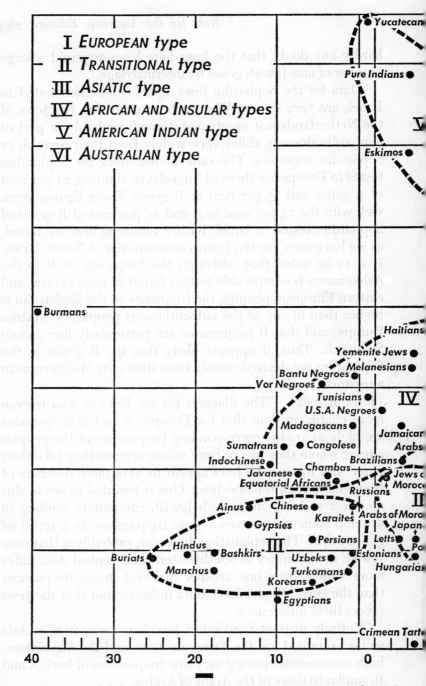

Chart by R. Kherumian: The ethnic division of the frequencies of the ABO system. Ordinates: the frequency, in percentages, of the O group; abscissas: the difference between the frequency of A and the sum of the frequencies B plus AB, i.e., A − (B + AB), placed to the right of zero when it is positive

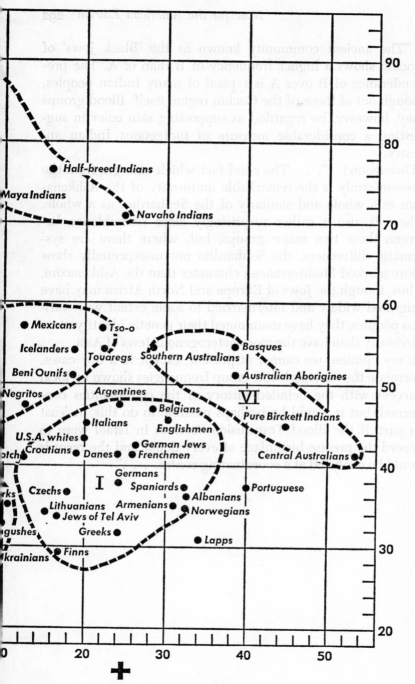

and to the left of zero when it is negative.

Each population is represented by one dot; thus the sum of the populations forms a group of dots that correspond to the six ethnic types (or races) indicated at the top of the chart.

"The ancient community known as the 'Black Jews' of Cochin shows a higher frequency of B than of A. The preponderance of B over A is typical of many Indian peoples, though not of those of the Cochin region itself. Blood groups may, however, be regarded as supporting skin color in suggesting a considerable measure of indigenous Indian ancestry."

(Discussion) ". . . The chief fact which emerges from the present study is the remarkable uniformity of the Ashkenazim as a whole and similarly of the Sephardim as a whole. There is also a rather surprisingly close resemblance between these two major groups, but, where there are systematic differences, the Sephardim not unexpectedly show more marked Mediterranean character than the Ashkenazim. Thus, though the Jews of Europe and North Africa may have migrated widely and intermarried to some extent with various peoples, they have maintained their genetic identity more obviously than have the more heterogenous Jews of Asia. . . . In my opinion, we cannot at present, except in a few cases, correlate the varying blood-group frequencies shown by local surveys with the detailed history of the communities concerned, but it would be perhaps possible to do this, at least in part, if the Blood Transfusion Services in Israel were to record the precise birthplace of every donor and the records could be analyzed at a coordinating center. . . ."

The Formation and Transmission of Jewish "Differential" Characteristics from the Viewpoint of Contemporary Biology

Considerations drawn from the history of the European Jews during the first thousand years after Jesus Christ, combined with the results of group serology, lead to the conclusion that their remote ancestry is essentially European. In this sense, the almost legendary formula of elementary-school textbooks in France: "Our ancestors the Gauls," is much less absurd, applied to young French Jews, than applied to young school-boys of equatorial Africa, for instance. But for several dozen generations, European Jews lived in the virtually total segregation of the ghetto, intermarriages with Christians having been quite exceptional before the nineteenth century. At the same time, behind the ghetto walls, there emerged the customs and manners, the mentality, and the very special aptitudes that we have often referred to in this work. We need hardly add that whereas the uniqueness of manners and customs have mostly disappeared with "assimilation," one can still recognize today certain Jewish aptitudes and mentality. (We shall discuss this point in a forthcoming volume.) Given these conditions, we must ask: in what way, from generation to generation, were these characteristics transmitted? Was it solely a transmission by environment and education, and do the Jews constitute a purely social phenomenon? Or does heredity ultimately intervene to some degree, in the incubator of the ghetto, permitting us to speak of an incipient differentiation, of a new "race" with definite biological characteristics of its own and only its own?

At the present time, geneticists are quite categorical on the matter: "acquired characteristics," whether physical or mental, are not transmissible by heredity. Insofar as they have been acquired by training or exercise, neither the robust muscles of the athlete or manual laborer, nor the agile brain of the intellectual or tradesman will in any way influence the make-up of their children, just as, to take an extreme example, a one-armed man (amputation being regarded as an "acquired characteristic") will father normal children. Human characteristics and predispositions, since they are determined by the whole of the hereditary pattern, do not depend in any way on behavior, on the "individual biography" of the direct ancestors. This is the verdict of Western genetics specialists. We are also aware of the tremendous amount of research done by the official U.S.S.R. scientists of the Lysenko school to demonstrate the contrary, to establish that living beings (of whatever realm), placed in better living conditions, biologically transmit from generation to generation the acquired gains and improvements. But this research, embracing so many polemics and such high hopes, has afforded no decisive results; even in the U.S.S.R. Lysenko was later severely criticized.

This might appear to settle the matter. But the Jewish "specificity" is so strong, so recognizable among the majority of Jews of the Dispersion, even after several generations of "assimilation," and the findings of science are still so fallible, so constantly readjusted and revised, that the question deserves further consideration. Especially since so many passions are involved—is there any need to explain why? There are few considerations to which a man is more sensitive than to those involving his parents and, beyond them, his ancestry and his descendants—in a word, to what is conventionally called his "race." We have recently seen how this vague and disputed concept could become the tribal divinity of a major European nation, with the catastrophic results familiar to us all. Consequently, the struggle against racism has shifted for some time to the foreground of the concerns of Western society, affording further reason to doubt the specialist. Would he not tend to interpret, to accommodate his theses to his secret or avowed political preferences?

Let us recall, then, what is definitely known. Hereditary traits—or at least physical traits—are transmitted from generation to generation by means of clearly defined material carriers, large complex molecules called *genes,* grouped in chains, called *chromosomes,* lodged in the nucleus of the reproductive cells (ovum and spermatozoon), each particular characteristic (for instance, eye color or skull shape or hereditary defect) being transmitted by a particular gene or a group of genes. There is no difference between a characteristic of "individual heredity" (variable within a given population, such as skull shape or freckles) and one of "racial heredity" (common, or presumably common, characteristics of the given population and often serving to define it as a race; for example, white or black skin). The characteristics and criteria of "racial heredity" are extremely few, corresponding at most to several dozen genes, while the total number of genes is in the tens of thousands. "What unites men is much more important than what separates them." Furthermore, contrary to popular assumption, these characteristics are never present uniformly in the whole of a given population. Hence, according to Jean Rostand:

"No problem is more difficult than *the problem of the races of man,* for we know no human group that can be considered as constituting a *pure race,* namely, one made up *exclusively* of individuals who possess certain genes that set them apart from individuals belonging to another group. It follows that the anthropologist with the help of the geneticist can only show that certain human groups differ relatively to the extent that they carry certain genes." [1]

[1] J. Rostand, *Human Heredity,* New York, 1961, p. 96. The author continues: "William C. Boyd says that a human race can be defined as a population that differs significantly from other human populations with respect to the frequency of one or more genes. His definition is rather vague and necessarily quite arbitrary, for in each instance we must decide whether

Such is the situation regarding physical characteristics, whose mode of transmission is unquestionable. As for mental or psychic characteristics, i.e., the strictly human ones, we must be much more cautious. Experimental proof is "obviously impossible, guinea pigs or fruit flies being useless here. As to simple observation, it does not usually permit a clear distinction between germinal or hereditary factors, and circumstantial or educative factors. Does a Bach give birth to a line of composers? He was the son of a court musician and taught his profession to his children. Are not the example of parents, environment, and family tradition enough in themselves to account for the musical contribution of a family in which, out of fifty-seven members, we find fourteen exceptional musicians; in six generations, we find scarcely two or three Bachs who are not endowed with some degree of musical talent." [2] To shed some light on these problems, a great deal of attention has been paid to the study of identical twins. In these cases, since the hereditary factors are necessarily identical, every observable difference theoretically stems from environment alone; but even these studies have not led to any entirely unequivocal body of knowledge.[3]

---

the difference in frequency is sufficiently pronounced and the differential genes sufficiently numerous to justify a racial distinction. But there is no other objective definition of human races."

[2] Andrée Tétry, "Hérédité ou milieu dans le psychique," *Synthèses,* May, 1950, p. 315.

[3] Andrée Tétry, in her study cited above, defines "the principles of the twin method." "The dissimilarities of identical twins necessarily derive only from the influence of environment: hence similar characteristics result from the influence of hereditary factors, and dissimilar characteristics from that of the environment. The differences between identical twins raised in unlike environments may be attributed to the environment, whereas the resemblances will derive from their heredity." After having tabulated the research done in this field, the author concludes: ". . . heredity thus exerts an essential influence on the psychic life; nevertheless, this influence seems to be less than in the case of physical characteristics . . . certain traits are hereditary; but social attitudes, especially, are largely a function of the environment; it is not always easy to discriminate between the influence of hereditary characteristics and the influence of environment or education."

In the last analysis, the question remains a highly disputed one.

As W. C. Boyd, one of the best specialists in this field, writes, summing up the latest research: "Klineberg, Dobzhansky and Montagu have stated that there is no clear evidence for the inheritance of mental traits in man, or for their being correlated with physical characteristics. With the second part of this statement we can agree without much more ado. The first part should probably be made somewhat less broad, for there is persuasive evidence that certain kinds of mental defects are inherited, and one is tempted to believe that genius, and perhaps other types of outstanding ability, are sometimes inherited, although this question is complicated by our ignorance of the extent to which environment plays a role. At any rate, there can be no doubt that great differences in mental ability do exist between certain individuals, although an adequate scale of measurement has not yet been devised, and it does not seem impossible that they are at least partly determined by hereditary factors. But we cannot assert that heredity does play any important role here without better data than those now available. We really do not know." [4]

Generally, we admit—or, more precisely, we postulate— that it is certain potentialities, certain predispositions, that are hereditary, and that education and environment will or will not permit them to be realized in this or that manner. So much for the question of individual heredity; and if we do not know much about it, as Boyd concludes, we know even less about racial heredity, where the already complex subject of hereditary character traits, aptitudes, etc., is further complicated by the question of how these are distributed among different human groups. Some authors, we shall see, categorically deny that they can be distributed with unequal frequencies, and their tests lead them to conclude the absolute equality of "races" from this point of view.

[4] William C. Boyd, *Genetics and the Races of Man*, Boston, 1950, pp. 13-14.

There remains, finally, the vast fringe of intermediate characteristics, half mental, half physical; in this category, in particular, belong the predisposition to "psychosomatic" illnesses, which are apparently determined (and also curable) by physical as well as by mental factors. We are very ignorant about this subject, too; yet this type of illness is found to be especially prevalent among Jews.

Now to return to the Jews. With respect to strictly physical characteristics, it is absolutely impossible to isolate any that occur among Jews with a specific frequency, thereby permitting us to categorize them. The myth of a Jewish "type" or "facial type" is certainly very persistent and in its way reflects an objective reality; but this reality corresponds to certain socially or professionally determined psychological attitudes, to certain forms of behavior, to a certain mimicry, so to speak, whose "acquired" character is incontestable. As to strictly hereditary characteristics, the confusion of Jewish types—blond or brunette, tall or short, brachycephalic or dolichocephalic—was already the despair of old-school anthropologists who were seeking a criterion impossible to find —and understandably, in view of what we have just said and what was said in Appendix A apropos of the subject of blood groups.

It is impossible to deny that the mental characteristics of the Jews offer much food for thought. Their intellectual and critical ability, expressed, for instance, by the percentage of recipients of the Nobel prize[5] and symbolized by those three shining lights of our time: Marx, Freud, Einstein (all German Jews!); their commercial and political dynamism; their extreme oversensitiveness; and the frequency of certain diseases among them. So many facts appeal to the imagination that at first glance it seems difficult to account for them on the basis of purely social factors. To clarify the subject, one

[5] Over 10% of the prizes (from 1895 to 1939, 21 Jewish recipients out of a total of 207); for Germany, over 30% (12 beneficiaries out of a total of 40 Germans), whereas the percentage of Jews in the chief European countries is less than 1%.

might pose the problem in such concrete terms as the following.

Let us assume that a whimsical prince, wanting to perform an experiment *in vivo,* made a large-scale exchange. Suppose he substituted a sufficiently large number (1,000 to 10,000) of newborn Jews from a ghetto for an equal number of newborn Christians selected from all strata of society, and arranged for the two groups to be raised as "Christians" and "Jews" respectively, in absolute ignorance of their true origins. After thirty years, would it be possible to distinguish any special characteristics whatsoever? Would the children of Christian origin, raised as Jews, furnish their quota of learned rabbis and shrewd tradesmen? Would those of Jewish origin, except for "statistically normal" exceptions, remain attached to their land or their trades?

The answer of the best contemporary specialists on the problem is that there would be no perceptible differences. As O. Klineberg, for example, writes, after having said that we must allow heredity its role in *individual* capacities:

"This is quite a different matter, however, from saying that *races* or *ethnic groups* differ in their psychological inheritance. For that there is no evidence. On the contrary, every racial group contains individuals who are well endowed, others who are inferior, and still others in between. As far as we can judge, the range of capacities and the frequency of occurrence of various levels of inherited ability are about the same in all racial groups. The scientist knows of no relation between race and psychology." [6]

Aren't these observations too schematic? Speaking as a cautious laboratory worker, Klineberg writes: "The scientist knows of no relation between race and psychology." Yet might there not be some imperceptible relationship that science at the present time is still unable to discover? This seems to be the opinion of Jean Rostand, for example, who writes:

". . . I do not exclude the idea that among racial groups

[6] O. Klineberg, *Race and Psychology,* New York, 1961.

there may be certain hereditary psychic differences that are too subtle to be revealed by ordinary tests. Still, this is only an impression, and I agree that we are not entitled to take such a differentiation into account so long as it has not been demonstrated by objective methods." [7]

And M. Rostand adds that the particular characteristics of the "Jewish mentality," if it could be demonstrated that they were hereditary, could only have appeared as a *mutation* (i.e., an accidental and spontaneous modification) of genes, then spread through the Jewish population as a result of natural selection. Admitting the possibility of mutations of the genes that determine mental predilections, it is certain that the circumstances of Jewish history were especially favorable to such selection in the ghettos. The continuous temptation of conversion, acting above all on the weak or the hesitant and inciting them to relinquish their Jewish allegiance, is an excellent example of natural selection. The practice of "reduction," an anachronistic eugenics invented in the eighteenth century by the Austrian government, which permitted only persons of strong and determined temperament to found a family, constitutes another, equally characteristic example.

This, then, is the only hypothesis modern genetics admits to explain a possible biological transmission of the "Jewish mentality." As for the other explanation that the uninitiated naturally think of—the hereditary transmission of acquired characteristics—we have seen how the geneticists regard it. To support their point of view, they cite both theoretical arguments[8] and the results of countless experiments on insects or animals.

[7] J. Rostand, personal communication to the author, September 4, 1952.

[8] "We simply cannot conceive of any way whereby a modification of the skin, muscles, or brain could be *inscribed* or registered in the germ cell, which contains neither skin, nor muscle, nor brain, nor even a rudiment of any of them.

"To be sure, it might be assumed that through the subtle influence of organic solidarity, a modification of the skin, for example, might entail a

Nonetheless, psychologists have reached other conclusions, derived from observations exclusively on the human being. Let us mention some of the most famous of these.

"Memory-traces" is what Sigmund Freud calls the "archaic" memories transmitted by inheritance. He resolutely passes over "biological fact, which at present absolutely rejects the inheritance of acquired characteristics. . . . Though we may admit that for the memory-traces in our archaic inheritance we have so far no stronger proof than those remnants of memory evoked by analytic work, which call for a derivation from phylogenesis, yet this proof seems to me convincing enough to postulate such a state of affairs. If things are different, then we are unable to advance one step further on our way, either in psychoanalysis or in mass psychology. It is bold, but inevitable. . . ." [9]

C. G. Jung, the Zurich psychiatrist who opposed so many Freudian concepts, speaks of "primordial images" or "archetypes"; but though the term is different, the idea is certainly the same, and Jung specifies: "It seems to me that their origin can be explained in no other way than by regarding them as the deposits of the oft-repeated experiences of humanity. . . ." [10] According to him, "the unconscious contains, as it were, two layers; first the personal, and secondly the collective. The personal layer does not go further than the earliest memories of infancy; the collective unconscious, on the other hand, all time before the actual dawn of infancy, that is, the residue of the life of the ancestors. . . ." [11]

---

general modification of the body, including the blood, and that in this way the germ cells might be slightly modified. But this does not explain how or why the modification would result in the identical reproduction of the parental modification in the succeeding generation.

"In short, while it may not seem impossible for a slight physical change to make its influence felt throughout the organism and even in the germ cell, it does seem impossible for the germ cell to 'photograph,' as Darwin once expressed it, the physical modification." (J. Rostand, *op. cit.*, pp. 104-105.)

[9] S. Freud, *Moses and Monotheism*, New York, 1955.

[10] C. G. Jung, *Two Essays on Analytical Psychology*, New York, 1953.

[11] C. G. Jung, *op. cit.* This author does not limit the existence of the

Is there, then, complete incompatibility between the more "materialistic" concepts of the biologists and the more "spiritualistic" concepts of the psychologists? We know how greatly the former reproach the latter for their too intuitive views and the insufficient precision of their methods.

Perhaps new discoveries in genetics will make it possible to reconcile them. This may come about, for example, by taking into account the special role that the mother seems to have in the transmission of hereditary factors. It has been possible to prove that in certain primitive creatures (protozoa, drosophila, etc.) and even, apparently, in the smaller mammals (mice) there is an additional method of transmitting characteristics, called *cytoplasmic* transmission, in which genes are not involved, the hereditary traits being transmitted by the mother alone, by means of particles lodged in the cytoplasm—the part of the ovule that surrounds the nucleus.[12] Even though there has not been any definite proof as yet that this occurs in the human race, it seems justifiable to postulate this possibility. This method of transmission seems to function particularly with regard to individual heredity; curiously enough, it confirms a traditional ruling found in the Talmud.[13]

Furthermore, an important role can be attributed to the influences which, transmitted by the placenta, affect the

---

"archetypes" to the human species: "Nothing prevents us, however, from assuming that certain archetypes are already present in animals; that they are involved in the peculiarities of the living organism itself, and are, therefore, immediate expressions of life whose nature cannot be further explained. . . . They behave empirically like agents that tend towards the repetition of these same experiences. For when an archetype appears in a dream, in a fantasy, or in life, it always brings with it a certain influence or power by virtue of which it either exercises a luminous or a fascinating effect, or impels to action." Let us add, in fairness, that Jung formulated his hypothesis before Freud did.

[12] On cytoplasmic heredity, see M. Caullery, *Génétique et Hérédité*, Paris, 1951, Chap. 11; and E. Guyénot, *L'Hérédité*, Paris, 1943, Chap. 22.

[13] According to the Talmud, in a mixed union, the child is regarded as Jewish if only the mother is Jewish, and is not Jewish if only the father is Jewish.

fetus during pregnancy—influences that we cannot call hereditary in the generally accepted sense of the word, and whose mechanism is still little known. We know, for example, that syphilis can be transmitted in this way ("precocious contamination"), and also an immunity acquired by the mother (which disappears soon after the birth of the child).

One may envision that some light will eventually be shed from this direction on the complex and disputed question of the transmission of mental characteristics. Also, it is probably a mistake to make a clear-cut distinction between "hereditary transmission" and "transmission by environment." Actually, between strictly genetic factors and external factors, educational and others, there appears to be a whole gamut of other possible influences, prenatal or immediately postnatal, not hereditary in the strict sense of the word, but functioning in a virtually unknown manner and contributing to the course of generations. From this point of view, the discontinuity caused by birth is more apparent than real. In such perspective, a psychological shock caused by the ritual of circumcision (which, as is known, the Jews alone practice several days after birth) may contribute to the formation of a "Jewish mentality"; similarly, the hunted existence of many a Jewish mother may serve as a prelude to the countless alerts and conscious shocks engraved on the Jewish memory in the course of centuries of persecution. This might well give rise to a perpetual "qui vive," a constantly lucid, vigilant alertness.

The most striking illustration of this state of constant vigilance and accessibility is the Jews' remarkable psychophysiological resistance to the effects of alcohol. This resistance is shown not only by traditional orthodox Jews—who had coined the saying, "the drunkard is a *goy*"—but by transplanted American Jews in completely new territory, and for the most part totally "assimilated" for several generations. Neither group feels any principle, ritual or otherwise, against drinking, and Jews sometimes drink a great deal; but in contrast to the patriarch Noah, they do not "discover their nakedness," that is, lose their lucidity and self-control, and for the most part, in comparison with non-Jews, do not suffer the various classic consequences of alcoholism. Heredity or environment? This is quite difficult to determine. Perhaps the nervous sensitivity of the Jews may be the price of this privilege; doubtless these two characteristics are closely linked. As has been noted, "There is no question that a people's relation to alcohol represents something very deep about it; so deep, however, that it is not easy to find a very good explanation of just what it is." [14]

In conclusion, let us note that a biologist as orthodox as the English J. B. Haldane postulates, in addition to heredity and environment, the existence of a possible "X factor," contributing to the formation of the personality, thus allowing for the exercise of human free will, with all the philosophical consequences this implies.

"If there is such a thing as freedom of the will in the more extreme sense, that comes under X. I regard it as unscientific to leave out X, if only for this reason, that if there is no such thing as X, if all differences between human beings are strictly determined, then it should be possible in the course of some centuries to prove that, let us say, 99.9 per cent at least

[14] N. Glazer, "Why Jews Stay Sober," *Commentary*, Feb. 1952. As for alcoholism and its consequences among the Jews, this author cites the following eloquent examples: "No matter what kind of ill effect from excessive indulgence we consider—alcoholic psychoses, alcoholism without psychosis, arrest for drunkenness, broken homes or marital unhappiness because of drink—we will not find many Jews affected.

"For example: in 1929-1931, Benjamin Maltzberg studied admissions to New York state hospitals for alcoholic psychoses, and calculated that the rate of first admissions for various foreign-born groups (per 100,000 in the population) was as follows: for the Irish, 25.6; Scandinavians, 7.8, Italians, 4.8, English, 4.3, Germans, 3.8, Jews, 0.5.

"In 1951, Robert Straus published a study of the religion of persons coming to clinics for treatment for alcoholism in eight cities; 1.6 per cent were Jews, though they formed about 7.5 per cent of the population of these cities.

"In 1941, a study was made of arrests for drunkenness in San Francisco; the rate for persons of Irish descent was calculated at no less than 7,876 per 100,000 in the population; for Jews, 27 per 100,000 in the population.

". . . The figures could be repeated *ad infinitum*."

of all differences of certain kinds are determined by differences of nature or nurture. To my mind a proof that 99.9 per cent were so determined would be very much more effective than an assertion on *a priori* grounds that 100 per cent were so determined. If therefore we leave X in our table we can say that in certain cases, for example that of skin colour, X is fairly small, and we may hope according to our philosophical views to prove either that X is negligible or considerable as regards differences of conduct. . . ." [15]

The inevitable conclusion, at the end of this long discussion, is that the role of heredity in the formation of Jewish mental characteristics is assuredly minor and that environment is the chief determinant. More precisely, the role of heredity seems to be at most that of a catalyst, operating only under certain conditions, which in this case are those of the Dispersion. This appears more clearly in the light of the enormous social experiment of Zionism than could be established by any laboratory experiments or psychological tests. Before our very eyes, the new generation of Israel, formed by a new environment, already, from a typological point of view, has little in common with its ancestors. But in many respects the young nation is still unique; hence, only future generations, still more detached and further removed from the Dispersion, will conclusively confirm or invalidate the various hypotheses that have been advanced.

[15] J. B. Haldane, *Heredity and Politics,* London, 1938, p. 43.

NOTES

1 Anti-Semitism in Pagan Antiquity

(1) This quotation, like those that follow below, is taken from Th. Reinach's *Textes d'auteurs grecs et latins relatifs au judaïsme*, Paris, 1895.

(2) Marcel Simon, *Verus Israël*, Paris, 1948, p. 241.

(3) Cosmas l'Indicopleuste, "Topographia Christiana," in Migne, *Patrologiae cursus completus*, series Graeca, Vol. 81, p. 172.

(4) Jean Juster, *Les Juifs dans l'Empire romain*, Paris, 1914, Vol. 2, p. 313.

(5) With regard to dating the Book of Esther, see especially Adolphe Lods, *Histoire de la littérature hébraïque et juive*, Paris, 1950, pp. 797-99.

(6) This speech is quoted by Philo of Alexandria. (Cf. Cohn and Wendland edition of the complete works, Leipzig, 1908, Vol. 3, Sec. 123.)

(7) *Lettres édifiantes et curieuses écrites des Missions étrangères*, Paris, 1773, Vol. 24, p. 62.

(8) Account of the Arab traveler Ibn Khordadbeh, "Le Livre des routes et des provinces," *Journal asiatique*, 1865, Vol. 5.

(9) *Lettres édifiantes et curieuses*, Vol. 18, p. 53.

2 Anti-Semitism and Early Christianity

(10) H. Lietzmann, *Histoire de l'Église ancienne*, Paris, 1950, Vol. 1, p. 58.

(11) Ch. Guignebert, *Jésus*, Paris, 1947, pp. 567, 573.

(12) J. Klausner, *Jésus de Nazareth*, Paris, 1933, p. 41.

(13) Tacitus, *Annales*, XV, 44; Pliny the Younger, *Epistolae*, X, 96-97.

(14) Cf. Marcel Simon, *op. cit.*, p. 128.

(15) H. Lietzmann, *op. cit.*, Vol. 2, p. 156.

(16) Cf. Marcel Simon, *op. cit.*, p. 153.

(17) Cf. Marcel Simon, *op. cit.*, p. 325.

(18) *Contra Celsum*, 4, 23; Migne, *op. cit.*, Vol. 11, p. 1,060.

(19) Aphraate, *Homelies*, 21, 1. (Cf. Marcel Simon, *op. cit.*, p. 119.)

(20) Migne, *op. cit.*, Vol. 46, p. 685.

(21) Migne, *Patrologiae cursus completus, series prima* [Latin], Vol. 25, p. 830.

3 The Western Jews in the High Middle Ages

(22) Cf. B. Blumenkranz, "Les Auteurs latins chrétiens du Moyen Age sur les Juifs et le judaïsme," *Revue des Études Juives* [cited below as *R.E.J.*], Vol. 109, 1948.

(23) Cf. R. Anchel, *Les Juifs de France*, p. 24, as well as all of Chap. 1.

(24) Gregory of Tours, *Historia Francorum*, V, 6.

(25) In Narbonne and in the old priory of Saint Orens in Auch. (Cf. E. Salin, *La Civilisation mérovingienne* . . . , Paris, 1950, p. 282.)

(26) From the way in which Pseudo-Fregedarius' chronicle relates this episode, it seems more symbolic than real. It was upon the urging of Heraclius, Emperor of Byzantium—that Byzantium where, as we have seen, Christian state anti-Semitism was constituted into a body of doctrine—that Dagobert took this measure.

(27) Account of the contemporary Arab traveler, Ibn Khordadbeh, "Le Livre des routes et des provinces," *Journal asiatique*, 1865, Vol. 5, pp. 512-15. Ibn Khordadbeh designates the Jewish tradesmen as Radanites. (Cf. also L. Rabinowitz, *Jewish Merchants . . . A Study of the Radanites*, London, 1948; and Simonsen, "Les Marchands juifs appelés Radanites," *R.E.J.*, Vol. 54, p. 141.)

(28) This refers especially to a passage of canon 50 of the Council of Paris of 829 (*"Si ergo Judei . . . sabbatum carnaliter custodientes eo die, nulla potentate terrena compellante, ab operibus ruralibus se abstinent"*). (*Mon. Germ. Hist.*, II, IIa, p. 643.)

(29) In chronological order:

1. *Ad proceres palati consultatio et supplicatio de baptismo judaicorum mancipiorum* (written about 824).

2. *Ad proceres palati contra praeceptum impium de baptismo judaicorum mancipiorum* (written about 826).

3. *Ad eumdem imperatorum de insolentia judaeorum* (written about 827).

4. *Ad eumdem imperatorum de judaicis superstitionibus* (collective memorandum of the bishops Agobard, Faova, and Bernard, annexed to the foregoing).

5. *Exhortatoria ad Nibridium episcopum narbonensem de cavendo convictu et societatae judaica* (written about 828). (Migne, *Patrologiae cursus completus, series prima* [Latin], Vol. 104.)

(30) "Amulonis Epistola contra judaeos," Migne, *Patrologiae*, Vol. 116, p. 141.

(31) Or, more generally, persecutions, except for their expulsion from Sens in 876 by Archbishop Anségise ("Chronique Odoranni," Migne, *Patrologiae* [Latin], Vol. 142, p. 771) and the annual vexations inflicted upon them in the Midi (Béziers, Toulouse) on the occasion of

the Easter holiday. It is true that at the period in question, the references to Jews in the chronicles are still quite rare; but this very scarcity of information, in a period whose sources have become numerous, confirms what we know elsewhere about peaceful cohabitation.

(32) Hebrew maunscript from Parma (No. 563 of the Rossi catalogue). As is often the case for Jewish sources, the date of the expulsion is not given, but the mention in the manuscript of Robert the Pious and Duke Richard makes it possible to assume the historicity of the event and to place it about 1010.

(33) Raoul Glaber, *Les Histoires,* Book 3, E. Pognon ed., Paris, 1947.

(34) Adémar de Chabannes, *Chronique,* Book 3, Chap. 47, Pognon ed.

(35) Pertz, *Monumenta,* II, 81, as well as Hebrew sources, which allow us to assume that the expulsion ordered by Emperor Henry II also occurred in other German cities. (Cf. Graetz, *Geschichte der Juden,* Vol. 5, p. 495, note 22.)

(36) Adémar de Chabannes, *Chronique,* Book 3, Chap. 52. The chronicler mentions an earthquake in Rome, caused by the sacrilegious practices of the Jews, but the coincidence of the event with the expulsions in the other cities is striking.

(37) *Würdtwein, nova subsida diplom.,* I, 127.

PART TWO | The Age of the Crusades

4 The Fateful Summer of 1096

(38) Thus Foucher de Chartres: "Who has ever heard of so many nations, of different languages, being united into a single army: Frenchmen, Flemings, Frisians, Gauls, Bretons, Allobrogians, Lorrainese, Germans, Bavarians, Normans, Scots, Englishmen, Acquitains, Italians. . . . Though divided into so many tongues, we all seemed so many brothers and near relations united in one spirit by the love of the Lord! . . ."

Other chroniclers (Guibert de Nogent, Raimond d'Agile, Robert le Noir) compare the Crusaders to the twelve tribes of Israel; they are, then, a collectivity to which its community has just been revealed.

(39) Orderici Vitali, *Historiae,* III, 495.

(40) Bouquet, *Recueil des historiens des Gaules et de la France,* Vol. 12, p. 411.

(41) Aronius, *Regesten,* No. 177. The chronicler Guillaume de Tyr also relates that the Rhenish Jews did not expect persecutions.

(42) This is how matters turned out in Trier, according to the account of Solomon bar Simeon. (Aronius, *Regesten,* No. 180.)

(43) Albert d'Aix, Book 1.

(44) Aronius, *Regesten,* No. 189.

(45) "Gest. abbat. Trudon," XI, 6, *Monumenta Germaniae Historia* [hereafter referred to as *M.G.H.*], *Scripta Sanctorum* [hereafter, SS], Vol. 10, p. 304.

(46) "Hermann opusculum de sua conversione," Migne, *Patrologiae* [Latin], Vol. 170, pp. 805 ff.

(47) Bouquet, Vol. 14, p. 642.

(48) Account of Rabbi Ephraim bar Jacob of Bonn. (Neubauer and Stern, *Hebräische Berichte über die Judenverfolgungen während der Kreuzzüge,* Berlin, 1892, p. 188.)

(49) *St. Bernhardi epistolae,* No. 365.

(50) Dom Gui Alexis Lobineau, *Histoire de Bretagne,* Paris, 1707, Vol. 1, p. 235.

(51) Léon Bloy, *Le Salut par les Juifs,* Chap. 7.

(52) "Annales Pragenses," *M.G.H.,* SS, Vol. 2, p. 120.

(53) "Annales Wirziburgenses," *M.G.H.,* SS, Vol. 2, p. 246.

(54) "Bernoldi chronicon," *M.G.H.,* SS, Vol. 5, p. 464.

(55) "Ekkehardi chronicon universale," *M.G.H.,* SS, Vol. 6, p. 208.

(56) "Hugonis chronicon," *M.G.H.,* SS, Vol. 8, p. 474.

(57) "Annales sax.," *M.G.H.,* SS, Vol. 6, p. 729.

(58) *Miracle de saint Hildefonse,* Langfors ed., Helsinki, 1937.

(59) *Les Miracles de Nôtre Dame,* Paquet ed., Paris, 1857.

(60) *Les Miracles de Nôtre Dame,* Miélet ed., Paris, 1929.

(61) "Disputoison de la Sinagogue et de Sainte Église," A. Jubinal, *Mystères inédits,* Paris, 1837, Vol. 2, p. 404.

(62) Migne, *Patrologiae cursus completus,* series prima [Latin], Vol. 214, 957.

(63) "Miracle de saint Nicholas et du Juif," *Early Mysteries,* Wright ed., London, 1939, pp. 11 ff.

(64) "Ludus de Antechristo de Tegernsee," W. Meyer, *Gesammelte Abhandlungen zur mitellateinischen Rhytmik,* Berlin, 1905, Vol. 1, pp. 150 ff.

(65) Cf. Hubner, *Promenade autour du monde,* Paris, 1873, Vol. 2, pp. 385-400; also Strack, *Das Blut im Glauben und Aberglauben der Menschheit,* Munich, 1900, p. 54.

(66) Cf. *Revue des Deux Mondes,* April, 1932, pp. 519-56.

(67) ". . . nullo modo sanori vos posse ab illo quo punimini verecundissimo cruciatu, nisi solo sanguine Christiano; sanguinem intelligentes christiani cuius libet . . ." Thomas Cantipratanus, *Bonnum univ.,* Colvenerius ed., Chap. 29, Sec. 23, pp. 304 ff.

(68) A. Jessopp and M. R. James, *St. William of Norwich,* Cambridge, 1896.

(69) Aronius, *Regesten,* No. 245.

(70) Jean des Preis, called d'Outremeuse, "Ly Myreur des Histors" in *Chroniques belges,* A. Borgnet ed., Brussels, 1864, Vol. 4, p. 403.

The chronicle, which dates from the fourteenth century, is in all probability a compilation of older chronicles that have not come down to us.

(71) At Gloucester (1168), at Bury Saint-Edmunds (1181), and at Bristol (1183). (Cf. Cecil Roth, *A History of the Jews in England*, Oxford, 1941, p. 13.)

(72) Neubauer and Stern, *op. cit.*

(73) At Lauda, at Bischofsheim, at Wolfshagen, at Haguenau, at Fulda. (*M.G.H.*, "Ann. Ephord.," Vol. 16, p. 31; "Gesta Senon Eccl.," Vol. 17, p. 178; Vol. 25, p. 324. See also the Hebrew source cited above.)

(74) "Golden Bull" of Frederick II. (Text published in *Zeitschrift für die Geschichte der Juden in Deutschland*, Vol. 1, 1887, pp. 137-44.)

(75) *Ibid.*

(76) *Ibid.*

(77) Élie Berger, *Les Registres d'Innocent IV*, Paris, 1884, p. 403.

(78) At Regensburg (1476), at Milan (1476), at Venice (1480); later (1496) expulsion from Styria and from Carinthia, on the same pretext. (Scherer, *Die Rechtsverhältnisse der Juden in den deutsch-oesterreichischen Ländern*, Leipzig, 1901, pp. 614-15.)

(79) Cf. *Endinger Judenspiel*, Karl von Amira ed., Halle, 1883.

(80) Cf. article "Bern," in *The Universal Jewish Encyclopedia*, New York, 1948, Vol. 2.

(81) P. Browe, "Die Hostienschändungen der Juden im Mittelalter," *Römische Quartalschrift*, 1926, Vol. 34, pp. 169-71.

(82) J. Trachtenberg, *The Devil and the Jews*, New Haven: Yale University Press, 1943, p. 125.

(83) Lateran Council, IV, Can. 67-70, Mansi, Vol. 22, pp. 1,054 ff. The other measures concerning the Jews dealt with abusive rates of interest collected by certain Jewish usurers, the exclusion of the Jews from public office, the case of converted Jews who continued to observe certain Jewish rites, and the cancellation of interest on Crusaders' debts to the Jews.

(84) Aronius, *Regesten*, No. 725.

(85) Cf. Cecil Roth, *A History of the Jews in England*, Oxford, 1941, p. 95.

(86) Cf. C. Margolioth, *Catalogue of Hebrew and Samaritan Manuscripts in the British Museum*, Vol. 4, pp. 402 ff.; Z. Ameizenowa, *Biblja Hebraiska XIV-go Wieku w Krakowie i jej Dekoracja Malarska*, Cracow, 1929; B. Italiener, *Die Darmstädter Pessach-Haggadah*, Leipzig, 1927.

(87) See in this connection Bernard Blumenkranz, *Disputations*, Minuit ed., Paris, 1955. (Work consulted in manuscript.)

(88) *Extractiones de Talmud*, a work composed by order of Eudes de Châteauroux; and Hebrew manuscript *Vikkuah Rabbenu Yehiel mi-Paris*. (Cf. I. Loeb, "La Controverse de 1240 sur le Talmud," *R.E.J.*, Vol. 1, 1880.)

(89) Von der Hagen, *Minnesinger*, Vol. 3, p. 342.

(90) Haupt, *Zeitschrift für deutsches Altertum*, Vol. 4, 2, p. 1,185.

(91) Von der Hagen, *op. cit.*, p. 431.

5   The Jewish Reactions

(92) Aronius, *Regesten*, Nos. 232-50.

(93) W. Roscher, *System der Volkswirtschaft*, Vol. 2, p. 335.

(94) For this quotation, as for those that follow, see J. Bernfeld, "Das Zinsverbot bei den Juden nach talmudisch-rabbinischen Recht," *Das Licht*, No. 8, Berlin, 1928; and J. Parkes, *The Jew in the Medieval Community*, London, 1938, p. 340.

(95) "Judaei, ut & eorum bona, olim Baronum fuere in quorum dominiis habitabant," *Statuts de Saint Louis*, 1270, Book 1, Chap. 129. (Cf. *Le Nouvel Examen de l'usage général des fiefs en France . . .* , by M. Brussel, counselor to the king, Paris, 1727, Vol. 1, p. 575.)

(96) *M.G.H.*, "Constitutiones et acta publica," Vol. 3, pp. 1 ff.

(97) H. Géraud, *Paris sous Philippe le Bel d'après des documents originaux, et notamment d'après un manuscript contenant le rôle de la taille imposée aux habitants de Paris en 1292*, Paris, 1837. It appears from this study that a Jewish taxpayer paid on the average as much as a Christian taxpayer, while a Lombard paid eight times more.

(98) Thus, a sum of 215,000 livres was collected in 1295 from the Jews of France. (Cf. Robert Fawtier, *L'Europe occidentale de 1270 à 1328*, Paris, 1938, p. 211.)

(99) Roger of Wendover, *Flores Historiarum*, Foxe ed., p. 231.

(100) Bouquet, Vol. 13, p. 315; Vol. 17, pp. 5-8.

(101) Laurière, *Ordonnances des rois de France*, Vol. 1, p. 44.

(102) Petit-Dutaillis, *Étude sur la vie et le règne de Louis VIII*, Paris, 1894, pp. 424-27.

(103) *Layettes*, Vol. 2, p. 192, No. 2083.

(104) *Geffroi de Paris, chronique rimée*, Lines 3121-27, 3162-65; Bouquet, Vol. 22, p. 119.

(105) Laurière, *Ordonnances des rois de France*, Vol. 1, p. 595.

(106) This is apparent in a rabbinical *responsum* that describes in some detail the commercial enterprises of the Jew Alexander of Andernach, murdered on a business trip to Koblenz. (*Responsa* of Eliezer ben Joel of Bonn, Book Or Zarua, I, 194; Aronius, *Regesten*, No. 345.)

(107) Decree of Emperor Frederick III, for November 6, 1445. The purpose of this decree was to forbid the Jews most of their commercial activities. (Cf. Scherer, *Die Rechtverhältnisse der Juden in den deutsch-österreichischen Ländern*, Leipzig, 1901, p. 473.)

(108) The Council of Vienna (1267), discussed on pp. 105 f., notes "the insolence of certain Jews who attract Christians to Judaism and cause them to undergo circumcision." (Council of Vienna, Can. 15-19; *M.G.H.*, Vol. 9, p. 702.)

(109) The *Memorbücher* (records of the persecutions) mention a certain number of proselytes. (Cf. Note 131.)

(110) Ottokar von Horneck, "Reimchronik," *M.G.H.*, "Scriptores rerum Austricarum," Vol. 3, pp. 782 ff. This author states that Emperor

Albrecht I demanded "his" Jews from Philip the Fair, and that the latter was obliged to hand them over, first despoiling them of all their goods. Evidently our chronicler exaggerated, since matters did not turn out this way; but there must have been some intervention, and it is significant that it could have been interpreted in this way.

(111) Voltaire, *Dictionnaire philosophique,* Paris ed., 1879, Vol. 3, p. 525.

(112) Montesquieu, *De L'Espirit des Lois,* XXI, 20, pt. II, p. 35.

(113) Cf. A. Neubauer, "Le Memorbuch de Mayence, essai sur la littérature de complaintes," *R.E.J.,* Vol. 4, 1882.

(114) Three Hebrew chronicles relate the events of the First Crusade: that of Solomon bar Simeon, that of Eliezer ben Nathan, and an anonymous chronicle. All three appear in Neubauer and Stern, *Hebraïsche Berichte über die Judenverfolgungen während der Kreuzzüge,* Berlin, 1892, whose text we follow.

(115) In this connection, see the introduction by M. Bresslau to the work by Neubauer and Stern referred to above:

"The connoisseurs of neo-Hebrew literature know that the medieval Jews avoided describing the details of non-Jewish worship by their usual names. In our chronicles, the following six expressions are the ones most frequently avoided: (1) 'Christ,' (2) 'Church,' (3) 'Holy Sepulcher,' (4) 'Christians,' (5) 'baptize,' (6) 'cross.' These were not mentioned, and opposite concepts were substituted for them; for instance, for (1) 'the hanged man,' 'the son of the criminal,' 'the hanged bastard'; for (2) 'house of corruption,' 'horror,' 'house of alien services'; for (3) 'their error,' 'place of shame'; for (4) 'the impure uncircumcised'; for (5) 'corrupt,' 'sprinkle with dirty water'; for (6) 'evil sign,' etc. Ultimately these expressions became typical and in a sense formal."

(116) Quoted from A. Darmesteter, "L'Autodafé de Troyes," *R.E.J.,* Vol. 2, 1881.

(117) Neubauer and Stern, *op. cit.,* pp. 106-107.

(118) M. Güdemann, *Geschichte des Erziehungswesens und der Kultur der abendländischen Juden,* Vienna, 1880, Vol. 1, p. 89.

(119) *Ibid.,* p. 30.

(120) *Or Zarua* of Rabbi Isaac ben Moses of Vienna, No. 416.

(121) Manuscript from the Oxford library, reproduced by M. Güdemann, *op. cit.,* Vol. 1, pp. 92-106.

(122) *Sachsenspiegel Landesrecht,* Homeyer ed., 1861, Vol. 3, p. 306, 7, Secs. 1-4. In this connection see the masterful study of Guido Kisch, *The Jews in Medieval Germany,* Chicago, 1949.

(123) *Sachsenspiegel,* Vol. 1, p. 63, Sec. 3.

(124) Cecil Roth, "The Medieval Conception of the Jew," *Essays in Memory of Linda M. Miller,* New York, 1938, pp. 171-90.

(125) "Dispute de Charlot le Juif et du Barbier de Melun," in Rutebeuf, *Le Miracle de Théophile,* by Gustave Cohen, Centre de Documentation universitaire, Paris, 1934.

(126) *Histoire littéraire de la France,* Vol. 23, p. 657.

(127) Von der Hagen, *Minnesinger,* Vol. 2, p. 259.

(128) Cf. "Philo-Lexicon," *Handbuch des jüdischen Wissens*, Berlin, 1938, plate 7.

(129) Thus the famous *Aaron fil diaboli* of the Forest Roll of Essex (1277). Similarly, the oldest English illumination showing Jews, which dates from 1233, shows them conspiring with devils. (Cf. J. Trachtenberg, *The Devil and the Jews*, New York, 1943.)

(130) St. Thomas Aquinas, "De regimine Judaeorum," Sec. 2, *Opuscule omnia*, J. Perrier ed., Paris, Vol. 1, pp. 213-14. The text probably dates from 1261.

PART THREE | The Century of the Devil

(131) Gottfried von Ensmingen gives the figure of 100,000 (*Gesta Rudolphi;* Bohmer, *Fontes rerum german.*, Vol. 2, pp. 144 ff.). Other details about Rindfleisch's persecutions are given in the *Annales Alt.* (Bohmer, p. 546), as well as by the Chron. Florianense (*Rerum Austriac. scriptores*, Vol. 1, p. 225). Furthermore, the *Memorbuch* of the Jewish community of Nürnberg contained the nominative list of over 5,000 victims who were killed in forty-one localities of Bavaria and Franconia between April and October, 1298. (Cf. *Das Martyrologium des Nürnberger Memorbuches*, S. Salfeld ed. Berlin, 1898, pp. 29-58.)

6 Background: The Fourteenth Century

(132) Rhymed chronicle attributed to Geffroi de Paris, Bouquet, Vol. 22, p. 119.

(133) Cf. H. S. Lucas, "The Great European Famine of 1315, 1316, and 1317, in *Speculum*, 1930.

(134) Continuer of Guillaume de Nangis (Bouquet, Vol. 20, p. 626). Concerning the "Pastoureaux" see also the chronicles of Saint Denis (Bouquet, Vol. 20, pp. 704ff.), the continuer of Giraud de Frachet (Bouquet, Vol. 21, pp. 54ff.), fragment of an anonymous chronicle (Bouquet, Vol. 21, p. 152), memoriali Iohannis to Sancta Victore (Bouquet, Vol. 21, pp. 671ff.), Bernardo Guidonis (Bouquet, Vol. 21, p. 731).

(135) *Shevet Yehudah*, chronicle of Ibn Verga, Wiener ed., Hanover, 1856.

(136) This, in particular, is the hypothesis of the historian Georg Caro (*Sozial-und Wirtschaftsgeschichte der Juden*, Frankfurt, 1924, Vol. 2, p. 188).

(137) J. Trachtenberg (*The Devil and the Jews*, New York, 1943, p. 101) indicates (without giving sources) a precedent in the canton of Vaud in 1308. Another seems to have occurred in Franconia in 1319. (*M.G.H.*, Vol. 12, p. 416.)

(138) Fragment of an anonymous chronicle. (Bouquet, Vol. 21, p. 152.)

(139) Cf. Robert Anchel, *Les Juifs de France*, Paris, 1946, pp. 87 ff.

(140) Wiener, *Regesten zur Geschichte der Juden in Mittelalter*, Hanover, 1862, Nos. 109, 123, 134.

(141) Aretin, *Geschichte der Juden in Baiern*, Landshut, 1803, p. 21.

(142) "Chronic. Zwetl.," *M.G.H.*, SS, Vol. 9, p. 683.

(143) Stobbe, *Die Juden in Deutschland während des Mittelalters*, Braunschweig, 1866, p. 169.

(144) A. L. Maycock, "A Note on the Black Death," in *The Nineteenth Century*, March, 1925.

(145) Königshoven, *Strasburger Chronik*, Schilter ed., Notes, pp. 1,031-40.

(146) Baronius, *Ann. eccles. ad annum 1348*, No. 33.

(147) Königshoven, p. 296.

(148) A. Colville, "Les Écrits contemporains sur la peste de 1348 à 1350," *Histoire Littéraire de la France*, Paris, 1937, Vol. 37, p. 404.

(149) Jean de Preis, called d'Outremeuse, "Ly Myreur des Histors," in *Chroniques belges*, Stanislas Bormans ed., Brussels, 1880, Vol. 6, p. 387.

(150) *Chronique de Simon von Grünau*, Perlbach ed., Vol. 1, p. 600.

(151) Conrad von Megenberg, *Das Buch der Natur* [about 1350], Hugo Schultz ed., Gräfswald, 1897, p. 92.

(152) Senkenberg, *Selecta*, Vol. 1, pp. 634 ff.

(153) L. Rothschild, *Die Judengemeinden zu Mainz, Speyer und Worms*, p. 9.

(154) J. Menczel, *Beiträge zur Geschichte der Stadt Mainz*, p. 24.

(155) Guido Kisch, *The Jews in Medieval Germany*, Chicago, 1949, pp. 41-44.

(156) Laurière, *Ordonnances des rois de France*, Vol. 3, pp. 473 ff.

(157) *Ibid.*, Vol. 6, p. 340.

(158) *Ibid.*, Vol. 6, p. 562.

(159) *Ibid.*, Vol. 7, pp. 225 ff., 589.

(160) *Ibid.*, Vol. 7, pp. 557 and 792. (There were two successive decrees, dated respectively April 4, 1392, and April 25, 1393.)

(161) *Ibid.*, Vol. 7, p. 675.

(162) "*Ir uns und das Riche mit Leib und mit gut an gehoert, und mugen da mit schaffen, tun und handeln, was wir wollen und wie uns gut dunchet,*" *Monumenta Zollerana*, Vol. 4, p. 110.

(163) E. Hecht, "Geschichte der Juden im Trier'schen," *Monatsschrift für die Geschichte und die Wissenschaft des Judentums*, Vol. 7, p. 182.

(164) Schreiber, *Urkundenbuch der Stadt Freiburg*, Vol. 2, pp. 358 ff.; Ulrich, *Sammlung jüdischer Geschichten in der Schweiz*, pp. 18, 118.

(165) Lacomblet, *Urkundenbuch für die Geschichte des Niederrheins*, Vol. 4, No. 177.

(166) Cf. J. Trachtenberg, *Jewish Magic and Superstition*, New York, 1939, p. 7.

(167) Élie Scheid, *Histoire des Juifs d'Alsace*, Paris, 1887, p. 74.

(168) J. Dietrich, *Revue d'Alsace*, 7th year, p. 408.

(169) Cf. Strauss, *Die Judengemeinde Regensburg im ausgehenden Mittelalter*, Heidelberg, 1932.

(170) Otto Stobbe, *Die Juden in Deutschland während des Mittelalters*, Braunschweig, 1886, p. 193. The author was a well-known specialist in medieval German law.

(171) Cf. Guido Kisch, "The Jewish Execution in Medieval Germany," *Historia Judaica*, 1943, Vol. 5, pp. 103-32.

(172) The *Magdeburg-Breslauer systematisches Schöffenrecht*, which dates from the fourteenth century, reads as follows (Vol. 3, p. 2, 38): ". . . with regard to money, the oath of the Jews is not admissible against Christians, and a Jew cannot cause a Christian to be sentenced with regard to money. . . ." (Cf. Guido Kisch, *The Jews in Medieval Germany*, Chicago, 1949, p. 262.)

(173) Cf. J. Scherer, *Die Rechtsverhältnisse der Juden in den deutsch-oesterreichischen Ländern*, Leipzig, 1901, p. 297.

(174) Israel Isserlein, *Responsa*, No. 235.

(175) Mansi, *Concilia*, Vol. 29, pp. 98 ff.

(176) Rabbi Lipmann Mülhausen, *Nitzahon* [written about 1410]. (Cf. note 233.)

(177) Cf. H. Graetz, *Geschichte der Juden*, Leipzig, 1864, Vol. 8, pp. 416 ff., note 3.

7 The Image of the Jew

(178) C. Lenient, *La Satire en France*, Paris, 1859, p. 193.

(179) *La Vallée des Pleurs*, Julien Sée ed., Paris, 1881, p. 67.

(180) Cf. in this connection the remarkable study by Jean Stengers, *Les Juifs dans les Pays-Bas au Moyen Age*, Brussels, 1950.

(181) *Ibid.*, p. 56.

(182) F. J. Child, *English and Scottish Popular Ballads*, Boston (n.d.).

(183) Geoffrey Chaucer, "The Prioress' Tale," *The Canterbury Tales*.

(184) Thus in the "Miracle de l'Agnolo Ebreo" in d'Ancone, *Le Sacre Rappresentazione*, Turin, 1872, Vol. 3, pp. 485 ff.

(185) See the exhaustive study by H. Michelson, *The Jew in Early English Literature*, Amsterdam, 1926.

(186) This comprehensive catalogue was made by M. Marcel Bulard in his masterful study *Le Scorpion, symbole du peuple juif dans l'art religieux des XIVe, XVe, XVIe siècles*, Paris, 1935, p. 42. M. Bulard has drawn mainly on the *Mystères de la Passion* by Arnoul Gréban.

(187) "Maria Himmelfahrt," in *Altdeutsche Schauspiele*, F. J. Mone ed., Leipzig, 1841.

(188) *Le Mistère de la saincte hostie, nouvellement imprimé à Paris*, A. Pontier, Aix, 1817.

(189) *Les Miracles de Notre-Dame, compilés par Jehan Miélot, secrétaire de Philippe le Bon, duc de Bourgogne*, H. de Laborde ed., Paris, 1929, p. 98.

(190) "Das Drama des Mittelalters," *Deutsche Nationalliteratur*, Fronig ed., Vol. 14, pp. 767 ff.

(191) *Mistère de la Resurrection de Notre-Seigneur, Jésus-Crist . . .* , Antoine Vérard ed., Paris (classification Res. y f. 15 of the Bibliothèque Nationale).

(192) We find the Church-Synagogue symbols on such great cathedrals of the thirteenth century as Notre Dame of Paris, Notre Dame of Rheims, and Saint Seurin of Bordeaux. (Cf. P. Hildenfinger, "La Figure de la Synagogue dans l'art du Moyen Age," *R.E.J.*, 1903, Vol. 47, pp. 187 ff.)

(193) See in this connection M. Bulard, *op. cit.*

(194) See E. Fuchs, *Die Juden in der Karrikatur*, Munich, 1921, pp. 114-21, and illustrations 6, 7, 8, 9, 15, and 16.

(195) H. Ch. Lea, *A History of the Inquisition of the Middle Ages*, New York, 1888, Vol. 3, p. 659.

(196) *Ibid.*, p. 648.

(197) Maurice Garçon et Jean Vinchon, *Le Diable, Étude historique, critique et medicale*, Paris, 1926.

(198) Thus in the *Judenrecht* of Breslau (collection Regulae juris "Ad Decus," late fourteenth century), two successive paragraphs which deal with sorcerers and heretics. (Cf. Guido Kisch, *The Jews in Medieval Germany*, Chicago, 1949, p. 360.)

(199) F. Vernet, "Juifs et chrétiens," *Dictionnaire apologétique de la Foi catholique*, Paris, 1913, p. 1,680.

(200) See the many engravings, chiefly of German origin, reproduced in Georg Liebe, "Das Judentum" (*Monographien aus deutschen Kulturgeschichte*, Leipzig, 1903), and in Eduard Fuchs, *op. cit.*

(201) See the article "Jude" in *Handwörterbuch des deutschen Aberglaubens*, Berlin and Leipzig, 1931, Vol. 4, pp. 808-18.

(202) *Ibid.*

(203) M. M. Gorce, "Vincent Ferrer," article in *Dictionnaire de Théologie catholique*, Paris, 1947, Vol. 15^2, p. 3,042.

(204) *Ibid.*, p. 3,038.

(205) H. Graetz, *Geschichte der Juden*, Leipzig, 1864, Vol. 8, p. 118.

(206) S. Dubnow, *History of the Jews in Europe* [in Russian], Riga, 1936, Vol. 2, p. 264.

(207) L. de Kerval, *Saint Jean de Capistran, son siècle, son influence*, Paris, 1887, p. 10.

(208) *Ibid.*, p. 125.

(209) *Ibid.*, p. 64.

(210) M. Brann, *Geschichte der Juden in Schlesien*, Breslau, 1896-1910, pp. 115-49.

(211) Abbé de Surrel de Saint-Julien, *Un grand bienfaiteur du peuple*, p. 156.

(212) E. Flornoy, *Le Bienheureux Bernardin de Feltre*, Paris, 1897, p. 70.

(213) *Ibid.*, p. 122.

(214) *Ibid.*, p. 129.

(215) "Hincmari remensis annales," *M.G.H.*, SS 504; Richeri, *Hist. Lib.*, Vol. 3, *M.G.H.*, SS Vol. 2, p. 996.

(216) J. Trachtenberg, *The Devil and the Jews*, New York, 1943, pp. 97, 238.

(217) A. Fürst, *Christen und Juden* (Strasbourg, 1892, p. 85), which refers to *Reconvenciones caritativas a los Professores de la Ley de Moyses* by Geronimo Feijoo y Montenegro (about 1750).

(218) E. Boutaric, *Saint Louis et Alfonse de Poitiers*, Paris, 1870, p. 87.

(219) "In the days of King Juan, son of King Henry, new sufferings accumulated. . . . And it was also decided that no Jew would be a surgeon or physician, except for the king's physician. . . ." (*Shevet Yehudah, Chronik von Salomon ibn Verga*, Wiener ed., Hanover, 1856, p. 180). (Cf. also F. Baer, *Die Juden in christlichen Spanien*, Vol. 1, p. 35, note 2.)

(220) I. Münz, *Die jüdischen Ärzte in Mittelalter*, Frankfurt, 1922, p. 51.

(221) *Ibid.*, p. 54.

(222) *Ibid.*, p. 55.

(223) *Ibid.*, p. 49.

(224) I. Kracauer, *Geschichte der Juden in Frankfurt am Main*, Frankfurt, 1925-1927, Vol. 3, p. 264.

(225) S. Krauss, *Geschichte der jüdischen Ärzte*, Vienna, 1930, p. 56.

(226) E. Flornoy, *op. cit.*, p. 136.

(227) *L'Incrédulité et mescréance du sortilège pleinement convaincues* by P. de l'Ancre, Counselor to the King in his Council of State, Paris, 1622, Treatise 8, pp. 446 ff.

(228) J. Huizinga, *The Waning of the Middle Ages*, New York, 1954, p. 168.

(229) Quoted in J. Janssen, *Die allgemeinen Zustände des deutschen Volkes beim Ausgang des Mittelalters*, Freiburg, 1887, Vol. 1, p. 396.

(230) Document quoted by J. Leman in *L'Entrée des Israélites dans la société chrétienne*, Paris, 1886, p. 11.

(231) Thus, for example, Rabbi Joslein ben Moses, in the manuscript *Leket Yosher*, Munich Library, fol. 88.

(232) Léon Bloy, *Le Salut par les Juifs*, Chaps. 20, 21, and 22.

(233) The last apologetic text by a German Jew is the *Nitzahon* (*The Victory*) of Rabbi Lipmann Mülhausen of Prague, who knew Latin and had read the Gospels. It was written about 1410. We must subsequently wait nearly two centuries to see publications of this kind reappear.

(234) Jean de Preis, called d'Outremeuse, "Ly Myreur des Histors," in *Chroniques belges*, Stanislas Bormans ed., Brussels, 1880, Vol. 6, p. 387.

(235) Guillaume de. Nangis, *Soc. de l'Histoire de France. Les grandes chroniques de France*, Vol. 8, p. 359.

(236) Meir of Rothenburg, *Responsa*, Prague, 1895, No. 517.

(237) Chaim Or Zarua, *Responsa*, Zhitomir, 1862, No. 14.

(238) Jacob Levi, *Responsa*, Cremona, 1556, No. 104.

(239) Israel Isserlein, *Responsa*, Venice, 1519, No. 198.

(240) Asher ben Yehiel, *Responsa*, XX, No. 20.

(241) Thus the *Sachsenspiegel*, the *Schwabenspiegel*, the *Deutschenspiegel*, and the *Glogauer Rechtsbuch* of 1386. (Cf. Guido Kisch, *op. cit.*, p. 120.)

PART FOUR | The Age of the Ghetto

8 Anti-Semitism in the Pure State: France

(242) Cf. Robert Anchel, *Les Juifs de France*, Paris, 1946, p. 125.

(243) *Les Regrets*, p. 116, line 8.

(244) Frippelipes, Marot's valet, to Sagon, Guiffrey ed., Vol. 3, p. 578, line 92.

(245) Epistle sent from Venice to Mme. la Duchesse de Ferrare. See C. A. Mayer, *Bibliographie des Oeuvres de Marot*, Droz ed., Geneva, 1954, Vol. 1, pp. 14, 64.

(246) *Journal de voyage de Montaigne*, Lautrey ed., Paris, 1906, pp. 223, 227, 254.

(247) *Le Coup d'essay de François de Sagon*, 1537, *Bibl. Nat.*, Rothschild bequest, No. 2,594.

(248) Bartoloccius, Vol. 4, p. 385.

(249) The narration that follows is for the most part based on the chronicle of Baptiste Legrain, *Décennie commençant l'histoire du roi Louis XIII*, Paris, 1619, pp. 182 ff. and pp. 404 ff. See also R. Anchel, *op. cit.*, p. 147.

(250) H. Sauval, *Histoire et Recherche des antiquités de la ville de Paris*, Paris, 1724, Vol. 2, p. 521.

(251) Isembert, *Recueil général des anciennes lois françaises*, Paris, 1821, Vol. 16, p. 76.

(252) Cf. M. Jacob, "L'Ascendance juive de Dacquin, médecin de Louis XIV," in *L'Univers Israélite*, No. 26, March 24, 1933.

(253) Malherbe, *Oeuvres*, Hachette ed., Paris, 1862, p. xxix of the Preface.

(254) "Catéchisme du diocèse de Meaux," in Bossuet, *Oeuvres Complètes*, Bar-le-Duc, 1863, Vol. 11, p. 443.

(255) *Catéchisme historique*, by M. Fleury, Prior of Argenteuil and Confessor to the King, Paris, 1766 (Lesson 19: "Des ennemis du Christ," and 27: "De la ruine de Jérusalem").

(256) Adrien Gambart, *Le Bon Partage des pauvres en la doctrine chrétienne et la connaissance du salut* . . . , Paris, 1652, p. 72.

(257) *Vie de Jésus-Christ*, written in the fifteenth century after Ludolphe le Chartreux.

(258) Father Boucher, *Bouquet sacré composé des Roses du Calvaire, des Lys de Bethléhem, des Jacinthes d'Olivet et de plusieurs autres belles Pensées de Terre Sainte*, Paris, 1620, pp. 644, 655.

(259) Dominique Auberton, *Récit véritable et miraculeux de ci qui a esté veu en Hiérusalem*, Paris, 1623.

(260) Bossuet, *Oeuvres oratoires*, Lebarq ed., Paris, 1913, pp. 158, 160, 161. Bourdaloue, *Oeuvres complètes*, Paris, 1822-1825, Vol. 2, p. 533; Vol. 9, p. 313; Vol. 11, p. 193. Fléchier, *Oeuvres choisies*, Brémond ed., Paris, 1911, pp. 31, 35. Massillon, *Oeuvres complètes*, Paris, 1911, pp. 31, 35. Massillon, *Oeuvres complètes*, Paris, 1823, Vol. 5 ("Sermons for Lent"), pp. 321, 337.

(261) Cf. *Le Bienheureux Grignon de Montfort* by E. Jac, Professor at the Faculté catholique d'Angers, Paris, 1903, p. 114.

(262) The works of the Blessed of Montfort with a study and notes by the Rev. Father Fradet (typescript), Beauchesne, Paris, 1929. The quotations are taken from the poem of the Passion "divided according to the days of the week: we witness the entire Passion, from the agony to the entombment" (pp. 57 ff.).

(263) E. Jac, *op. cit.*, p. 229.

(264) Lucien Romier, *Le Royaume de Catherine de Médicis*, Paris, 1922, p. 263.

(265) All the items that follow may be found in the collection of "Mazarinades" in the Bibliotheque de l'Arsenal in Paris, They are in Vol. 8⁰ H 7,667 and Vol. 8⁰ 7728 of this collection.

(266) Complete title: *Monitoire publié par toutes les Paroisses de la ville de Paris contre les Juifs de la Synagogue, le 1er jour de septembre 1652, pour avoir cruellement martyrisé, assassiné, et tué un notable bourgeois de ladite ville de Paris.*

(267) *Récit naïf et véritable du cruel assassinat et horrible massacre commis le 26 août 1652 par la Compagnie des Fripiers de la Tonnellerie commandée par Claude Amant, leur Capitaine, en la personne de Jean Bourgeois, marchand épinglier ordinaire de la Reyne, Bourgeois de Paris, âgé de trente-deux ans.*

(268) *Examen de la vie des Juifs, de leurs religion, commerce et trafic dans leur Synagogue.*

(269) *Relation véritable de ce que s'est passé au meurtre d'un jeune garçon fils d'un marchand épinglier de la rue Saint-Denys, nommé Bourgeois.*

(270) *Response des principaux de la Synagogue présenté par Articles aux Notables Bourgeois de Paris, où il monstre leur Ordre, leur Reigle, leur Loy et leur Procez avec le complaignant.*

(271) *L'Assemblée des Fripiers en la maison d'un officier de leur compagnie,*

pour adviser aux moyens de remédier à la cruanté de leur grand crime, suivant le Monitoire, qui se publie contre eux par les Paroisses de Paris où, ne trouvant pas de remèdes assurés, un d'entre eux, nommé Jean Lalloué, s'est jetté dans un puits par désespoir: et aussi avec le refus de la somme d'argent qu'ils ont offert à Son Altesse Royale pour tascher d'estouffer cette action barbare.

(272) *Relation véritable de l'horrible assassinat commis par les fripiers de la nation judaïque en la personne d'un bourgeois de cette ville de Paris, le 26 août 1652.*

(273) *La Synagogue mise en son lustre, avec l'épitaphe de Bourgeois pour mettre sur son tombeau.*

(274) Claude Veiras, *La Fureur des Juifs dédiée à Messieurs de la Synagogue.*

(275) *La Cruauté de la Synagogue des Juifs de la dernière génération, de plus le jugement de Minos rendu à l'âme du pauvre massacré aux Champs-Élysées, le repos des âmes heureuses,* P.A.R.C.C.A.M.B.D. R.T.A.P.

(276) *Le Jugement criminel rendu contre la Synagogue des Fripiers portant que ceux de leur nombre qui se trouveront circoncis (qui est la marque de la juiverie) seront chastrez vie à vie, afin que la race en demeure à jamais esteinte dans Paris.*

(277) J. Savary des Bruslons, *Dictionnaire du Commerce,* J. Étienne ed., Paris, 1723, Vol. 2, p. 923.

(278) Factum serving as a response to the book entitled "Abrégé du procès fait aux Juifs de Metz" in *Bibliothèque critique ou Recueil de diverses pièces critiques . . .* , Sainjore ed., Amsterdam, 1708, p. 109.

(279) *Cérémonies et coutumes qui s'observent aujourd'hui chez les Juifs.* Translated from the Italian of Leon of Modena, Rabbi of Venice . . . , by the Sieur de Simonville, Paris, 1681.

(280) Letter to Monsieur J.H., in R. Simon, *Lettres choisies,* Amsterdam, 1720, Vol. 1, p. 235.

(281) *Pensées,* Brunschvicq ed., p. 590, also pp. 592, 593, 630, and 640.

9   Anti-Semitism in the Pure State: England

(282) Cf. the two excellent and complementary doctoral theses: *The Contemporary Jew in the Elizabethan Drama,* by Jacob Cardozo, Amsterdam, 1925; and *The Jew in Early English Literature,* by Hijman Michelson, Amsterdam, 1926.

(283) Cf. Michael Adler, "The History of the Domus Conversorum," in *Jews of Medieval England,* London, 1939, pp. 306-79.

(284) Cf. Cecil Roth, *A History of the Jews in England,* Oxford, 1941, pp. 131-32.

(285) *Ibid.,* pp. 136-38.

(286) *Ibid.*

(287) Cf. D. Kaufmann, "Une consultation de Jacob Rafaël Peglione de

Modène sur le divorce de Henri VIII," *R.E.J.*, Vol. 30, p. 309; and by the same author, "Jacob Mantino," *R.E.J.*, Vol. 27, p. 30.

(288) Murray, *A New English Dictionary*, Vol. 5, p. 576.

(289) Cf. Cecil Roth, *op. cit.*, pp. 149-54, where numerous examples are cited.

(290) Cf. W. K. Jordan, *The Development of Religious Tolerance in England*, London, 1938, Vol. 3, p. 209.

(291) Cf. M. Ashley, *Oliver Cromwell*, London, 1934, p. 268; and L. Wolf, "Cromwell's Jewish Intelligencers," in *Essays in Jewish History* (posthumous), London, 1934, p. 91.

(292) Cecil Roth, *A Life of Menasseh ben Israel*, Philadelphia, 1945, pp. 249, 346.

(293) William Prynne's preface to his pamphlet, *A short Demurrer to the Jews' long discontinued Remitter into England*, 2nd ed., London, 1656.

(294) *A Narrative of the Late Proceedings at Whitehall Concerning the Jews . . .* , London, 1656. (Cf. *Harleian Miscellany*, London, 1810, Vol. 6, p. 445.)

10 Activated Anti-Semitism: Germany

(295) Jacob Wimpheling, *De arte impressoria*, fol. 2 of the manuscript (quoted in J. Janssen, *Die allgemeinen Zustände des deutschen Volkes beim Ausgang des Mittelalters*, Freiburg, 1887, Vol. 1, p. 9).

(296) Quoted in H. A. Mascher, *Das deutsche Gewerbewesen von der frühesten Zeit bis auf die Gegenwart*, Potsdam, 1866.

(297) Quoted in J. Janssen, *op. cit.*, p. 399.

(298) *Doctro Johannes Reuchlin tütsch Missive, warumb die Juden so lang in Ellend sind*, 1505. (Cf. L. Geiger, *Johannes Reuchlin*, Leipzig, 1870.)

(299) This quotation, like those that follow, is taken from the work by J. Janssen cited above, pp. 400-406.

(300) *Ibid.*

(301) *Ibid.*

(302) *Ibid.*

(303) Pierre de Froissart, *Lettres* (L. 21), Lyon, 1527.

(304) *Augenspiegel*, fol. 32b.

(305) Cf. L. Geiger, *op. cit.*, p. 374.

(306) Letter from Erasmus to Pirkheimer, November 2, 1517; letter to Reuchlin, November 15, 1517. (Cf. L. Geiger, *op. cit.*, p. 342.)

(307) *Gegen die Juden und ihre Lügen*. In this connection see R. Lewin, *Luthers Stellung zu den Juden*, Berlin, 1911.

(308) "Les Mémoires de Josselman de Rosheim," French translation of S. Schwarzfuchs, *F.S.J.U.* (quarterly review), Paris, October, 1954, p. 23.

(309) Heinrich Bornkamm, *Luthers geistige Welt*, Lüneburg, 1947, p. 35.

(310) "Les Mémoires de Josselman de Rosheim," *loc. cit.*

(311) Cf. S. Stern, *The Court Jew*, Philadelphia, 1950. Apropos of the Court Jews, see also Peter Alldag, *Der Hofjude*, Berlin, 1938 (a work of Nazi inspiration), as well as the chief works on Jewish history.

(312) The *Judenstättigkeit* of the Jews of Frankfurt and their *Kleiderordnung* have been reproduced in J. G. Schudt, *Jüdische Merckwürdigkeiten*, Frankfurt and Leipzig, 1714-1718, Vol. 3, pp. 119 ff.

(313) *Mitteilungen der Gesellschaft für jüdische Volkskunde*, Hamburg, 1899, Vol. 3, pp. 29 ff.

(314) Jacob and Wilhelm Grimm, *Deutsches Wörterbuch*, second section of Vol. 4, Leipzig, 1877, p. 2,353.

(315) These works both appeared in 1681, the first in Nürnberg and the second in Altdorf.

11 Poland: the Autonomous Center

(316) Aronius, *Regesten*, No. 724.

(317) Quoted in S. Dubnow, *History of the Jews in Europe* [in Russian], Riga, 1936, Vol. 3, p. 290.

(318) Cf. S. Dubnow, *op. cit.*, Vol. 3, p. 323.

(319) "Zawsze dla nas chlopkov bieda: musim karmic pana, ksiedza, zyda." (S. Adalberg, *Księga przyslow* . . . , Warsaw, 1894, No. 58.)

(320) "Chlop zarobil, pan wydal, a zyd skorzystal." (*Ibid.*, No. 56.)

(321) "Zyd, Niemiece, diabel trzeci, jednej matki dzieci." (F. Korab-Brzozowski, *Przyslowia polskie*, Cracow, 1896, No. 191.)

(322) Nathan Hannover, in the introduction to his chronicle of persecutions, *Yeven Metzulah*, Venice, 1653.

(323) N. Kostomarov. *Russian History* [in Russian], St. Petersburg, 1880, Vol. 2, p. 230.

(324) Quoted in S. Dubnow, *History of the Jews in Russia and Poland*, Philadelphia, 1946, p. 188.

(325) "Multitudes in Poland, Lithuania, and Prussia by the late wars by the Swedes, Cossacks, and others being driven away from them. Hence their yearly Alms to the poor Jews of the German synagogue at Jerusalem hath ceased, and of 700 widows and poor Jews there, about 400 have been famished, as a letter from Jerusalem to their friends relates." (*Harleian Miscellany*, Vol. 7, p. 579. See also D. Kaufmann, "Le Rachat de Juifs prisonniers durant la persécution de Chmielnicki," *R.E.J.*, Vol. 25, p. 202.)

(326) The Ukrainian priest Goliatovski, in his book *The True Messiah*, written in 1667 and published in 1672.

(327) G. G. Scholem, "Le Mouvement sabbataïste en Pologne," *Revue de l'Histoire des Religions*, January, 1953, Vol. 143, p. 48.

(328) G. G. Scholem, "Le Mouvement sabbataïste en Pologne," *Revue de l'Histoire des Religions*, April, 1953, Vol. 143, p. 216.

(329) Quoted in S. Dubnow, *History of the Jews in Europe* [in Russian], Riga, 1936, Vol. 4, p. 144.

(330) *Shibkhe ha-Besht* [Eulogy of BEShT or Legend of BEShT], published at Kopyss in White Russia in 1815.

(331) G. G. Scholem, *op. cit.*, p. 231.

(332) Quoted in S. Dubnow, *Geschichte des Chassidismus*, Berlin, 1931, Vol. 1, p. 191.

(333) *Ibid.*, Vol. 2, p. 300.

(334) From R. Elimelech of Lyssensk in his treatise, *Noam Elimelech*, published in Lvov [Lemberg] in 1788.

(335) From R. Baruch of Miedzyboz, grandson of BEShT. Quoted in S. A. Horodezky, *The Hasidim and Hasidism* [in Hebrew], Berlin, 1923, Vol. 3, p. 15.

(336) From Rabbi Jacob Isaac of Lublin. Quoted in S. Dubnow, *Geschichte des Chassidismus*, Berlin, 1931, Vol. 2, p. 236.

(337) Quoted in S. Dubnow, *History of the Jews in Europe* [in Russian], Vol. 2, pp. 238-39.

(338) Quoted in G. G. Scholem, *Major Trends in Jewish Mysticism*, New York, 1941, pp. 349 f.

(339) S. Dubnow, "The Pogroms of Vochtchilo," *Voskhod* [periodical in Russian], 1889, Vol. 1.

(340) Michael the Neophyte's work written in 1716, first circulated in manuscript. It was reproduced *in extenso* in the work of Canon Pikoulski, *Jewish Wickedness* (*Zlosc zydowska*, Lvov [Lemberg], 1760), which became the veritable breviary of Polish anti-Semitism.

(341) During the Beilis trial in Kiev (1912), the last major trial for ritual murder, the experts for the prosecution based their memoranda and reports on the account of Michael the Neophyte.

(342) Quoted in S. Dubnow, *History of the Jews in Europe* [in Russian], p. 93.

12 The Case of Russia

(343) This is the chief reason why certain historians have attempted to identify this Skharia, who appeared from Lithuania about 1470, with the Zechariah or Skharia of Crimea, who was active some fifteen years later. This, in particular, was the opinion of E. Panov, author of the best study to date on the heresy of the Judaizers (*Review of the Ministry of Public Instruction* [in Russian], Nos. 189-91, St. Petersburg, 1877). But S. Dubnow, for instance, was of the contrary opinion.

(344) E. Panov, *op. cit.* (No. 343), No. 191, p. 16.

(345) Joseph of Volotzk, in his *Prossvietitel*, in E. Panov. *op. cit.*, No. 189, p. 38.

(346) Joseph of Volotzk, in his letter to Nifonte, bishop of Souzdal, quoted

by S. Soloviev, *History of Russia* [in Russian], Moscow, 1855, Vol. 5, p. 257.

(347) Paulus Iovius Novocomensis, *Study of the Russian State* [in Russian], St. Petersburg, 1908, p. 268.

(348) Quoted in I. Hessen, *History of the Jewish People in Russia* [in Russian], Petrograd, 1923.

(349) Cf. Sh. Ettinger, "The Muscovite State and Its Attitude toward the Jews," *Zion* [periodical in Hebrew], Nos. 3-4, Jerusalem, 1954, p. 139.

(350) *Ibid.*, p. 141.

(351) A. Nartov, *Stories of Peter the Great* [in Russian], Imperial Academy of Sciences, St. Petersburg, 1891.

(352) From the Imperial Russian Archives. (Cf. *Stories and Writings about Peter the Great* [in Russian], St. Petersburg, 1898, p. 92.)

(353) Quoted by Kostomarov, *Russian History*, Vol. 2.

(354) Cf. S. Dubnow, *History of the Jews in Europe* [in Russian], Riga, 1936, Vol. 4, p. 130.

Index